Connecting in San Francisco

693 Great Places to Enjoy Yourself and Meet New People

by
Ruth B. Harvey, Ph.D.
Diane R. de Castro

OFFTIME PRESS
San Francisco, CA

Connecting in San Francisco:
693 Great Places to Enjoy Yourself and Meet New People

Please note that the information herein was obtained from sources available to the public. It is subject to change. Although the authors and publisher have exhaustively researched all sources to insure the accuracy of information contained in this book, they assume no responsibility for errors or inaccuracies. Any slight of people or organizations is unintentional. It is recommended that organizations be contacted before making arrangements to attend events.

Publisher's Cataloging-in-Publication

Harvey, Ruth B.
    Connecting in San Francisco : 693 great places to enjoy yourself and meet new people / by Ruth B. Harvey & Diane R. deCastro. —
1st ed.
    p. cm.
    Includes index.
    ISBN: 0-9643708-2-4

    1. San Francisco (Calif.)--Guidebooks. 2. Social networks--California--San Francisco--Directories. 3. Leisure--California--San Francisco--Directories. I. Harvey, Ruth B. II. Title.

F860.S33D43 1997   917.94'610453
                         QB197-41014

Library of Congress Catalog Card Number: 97-92484

Layout & Graphic Design: Janet Gala
Cover Design & Illustration: Carter Design
Editors: Kathy Sheehan, Aimee Minarik, Madeline Sunley

This book is available at special quantity discounts on bulk purchases. For information contact Offtime Press (415) 292-5230
41 Sutter Street, Suite 1763, San Francisco, CA 94109

Contents

Contents

Contents

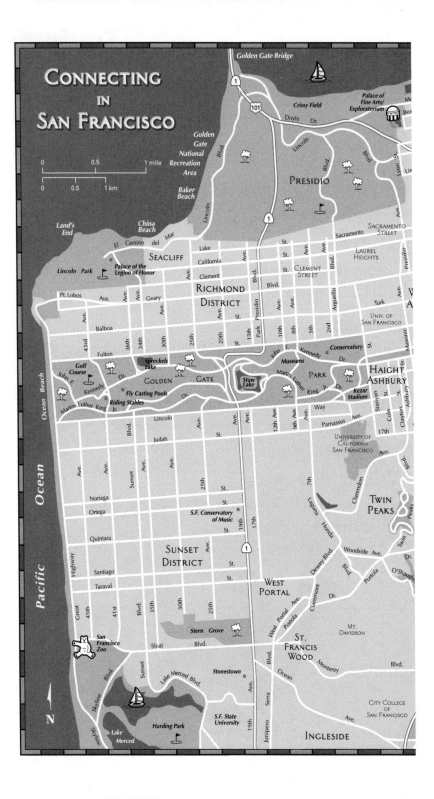

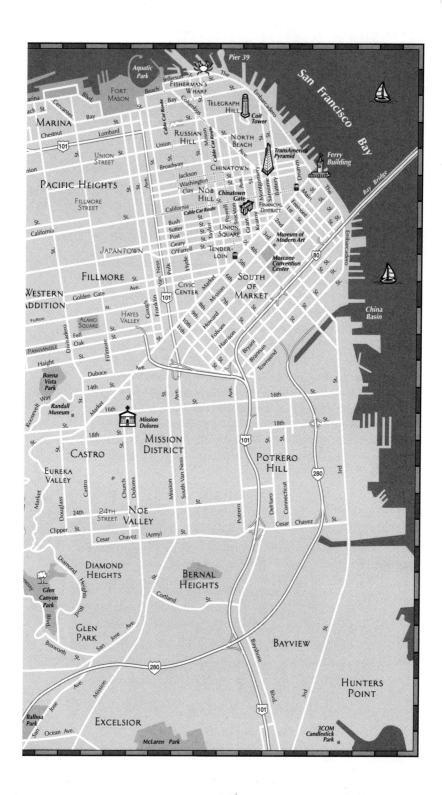

Acknowledgements

People who worked (hard) on this book

Janet Gala (Graphic Artist & Layout) for her fine sense of design,
and hours and hours of dependable time

Cherie Carter (Cover Artist) of Carter Design, for creativity (and
flexibility) in cover design

Kathy Sheehan, Madeline Sunley & Aimee Minarik, Editors, for sharp
eyes and careful attention, even at a moment's notice

Kristin Bergstrom & Sheila Semans (Carto Graphics) for geographic
artistry & details

Bonnie Martin (Image-in-Focus) for professional skill & humor

Valerie Camarda (Marketing Sense) for being the marketing doctor.

From Diane

Peter for understanding and love

Mom for life

Family and old friends for their continued support

Ruth for her sense of humor and my guardian goddess angel.

From Ruth

Jim, again, for patience, loving support and best common sense

The Queen Street Group for nurturance and ongoing connecting ideas

Family and old friends for their continued support

Diane who was trustable, fun and a strong partner.

Diane and Ruth at the peak

Foreword

Serendipity and the Computer Age

For those of you who are enjoying this book, you might be interested in how it emerged.

It began in Toko's (a store) when Ruth (never the shy one), here on vacation, jumped in on Diane's (private) conversation about wishing to find compatible friends in the area. Having just got her head above water from finishing a degree program, she was looking both for new people to enjoy *and* a challenging work project. Ruth was looking for a way to do one of her **Connecting** books in San Francisco. "Funny you should say that...," and we were off and running. A week later we were on the phone, wondering if we were crazy to embark on such a big project with someone we didn't know. But each of us had a gut feeling that this was the right person to work with and that serendipity was in evidence (again!).

In Sept 1996, Diane began a full-time commitment, accumulating hundreds of exciting interactive activities and groups in S.F. We met in December to format and cluster the material and spent our first real time together. We found out we really liked each other! (Whew!) The material was fabulous—Ruth was impressed out of her mind. And Diane was having a great time meeting new people.

During the next six months, our email flew fast and furious as Diane sent files to Ruth who reviewed and edited. We established a private chat line for cheap one-on-one online conversations and "met" regularly at nine (noon for Ruth) on Tuesdays. We sent thousands of email about everything from data base changes to comforting words to "Where the hell are you!—in cyberspace? I *need* you!" Diane kept finding more and more great activities, overfilling our planned number, until Ruth called a definite HALT! Prose writing pulled Ruth into the circuit full-time in June, Sheehan in Seattle began her edits, sent through email as usual, and a San Francisco **Connecting** book was about to be born.

A final get-together in July found Diane on a computer in one room, Ruth on a computer in another and Bonnie making final accuracy calls in yet another. From 7am to midnight we worked, with breaks for sushi and shopping and lots of (real) talking and laughing. With Diane in the lead, Ruth couldn't get over what a fabulous city San Francisco is and what wonderful things there are to enjoy.

We think it looks like a great book. We loved doing it, and becoming such good friends. We hope you find good friends in the places you discover in these pages.

Tai Chi enthusiasts in Washington Square.
Photo by Mark Downey. Courtesy of the S. F. Conv. & Visitors Bureau

Introduction

Finding the People You Want to Meet By Choosing the Activities You Love

INTRODUCTION: The Short Version

Here is an outline of the philosophy of this book for those of you who want to speed read to the key points.

1. There are many great places to enjoy yourself and meet new people in San Francisco.

2. There are wonderful people to meet in those places.

3. You have a much greater chance of meeting compatible people if you find them while doing your favorite activities.

4. You can identify people with the personality traits you seek with greater accuracy if you go to a group that has a focus and meets regularly.

5. To maximize happiness and add balance to your life, get involved in interest-based activities that you love. Find "your" communities and have fun!

The Introduction that follows elaborates on these ideas and is a **mini-workshop** (based on Ruth's Social Interaction Workshops) on how to develop a great social life.

INTRODUCTION: The Long Version

This book is for people who want to get off the couch and out of the house to join others who are enjoying life's healthy pleasures. That includes single people as well as those who are attached, people who are new to the area, and people from 15 to 100 years of age. This book is also for long-time San Francisco residents who love socializing and need new ideas for things to do and places to go.

It is our belief that more than ever we all need to take our free-time activities seriously. Because society is mobile and people are in constant transition—changing jobs, changing geographic locations, even changing families—more of us experience feelings of isolation and disconnection than ever before. It is important to continually develop new interests and build our reference groups, networks of people where we feel we belong.

Introduction

The Connecting Workshops

The activities in this guide were selected because they support interaction and connection between the people who do them. They were found in public sources: fliers, brochures and notices from local papers and magazines which listed places to do things with other people. Others were passed to us word-of-mouth from people who love *their* outside activities and interests ("You *have to* include the Royal Scottish Folk Dancers!"). Originally the collection was started, organized and handed out to Ruth's workshop participants who were looking for effective ways to discover places to meet people of interest, both friends and romantic partners. In fact, it was the workshop participants who suggested that the lists be printed in book form.

The workshops were attended by people **new to the area**, both single and attached, who already had identified interests. They wanted to know where to find people their age and who participated in their favorite activities. They were curious to know about events in the city and where interesting people gathered. Some people wanted to locate groups who like sketching and painting, some were looking for a bridge game. Others wanted to find groups that love snow camping or rowing on the Bay. All wanted good, current information about these things as well, as the best resources for keeping up with what is happening in San Francisco.

Long-time San Francisco residents attended to **expand their repertoire** of exciting new interests. They needed a nudge to try acting in a play, reading in a poetry writing group—or swing dancing. Even with their busy lives, they were ready to grow and do something new. And they knew the time was now.

Identifying specific places to go was especially important to the **single** participants who believed the answer to finding romantic relationships was in knowing *where* to go to find the people right for them. This makes sense. Finding the right place(s) to go helps a lot. It is hard to find the people you want to meet in a laundromat or grocery store, even if you have great people-meeting skills! (How do you start *that* conversation? "Excuse me, are you *really* going to mix your whites with your darks?" or "Are you aware of all the ways you can use Bok Choy?")

No, it is clear that the best chance of finding people who have *durability* as friends and loving partners is in places where you share common interests. For starters, you know that they independently chose an activity that you really enjoy. If the relationship continues, you already have an important bond. You also know more about someone's personality when you have been involved together in a mutual activity for awhile because you've had a chance to see how they act in different situations. Your interest in them will be based on more than just looks. And, speaking of interests, don't you think you are your most interesting and attractive self when you are enthusiastically involved in something you love to do? Isn't that "the you" that you would like people to be attracted to and get to know? One last point: When two people are doing a purposeful activity, people-meeting skills pretty much take care of themselves. You just feel more natural approaching someone when you have an activity-based reason to talk to him/her, rather than having to start with a free floating opener, like the infamous "So, what's your sign?"

The workshop participants wanted to expand their boundaries even though it could be risky. They knew it's never too late to explore new interests and were reaching out to find new people-sharing activities. They knew that having a successful social life was related to feeling happy.

Happiness and Choosing the Activities You Love

What the participants were saying affirmed the ideas in a book called *Flow* (Csikszentmihalyi, M., 1991). The research in this book concludes that people are happiest when they are immersed in something they love, when they are so involved that they are oblivious to time and their surroundings.

This point emphasizes the powerful influence of people's activities on their feelings, attitudes and general disposition. *What* people are doing and the rewards and risks of that activity, *who* they're with and the kinds of interaction they're having, influence how they feel about themselves and life in general. This means you can alter moods of boredom, frustration, self-deprecation, loneliness and create hopefulness, excitement and vitality by paying attention to your schedule of activities!

With all this, it's interesting how little attention many of us pay to developing interests and activities we could enjoy. In the workshops, there is an interest list to jog participants' memories of activities they liked at some time in their lives. Here is a brief version of that list.

Introduction

Activities Sheet

Acting	Coin Collecting	Political Activities
Archery	Computers	Running
Architecture	Cooking	Sailing
Astrology	Discussion Groups	Science Fiction
Backpacking	Environmental Studies	Sculpture
Ballroom Dancing	Filmmaking	Singing
Basketball	Fly Fishing	Skiing
Bicycling	Galleries	Social Groups
Billiards	Gardening	Swimming
Bird Watching	Golf	Swing Dancing
Blues	Hiking/Walking	Tennis
Bookstore Browsing	Inline Skating	Theater
Camping	Kite Flying	Vintage Cars
Canoeing	Martial Arts	Volunteering
Card Games	Motorcycling	Weaving
Cat/Dog Lovers	Painting/Drawing	Wine Tasting
Ceramics	Personal Growth	Windsurfing
Chess/Go	Photography	Woodworking
	Play/Poetry Readings	Yoga/Meditation

Exercise: Circle the interests that stimulate a spark. Once you've identified them, look through the book to get leads about where they might be taking place. Call to have a friendly chat with the contact person to get a picture of what the group actually does, who goes there, what kind of commitment you have to make, and other questions that matter to you. Most groups are pleased to discuss their activities, and they welcome new participants. You can also ask them about other groups focused on similar interests.

Introduction

Balancing Your Activities Choices

Everybody talks about achieving balance in their lives. Usually they mean having a balance between income-producing work, free time activities and family responsibilities.

This section, however, is about the balance in your free time activities. There are a number of dimensions that describe the interests you are choosing. If you keep them in mind when organizing your activities, you should maximize the pleasure they give you.

(1) **Using many parts of ourselves.** The first type of balance relates to our personal make-up: We all have personalities very rich and multi-faceted, that include many qualities.

We have a *serious thoughtful* side that reflects and
contemplates important questions.

An *adventurous side* where we are exhilarated by the
challenge of hiking a mountain or sailing a storm.

A *comic, silly, playful side* that loves to goof off and feels
like a child, ten years old.

An *intellectual side* that loves to analyze and play with
ideas and possibilities.

A *flirtatious, sexy side* that loves courtship games.

A *soft romantic side* that loves candles and illusion.

A *curious, tenacious part* that won't let go of a problem
until it is resolved.

And on and on.

We need to exercise as many qualities of our personalities as we can. When we use only a few parts of our personality to the exclusion of others, we may become lethargic and bored and possibly depressed. Although we may feel bored with the world and our friends, we may be, in reality, bored with ourselves. If we slide into filling our time with the same-old, same-old things, we stop expanding. We stop looking at new places in the world, stop seeking out new people and *using new parts of ourselves.*

Introduction

It's demoralizing to spend most of our time doing things that don't really interest us but are what other people think we should be doing. We feel sluggish when we only seem to have time for what we *have* to do and no time to do what we *want* to do.

That's when it's necessary to be actively involved in expanding our knowledge of places to go and things to do to give us vitality and enthusiasm, that "can't wait to go" feeling. We need to search for experiences that arouse curiosity, adventure and a deep, sincere interest.

Exercise: Choose activities that appeal to different sides of yourself. Here are some examples of how interests could be divided into three basic personality parts.

Physical	Intellectual	Cultural
hiking	word games	opera
tango	book discussions	acting
sailing	world affairs discussions	sketching
biking	stamp collecting	wine tasting

It's easy to get out of balance in favor of one type of activity. We might spend all of our time doing outdoor events, and undervalue the side that loves good discussions and singing. When this happens, we restrict the types of people we meet and lose touch with valuable parts of ourselves, parts we really enjoy. When we feel out of balance and notice a feeling of "missing something," we know it's time to look at the ways we're spending our time.

(2) **Ongoing activities** *or* **one-time events.** Another type of balance has to do with the way the activities are organized. Some activities are one-shot events, such as the annual **Sing-It-Yourself Messiah,** while others are ongoing with a regular core of people, like the **Anything Goes Chorus** at the Community Music Center.

Introduction

This is a pretty important distinction. People, especially single people, often complain that they go out and don't meet anybody they like, thus drawing the conclusion there is no one "out there" to meet.

If you ask where they are going, you find out that they are going to various one-time events over and over. When they *do* talk to people, their conversations are often brief and the subject matter is not especially important to either person. How do they know *whom* they have met? Ongoing activities, on the other hand, give you a chance to get to know someone and develop a relationship based on something more than just first impressions.

(3) **Activities with structured interaction** *versus* **ambiguous format.** One-time events are fun too, especially if they have a focus. This brings us to the next important characteristic of these activities: How *structured* are they? Some are very organized around the activity. You are there to do something and that is what you do. If you attend a swing dance class you will team up with a partner, receive instruction and dance together. Even though it might be only one class, you have a chance to see if you enjoy the dancing without making a major commitment and you can participate in engaging interaction with some of the other dancers.

There are times when time is tight and spontaneity is your first priority in deciding how to spend your day/evening. That's usually when you go to activities that are more loosely structured, such as **First Thursdays** or the wonderful street fairs and jazz festivals San Francisco regularly offers. Although these activities provide a focus that everyone shares (e.g. art, jazz), it can be tough to find compatible others because a way to talk with new people is not built in, as it is when you take a walking tour, for example. You have to take a lot of initiative to meet someone. ("The walk across the dance floor is the longest mile," one young man reported.) Although loosely structured one-time events are the easiest places to go to socialize without advance planning, unfortunately they are the least likely venues to find the relationships we are looking for.

(4) **Risky and Exciting** *or* **Familiar and Comfortable.** Your psychological safety/excitement continuum is another dimension to keep in balance when choosing an activity. This is a dimension that changes from day to day. Some days you feel that you can handle anything (or anyone). Other days you feel you just want to be in the bosom of familiar friends. It's important to take a reading of your risk tolerance

Introduction

and choose accordingly. You'll want to include activities all across this scale—on one side things that expand your boundaries and are therefore more risky, and on the other things that are familiar and nurturing. If you only go places that feel completely safe (from rejection, for example) your social life can feel flat. Activities that include a stimulating challenge and an adventure, such as an inline skate class or learning to throw a pot, are important to keep the roses in your cheeks.

Your Social Goals

Suppose you have identified your interests and have been going to a lot of places to do them—but you're not finding the people who interest you. Although they are people you like, they are not the community (or person) you are looking for.

The next step in this process is to define your social goals. Whom do you really want to meet? This is a tricky question, but one that has to be addressed directly in order to choose the places that will satisfy you.

First of all, how do we **describe the people we're looking for** in a way that helps us find them? Often we describe them by detailing the personal traits we want them to have. But how do we *find* them? It certainly would be nice if we knew the places where the sweet people were, where the sensitive people were, the kind, considerate and good-looking people were, and best yet, where those who had *all* of these qualities hung out! Unfortunately, we do not know those places. However, we do think that interest-based activities attract people with certain types of personality characteristics, don't you? So looking at where they spend their discretionary time may provide one of the best clues we have to find the people we like. If someone physically fit appeals to you, try outdoors activities. If you want someone who loves ideas, try world affairs groups or book clubs. Someone who cares about political change? Look in political organizations. People who are nurturing? Look into care-taking volunteering, and so on.

Secondly, be **clear with yourself about who you are looking for**. Is it friends, romantic partners, biking buddies or a sailing group? Analyze where those people might be and make a commitment to keep looking until you find them. If you wish to go with a group that shares your social conscience, look into community service activities and try them. If you are looking for a spouse or significant other, think about where people appropriate for long-term relationships might be. Check groups for singles with a special-interest sub-group, and then go with the idea of having fun while you look. If you want to find people who love books and ideas, make a promise to explore various book discussion groups until you find the one you want. Diane loves style and culture. She found the **San Francisco Hat Society** and the **DIVA's** (Women who love Italian culture). Ruth wanted to find women friends who enjoy outdoor activities, especially golf (**Executive Women's Golf League**). But a tall ship sailing group worked for her, too. The clearer you are, the more specific your search can be and the more likely it is that you'll find your people.

Third of all, **watch out for perfectionism.** You certainly are entitled to be as much of a perfectionist as you wish, but the higher your standards, the fewer people will make it through your filters. You'll need to weigh the importance of finding friends or partners to do things with against your expectations for the people you find.

There are many interest groups that are specifically for certain populations. They might be for certain ages, religious denominations, sexual preferences, races and genders. When you know who you want to meet, you can make more of an effort to go places you love where you think they might be.

Suggestions to Help You Get Going (or, Dealing with Your Resistance)

1. Do whatever you need to do to **commit** to finding great places for yourself that offer activities and ongoing community. To find what you are looking for, you will have to invest time and energy and be optimistic that you *will* find what you want—eventually. You will have to evaluate each situation. When one place you try doesn't work for you, try another and hang in there knowing that you're getting closer to the places where you really want to spend time and belong.

2. **Collect Information and Make a List.** Call and write for catalogs, fliers and brochures. Organizations love to send information to prospective members. Scan the local papers frequently. Every week you'll find new activities that sound interesting. Write down the activities and

Introduction

groups that appeal to you even if you are not quite ready to go. Look at them often. Try the easiest one, then one a little harder, and so on. Keep a notebook about the ones you liked. Talk to people and ask them where they go to have fun and meet people they like. Go with them!

3. **Confront your myths—demons and expectations**—about the people who are socializing in the places you'd like to go. Hold them to the cold light of day and see them realistically. Look at these black and white examples: "Everybody who goes to singles groups is bottom of the barrel, desperate or secretly married;" or "The love of my life is waiting for me at this event. If she's not there tonight, I'm never going again." These attitudes may sound pretty silly on paper, but negative attitudes that keep you in your living room often sound this way and operate underground. It is only when you become aware of them, and talk to yourself about them, that you will defuse them. Then you'll have the freedom to go out and enjoy the people you meet.

4. **Plan.** Choose places that look good and feel safe. Make sure you go with someone you can trust, but who will give you space if you want it. Discuss it before you go. You might want to drive your own car so you have the assurance that you won't be stuck in a situation. Find an outfit you feel really good in (women *and* men) and have it ready ahead of time. Know your familiar excuses to cop out and plan a self-talk response to them.

Hot Tips for Socializing

Try to be **open to people who don't fit your favorite visual stereotype** at first. You would be surprised at the qualities people have underneath the image. The most successful approach in socializing is an attitude of liking people. Sounds corny? Well, watch people in social situations. Who would *you* want to talk to? What does this attitude look like? You can't even begin to *like* someone without *looking* at them, *listening* to them, and *enjoying* them for what they are. You will be projecting interest and energy and a general good humor about the situation.

Introduction

Try to **get into the activity.** This is important. You are there to have as much fun as you can. To be immersed, to get into *Flow*, act as if this was the thing you always wanted to do! Give yourself a chance to stop observing yourself ("Look how stupid I look.") and into the game. It is the only way to find out if this is something you could really enjoy.

Not only that. Research shows that you are most attractive and interesting when you are engaged and interested in what's going on, in something outside of yourself. You are more approachable and people feel more comfortable with you—which is what they want to feel.

Pay attention to cues when you want to approach someone. What did they say or do in the group that interested you? Comment on it or ask about it. You can also look for identifying information such as jewelry or logos on T-shirts that tell you what this person cares about, and remark on it.

Use the group activity to get in connection with people there. Offer to join someone in a project, or ask for help in learning something the group is doing. When Ruth goes to a Swing Dance she always asks an expert to dance one dance with her so she can get the feel of how it's supposed to feel. She's never been turned down, even though they may have regretted it while dancing! If you *want* to be involved, most people will extend themselves to help you in a gracious manner. Remember that chatting with someone is not a commitment!

Learn to deal with rejection. You are going to get slighted, rejected and disappointed. Sometimes you'll feel fearful that you do not belong. Most of the time it's just part of the game. Everybody gets rejected, and the more you are in contact with people, the more it happens. You need to work on how not to take it personally. Learn about this by talking to friends, reading about it, and taking workshops where it is addressed. We all need armor and strategies to stop fears about rejection from keeping us home.

Keep in mind that many people feel anxious and awkward. There is a common human concern called the "on stage" phenomenon in which you are sure that everybody is looking at you with a very critical eye. Usually the criticism you think they have is the one you have about yourself. Although someone *may be* looking at you, his(her) main concern is usually how *he(she)* is being evaluated by the crowd. Knowing that others are uneasy about the impression they make on you often makes it easier for you to relax.

Introduction

Sometimes the "on stage" feelings are labeled as shyness, as in, "I'm too shy to try that." We want to talk for a minute about shyness. Most people are shy sometimes, especially in unfamiliar situations when they don't know anyone. The feeling is based on not knowing what in the world to do or say, and to whom. One of the reasons for this book is to encourage people who are moderately reserved to go places that liberate their natural friendliness. Many times shyness is more related to the situation than the person. Test this out by being aware of your fluttering anxiety when you go places of different risk value to you. Do you notice your shyness level change?

Finally, give yourself **permission to leave** at any time when you have given an event a fair shot and you know you aren't having a good time. It's much easier to *go* when you know you don't have to spend hours and hours feeling miserable if what sounded great turns out to be lousy. There are lots of great places for you out there and many that do not work at all. That's OK—go sort them out!

The process of finding new interests, new places to have fun and new people to join with *is* exciting. Like any challenge it takes thought, energy and nerve. You'll learn a lot about yourself—things you do not know right now. It is about your own self-development, regardless of whether you have an intimate partner, children or close friends. One of the best things about it is that the skills you learn while exploring this great city will *always* be with you, no matter what happens to you or where you are. This is a golden opportunity!

How to use this book

1. This guide contains an overview of participatory activities in a number of interest categories. It does not include every group and activity in San Francisco. (There are many, many more!) It is meant to provide you with kick-off material to get you thinking and started on your unique search.

2. Places close down. They change structure and focus. Contact people change. Please call before you set out. Diane worked very hard to have phone numbers current to time of publication, but some will change even while this book is at press.

It was very hard to accept the discontinuation of several groups, like the San Francisco Macintosh Users Group. One or two are still included in this guide with a note about their possible discontinuation. We hope if enough people show an interest in their events, they might remain intact or start up again.

3. Note that there are sometimes two phone numbers and two addresses in one listing. When that is the case, the first address-phone number is that of the organization, and the second is that of the place where the activity is held. You should **call** the organization to find out more about the group and details of the events, but you should **go** to the location address.

The listings information follows the standard format below.

Activity Type

Organization Name
Organization Address
Organization Phone   *Organization Email*   *Organization Web site*
Activity Location (if different from Organization address): Address & Phone

Comments about the Group

☀ Date   ⏰ Time
☎ Contact Person
💰 Cost

Windsurfers catch the wind off Fort Mason Center. Photo by Carol Simowitz in conjunction with the S.F. Conv. & Visitors Bureau.

Golden Gate Sport & Social Club hosts a party at Marina Central.

Art

Art Lovers of Nature • Art of Cultures
Book Arts • Classes • Gallery Programs
Lectures & Discussions • Resources
Young Professionals' Art & Social Clubs

Art

The San Francisco Center For The Book
Suminagashi: Japanese Marbling workshop, Robin Heyeck, instructor

A painting party at the Stroke of Genius

Artists and art-lovers are drawn to San Francisco to enjoy a rich visual landscape. Charming residences, dynamic architecture and lush landscaping in gorgeous natural surroundings set the stage for an active artistic community. If you're an aficionado of the arts, you're in the right place!

There are two ways to share art experiences with other people: 'Making art' and 'Looking at/Discussing art.'

In making art, maybe the biggest thing we need to learn is that we don't have to be "good at it." In that way it's like singing and dancing— we've been taught that if you aren't really "good at it" ("good" being what your art teacher pronounced after you did a picture), then you have no business doing it. Many of us never allowed ourselves to play around with soft drawing pencils, water colors or those nifty pastel chalky crayons you see in the expensive art stores. The message has been, "Live your life without doing art because you don't do it 'right.' "

Wait a minute!

If you like it, do it! Do it just because making art is fun and fulfilling. Do it because the product is a unique expression of yourself. Do it to find the artist in you and add creative balance to your life. Or do it for whatever reason you want.

Besides, while you are having fun getting involved in ART, you will find yourself in the company of others who are enjoying it as well. You'll find people who also are embarrassed that they don't do it "good enough," people who love color for the sheer beauty of it, people who also strive to brush a soft peachy shadow on the apple. You'll all want to talk about what is happening with your artwork in the class, and, painting side by side, you'll form a community around that activity.

The best news is that there is a *wide* variety of exciting classes in the Bay Area for learning how to do all kinds of art. A notable example is the **Sharon Art Studio**, which is part of the cultural division of the **San Francisco Recreation and Park Department**. For a low fee, you can take classes there in Drawing, Painting, Metal Arts, Leaded Glass, Jewelry Making and much more. **The San Francisco Art Institute** offers an Extension Education Program that meets on Saturdays and weeknights (just right for the time-challenged 9-5 worker) and includes such classes as Photography, Figure Drawing, Etching, Color Theory and Three-Dimensional Collage.

Looking for the illustrator in you? Create your own cartoon characters and super heroes (YES!) at the **Cartoon Art Museum** in an ongoing Saturday afternoon class where you can drop in when you want to have some drawing fun. If you're a museum member, it's free, otherwise the class is offered for the price of museum admission. A great place to get involved in ceramics is at the **Clay Studio** where they teach advanced potters as well as novices like us. Or knit, weave and crochet your way to creating one-of-a-kind fiber arts at **Atelier Yarns**. New classes start monthly and beginners are encouraged to give it a try in a comfortable environment where small classes insure plenty of personal attention.

The city's colleges and universities (such as **City College** and **San Francisco State**) and art schools (such as the **Academy of Art College,** the **San Francisco School of Art,** and the **California College of Arts and Crafts**) offer both unusual and traditional classes including Basic Drawing, Illustration, Chinese Brush Painting, Metal Arts and Fine Art Printmaking. Classes are held on a semester basis and require advance registration.

There are some terrific free classes offered for Seniors through the **Older Adults Department** at **City College.** They don't require registration and are open on a drop-in basis. Seniors will also want to check out the many fine art classes sponsored by senior centers throughout the city.

Taking a class is a structured way for someone to commit to making art and developing an artistic side to his(her) personality. So if you've been looking longingly at your neighborhood art group, choose your medium and jump in! Once you get going, you'll be surprised where it takes you. We'll watch for your Opening!

Looking at art, wonderful as a solitary experience, is also an exciting way to connect with others. Just looking together and realizing the beauty you all see can be a great thing to share. And there is so much to talk about. You can have terrific discussions about the historical context, the lines, the artistic unity, or general observations ("What IS it?" or "I could do that.").

As with making art, the knowledge or skills you possess are not the issue. Loving art is not an IQ quiz. Anybody can love what they see.

Artists do art for everybody, not just other artists or Ph.D.s in Art History. Of course, like anything else, the more you know, the more dimensions you may enjoy, but we all can appreciate art at *any* knowledge level. One bonus of being open to enjoying art is that there are lots of others who are interested too, whose company you may well enjoy, if only when you feel like going out to look at and discuss art.

Where to start? The major art museums including the **California Palace of the Legion of Honor, M.H. (d)e Young Memorial Museum, Asian Art Museum of San Francisco** and the **San Francisco Museum of Modern Art** all have exceptional programs, gallery events, lectures and receptions that promote sharing art with others. Be sure not to overlook the programs offered by smaller venues including the **111 Minna Street Gallery** where art viewing and California wine come together in a hip performing arts club and wine bar.

San Franciscans are an intelligent crowd who love to learn through discussion. There is a plethora of art-based discussion groups, many of which target specific genres. For example, the **American Decorative Arts Forum of Northern California** sponsors monthly lectures for those interested in historic artifacts (furniture, silverware and other everyday useful items) from a bygone American era. Photography lovers can take part in one of many events organized by the **Friends of Photography.** Or you could join the informal **Wilder Art** group that encourages artistic types to explore and interpret nature as an art form.

San Francisco has scads of terrific galleries, shows, programs and organizations that showcase fine art. Two programs that strike us as outstanding for meeting other enthusiasts are:

First Thursday, which takes place downtown on the first Thursday of every month. Many galleries open their doors to the general public for art viewing and receptions. You'll make your way from gallery to gallery along with many others whose priorities include setting aside a Thursday night for art observation. Good conversations and friendships have been known to develop out of these evenings. However, even if that doesn't happen to you, what *will* happen is a chance to see some fine artwork by outstanding local artists.

The **Contemporary Extension of the San Francisco Museum of Modern Art** involves a friendly and energetic group of young professionals who share an interest in modern art. There are many single people as well as couples who attend special museum openings, tours and lectures, visit artists' studios, view private collections and enjoy relaxed conversations at cocktail receptions. It's a great way to get to know others who share your enthusiasm in a less formal, more social, context.

The activities listed in this chapter are ongoing with a somewhat regular group attending. There are also scores of one-night events open to the public, listed regularly in the *SAN FRANCISCO BAY GUARDIAN,* the *San Francisco Chronicle's Sunday DATEBOOK* and *SF WEEKLY.* They can also be found described on a myriad of posters hanging in store windows around town. At one-night events you can meet a variety of new people who have just begun to discover the world of the arts. You may be one of them!

Art Lovers of Nature

WilderArt
(415) 648-0850

An informal gathering of painters, photographers, dancers, musicians, poets and other artistic types who meet several times a year to express and reflect on their visions of nature as an art form.

☏ Ward Ruth

Art of Cultures

Center for African & African-American Art & Culture
762 Fulton Street, San Francisco, CA 94102
(415) 928-8546   caac@aol.com   http://www.caaac.com

The Center is dedicated to promoting, enhancing and supporting African and African-American art and culture. Stop by the last Monday night of the month for free jazz or take part in one of the many interesting workshops, such as Capoeira Drumming or Silk Screening and Design. The Library and Archive is available for research.

Galeria de la Raza/Studio 24
2857 24th Street, San Francisco, CA 94110
(415) 826-8009   galeria@thecity.sfsu.edu

This 26 year-old community art gallery highlights the cultural traditions and art forms of the Latino culture. Exhibitions, lectures, artisan demonstrations, poetry readings and artist receptions are scheduled throughout the year.

💰 $35/year membership

Irish Arts Foundation

44 Page Street, #404B, San Francisco, CA 94102
(415) 252-9992   IAF@iaf.org   http://www.iaf.org/~iaf/
Activity Location: New College of California, 776 Valencia Street

In its second year, the New College of Irish Studies Program offers courses that explore the history, language, customs, rituals and traditions of the Celts. The Irish Arts Foundation also sponsors the SF Celtic Music & Arts Festival, Cinemagael: A Celebration of Irish Film, and other informal events.

Society For Asian Art

Asian Art Museum in Golden Gate Park, San Francisco, CA 94118
(415) 379-8805

If you are an Asian art enthusiast you will marvel in the high quality educational and cultural programs offered. Exhibitions such as "Splendors of Imperial China," as well as study groups that discuss topics like "Identifying and Evaluating Ming and Ching Jades" will interest the novice as well as the sophisticated collector. Look for the opening of the Asian Art Museum at its new location on Larkin Street across the plaza from City Hall.

💰 $40/year membership+museum membership

The Polish Arts and Culture Foundation

1290 Sutter Street (at Van Ness Avenue), San Francisco, CA 94109
(415) 474-7070

For over 30 years the Foundation has promoted and celebrated Polish history and culture. The monthly forum meetings, folk dancing classes, the Polish Art Gallery, the research library and other scheduled lectures and events are open to all. Polish language tutoring is also available.

☼ Tuesday, Wednesday, and Friday   ⏰ 12-7pm
💰 $50/year membership

Book Arts

The San Francisco Center For The Book

300 De Haro Street, San Francisco, CA 94103
(415) 565-0545   info@sfcb.org

A fine organization that promotes "the art of the visible word" realized by the writing, production and craftsmanship of books as an art form. These one/two-day classes are in-depth and worthwhile. Learn in "Basic Book" about fundamental soft type setting, letterpress printing and binding. The workshop "Fore-Edge Painting" includes a demonstration of hand gilding 23-carat gold leaf. More than 20 free receptions, readings and lectures are held throughout the year.

☎ Kathleen Burch

Classes

Atelier Yarns "Fiber Arts"

1945 Divisadero Street, San Francisco, CA 94115
(415) 771-1550

Take a class or a series of classes in knitting, weaving, spinning, crochet and dyeing. New classes start monthly and run for four consequtive weeks. This is a great way for men and women to learn how to create beautiful and original textured art works.

☼ Saturdays   🕐 9-11am
   & some weeknights   7-9pm
☎ Grace
💰 $65/4 week class

Art

Cartoon Art Museum "Explorations in Cartooning"

814 Mission Street, San Francisco, CA 94103
(415) 227-8666

You want to have some real fun? Create your own cartoon characters and superheroes (!) in a comfortable environment. No experience is necessary and the resident artist provides expert help. "Cartooning 101" is a great activity for all ages, not just kids! (This wonderful spot was on the endangered species list as this book went to print.)

☼ Saturdays   ☎ 2-4pm
☎ $4/adult; $2/kids

Center For Public Glass Art in the Bay Area

1750 Armstrong Street, San Francisco, CA 94124
(415) 671-4916   publicglas@aol.com

Public Glass has brought the excitement of molten glass art to the city. This non-profit, fully equipped hot glass facility offers classes in glass blowing, hot glass casting, slumping, fuse casting and other glass arts. It is located in 5000 square feet of space in the artistic center of San Francisco's Bayview Hunter's Point area. Less than five blocks from 3Com Park, it is easily accessible by the #15 Muni line. Visitors are welcome to observe this dramatic art process.

☎ Bob
💲 Sliding Scale

City College of San Francisco

50 Phelan Avenue, E200, San Francisco, CA 94112
(415) 239-3000   http://www.ccsf.cc.ca.us
Activity Location: Mission Campus, Fort Mason Site and other campuses

You can sign up for many classes at this fine school including Figure Drawing, Watercolor and Acrylic Painting, Sculpture, Ceramics, and many more. Call for the schedule of classes offered each semester.

💲 $13/credit hour for California residents

Galileo Gem Guild

(415) 863-7618

Activity Location: The Randall Museum, 199 Museum Way
(415) 554-9600   *http://www.wco.com /~dale/randall.html*

This group is for the gem, mineral and jewelry making hobbyist. Stop by and informally meet members or learn the basics of cutting and polishing gemstones in one of the reasonably priced classes sponsored by the Guild. Wear your "grubbies" to class.

☼ Tuesday, Thursday & Saturday   ☏ 10am-1pm; 7-9:45pm
☎ Ken

Precita Eyes Mural Arts Center

348 Precita Avenue, San Francisco, CA 94110
(415) 285-2287

The Center offers ongoing, drop-in workshops and classes for artists of all levels. If you're interested in mural painting, take a Community Mural Painting workshop and learn collaboration techniques, theme development, preparation, transfer and painting, with hands-on involvement. The workshop meets three evenings at Precita Eyes and four days on-site.

☼ Saturdays
💰 $5/session; $30/membership for 10 classes

Ruby's Clay Studio & Gallery

552 A Noe Street, San Francisco, CA 94114
(415) 558-9819

An excellent pottery and sculpture studio offering workshops, lectures, exhibits and classes such as Wheel Throwing and Handbuilding. Take part in a lecture that explores firing and glazing techniques. Call for a catalog.

💰 About $185/series of classes

San Francisco Art Institute, Extension Education

800 Chestnut Street, San Francisco, CA 94133
(415) 749-4554   yap@sfai.edu   http://www.sfai.edu

This excellent art institution offers a comprehensive variety of 10-week classes designed for the dabbler, busy professional (Saturday classes) or serious full-time art student. Just a sample of classes offered are Beginning Painting, Color Photography, Fine Art Filmmaking, Three-Dimensional Collage, Figure Drawing and Fine Art Filmmaking.

☼ Saturdays
☎ Ariege Arseguel

San Francisco School of Art

667 Mission Street, San Francisco. CA 94105
(415) 543-9300

For all of you who have ever wanted to learn how to draw, paint, sculpt, study color perception, work in mixed media/collage and printmaking, this excellent and respected school is run with you in mind. Beginners are encouraged to attend. Many of the students are full-time employed professionals from various fields who take classes to relax and exercise their creative spirit. Afternoon, evening and Saturday classes are offered for convenience.

☎ Bruce Tessler
💲 About $195/credit hour

Sharon Art Studio

501 Stanyan Street, San Francisco, CA 94117
(415) 753-7004
Activity Location: Arts & Crafts Division, McLaren Lodge, Golden Gate Park

Offered by the San Francisco Recreation & Park Department, these classes cannot be beat for the quality and price. Drawing, Painting, Glass Cutting, Ceramics, Metal Arts and Jewelry Making are just a sample of the classes offered. Classes meet from seven to ten times.

☎ Caroline
💲 About $50-$120

Stroke of Genius

2326 Fillmore Street, San Francisco, CA 94115
(415) 776-2529

It's easy and a lot of fun to be part of a roomful of people painting dinner plates, flower pots, vases and other assorted items. Just buy the piece you want to paint and the rest is up to you. Meeting others is natural and you leave with a handmade, personalized object of art. Some instruction available.

☀ Open 7 days
☎ Jennifer
💰 $7/hour plus supplies

🕐 Open until 9pm Tuesdays, Wednesdays, & Thursdays

The Clay Studio

743 Harrison Street, San Francisco, CA 94107
(415) 777-9080

Premier pottery studio offering beginning, intermediate and advanced classes in Ceramics, including Handbuilding and Pottery-on-the-Wheel. Take part in this friendly and relaxed environment which promotes learning and creativity. For the professional artist there are 32 individual work spaces available for the production and promotion of ceramic art.

💰 About $165

The Randall Museum

199 Museum Way, San Francisco, CA 94114
(415) 554-9600   *http://www.wco.com/~dale/randall.html*

Many wonderful interactive classes are offered including B&W Photography, Joy of Drawing I & II, Handmade Papermaking, Adult Ceramics, Jewelry Making for Lapidary and many more. Call for a catalog for specific dates, times and costs.

💰 About $45; classes meet 6-9 times

Art

Gallery Programs

111 Minna Street Gallery

111 Minna Street, San Francisco, CA 94105
(415) 974-1719

The artists and art-loving crowd make this place special. A combination arts club and California wine bar, this is the right place for anyone interested in fine and performing arts. Stop by and look at the latest exhibit and ask for a list of upcoming events which may include films sponsored by the Film Arts Foundation.

☎ Eiming Young

San Francisco Art Dealers Association "First Thursdays"

1717 17th Street, San Francisco, CA 94103
(415) 626-7498   *http://www.artline.com*
Activity Locations: Galleries around Geary, Sutter & Grant Streets
(415)626-7498

Many galleries stay open late, greeting visitors with refreshments and lively activity. This Thursday night activity invites a crowd for art and socializing. There are 31 member galleries who participate, including the Braunstein/Quay Gallery (250 Sutter), Edith Caldwell Gallery (251 Post), Catharine Clark Gallery (49 Geary) and the Erickson & Elins Gallery (345 Sutter). For a complete listing visit the web page or give them a call.

☼ 1st Thursday/month   ☎ 5-7:30pm
☎ Beth Beasley
💰 Free

Lectures & Discussions

Achenbach Graphic Arts Council

California Palace of the Legion of Honor–Lincoln Park,
San Francisco, CA 94121
(415) 750-3676   *http://www.thinker.org*

One or two events each month are presented for members, but non-members can attend. From gallery walk-throughs to visiting artists' studios, this is a valuable way to learn more about prints, drawings, photographs and other works of art on paper.

🖐 $50/year membership

American Decorative Arts Forum of Northern California

M.H. de Young Memorial Museum, San Francisco, CA 94118
(415) 431-6930

Activity Location: M.H. de Young Memorial Museum, Golden Gate Park

Join this group for insightful lectures by informative guest speakers including post-lecture receptions and mini-exhibitions from members' collections. Day and weekend tours and trips are organized periodically.

☼ 2nd Tuesday/month   ⏰ 8pm
🖐 $40/year membership

California College of Arts and Crafts

450 Irwin Street , San Francisco, CA 94107
(415) 703-9520   *enroll@ccacsf.edu   http://www.ccacsf.edu*

Take part in the excellent programs, including monthly lectures and discussions ("Gutenberg to the Golden Age of the Poster"), exhibitions, symposia, artist receptions and much more. Call for an upcoming events calendar.

🖐 Free or inexpensive

Art

Capp Street Project

525 2nd Street, San Francisco, CA 94107
(415) 495-7101　　　　　　　*http://tesla.csuhayward.edu/cappstreet*

An unique opportunity to experience installation art where an entire open space is used as a canvas for creativity. You'll be amazed to see how the space is transformed every several months. Stop by and see the current exhibit and check out the forum led by the resident artist.

☀ Tuesday-Saturday　　　　　　　☎ 12-6pm
💰 Free general admission; $35/year membership

Center for the Arts Yerba Buena Gardens

701 Mission Street, San Francisco, CA 94103
(415) 978-2787　yerbamembr@aol.com　　　*http://www.yerbabuenaarts.org*

The Museum offers ongoing lectures, tours, readings, workshops and film and video programs. Become a museum member and be privy to special events.

💰 $35/year membership

San Francisco Art Institute

800 Chestnut Street, San Francisco, CA 94133
(415) 749-4588　　　　*yap@sfai.edu*　　　　*http://www.sfai.edu*

An excellent way to spend an entertaining and informative evening. Call for a schedule of upcoming events.

☎ Ariege Arseguel
💰 $6

San Francisco Ceramic Circle

P.O. Box 15163, San Francisco, CA 94115
(415) 750-3600
Activity Location: California Palace of the Legion of Honor , 100 34th Avenue
(415) 750-3600

Get involved and learn more about the collection and appreciation of fine pottery and porcelain. As an expert you can share your knowledge with other enthusiasts. New members are always welcome to join this group which is affiliated with the Fine Arts Museums of San Francisco.

💰 $25/year membership

SF Camerawork

115 Natoma Street, San Francisco, CA 94105
(415) 764-1001

This fine, nonprofit artist's organization brings you into the world of contemporary photography and related media through exhibitions and programs. Everyone is encouraged to stop by and view the latest exhibition and browse the bookstore.

☼ Tuesday-Saturday   ⏰ 12-5pm
💰 Free general admission; $40/year membership

The Friends of Photography
Ansel Adams Centers for Photography

250 4th Street, San Francisco, CA 94103
(415) 495-7000   seefop@aol.com

This fine photography museum offers the best in historical and contemporary works as well as outstanding programs. A sampling of the ongoing events include exhibitions, seminars such as "The Art of the Fine Print: Black-and-White Darkroom Technique," and lectures. Be sure to check-out the "Snapshots" series of lunchtime talks .

☼ Tuesday-Sunday   ⏰ 11am-5pm
💰 $35/year membership

Resource

SOMAR - South of Market Art Resource

934 Brannan Street, San Francisco, CA 94103
(415) 552-2131

Are you an artist looking for support to produce your work? This resource center provides space, special equipment and help in professional planning to help artists bring their art to life. With a gallery for exhibitions, a theater for performance, a dance studio and rehearsal space (and more), this is an excellent place to see and experience fine local art. Pick up a detailed flyer of their events and check the listing board when you're at the center.

Art

Young Professionals' Art & Social Clubs

The San Francisco Museum of Modern Art (SFMOMA) "Contemporary Extension"

151 3rd Street, San Francisco, CA 94103
(415) 357-4086   *http://www.sfmoma.org*

Join this friendly and energetic group of young professionals, between 25 and 40, who are interested in modern art. Some of their wonderful activities include special museum tours, visiting artists' studios, viewing private collections, cocktail receptions, and the annual Beaux Arts Ball.

☏ Marjaneh Moghimi
💲 $50/year membership + museum membership

Contemporaries: The Young Professionals Auxiliary of The Jewish Museum San Francisco.

121 Steuart Street, San Francisco, CA 94105
(415) 543-2090 ext.213   jmsf21@aol.com

This exciting group of Jewish young professionals hosts art-related social events to promote education, fund-raising, and membership in the Museum. Past programs have included the photographic exhibition, "Russia in Black & White," a private screening of "Taxi Blues," and a "Summer Gallery Walk" including a cocktail party. Sounds like fun!

☏ Natasha

Cheap or Free

Cheap or Free

San Francisco School Of Circus Arts-Flying Trapeze Class
Photograph by Alyson Boell

Cheap or Free

Although San Francisco is an expensive city (It costs money to live in Paradise!), you can do the things you love without spending a bundle. Most of the things listed in this guide are reasonably priced to downright cheap, but this chapter highlights activities that are more than great deals. They are places where getting together for learning and self-expression, laughter and fun, are not governed by the boundaries of money. Taking a walk or riding your bike through Golden Gate Park, the Presidio or along Ocean Beach are unparalleled activities—and they are free.

Tell the truth: have you been to the new **Main Library** since it opened? If not, look forward to discovering an architecturally and technologically superior wonder. Have you wandered through a sampling of the forests of the world at the **Strybing Arboretum?** Have you seen the Impressionist or Modern art at the **Palace of the Legion of Honor** (2nd Wednesdays/month) or the **SF MOMA**(1st Tuesdays/month) on their monthly free admission days? Try jumping onboard the **Red & White Fleet** (Pier 431/2) and cruising the Bay to Sausalito, Angel Island or Tiburon for an afternoon for about $11 round-trip. So much pleasure for so little money!

Skimming through this chapter you can see that there are outdoor activities like the **Ferry Plaza Farmers' Market** and cultural events like noontime concerts at **Old St. Mary's Cathedral**—but then maybe you already knew about these! However, *did* you know about the **San Francisco School of Circus Art's** weekly juggling night for only $2? And did you know that you can try inline skating by taking the free Saturday morning class offered by **Marina Skate & Snowboard?** How about learning croquet with the **San Francisco Croquet Club?** It's the largest, non-profit club of its kind on public turf in America and the home of the San Francisco Open Croquet Tournament. Start with a free class and you just might be the next SFCC croquet champion!

Some Cheap or Free events are only once a year–like the **San Francisco International Motorcycle Show** in January. Sample ethnic food, music and dance in February during the three-day **Russian Festival.** **Tulipmania** offers free tours of the City's largest tulip plantings in March. Take part in the 40-plus years tradition of the **San Francisco International Film Festival** in April. Get your costume ready for the

Cheap or Free

annual **Bay to Breakers** race in May and your float for the **Lesbian, Gay, Bisexual and Transgender Pride Celebration Parade** in June. Be sure to make your way down to the Hyde Street Pier for the annual **Fourth of July Fireworks Celebration.** Find your place on the lawn for the **San Francisco Shakespeare Festival** held on Labor Day weekend. Enjoy the **San Francisco Blues Festival** in September and jump around at **Reggae in the Park** in October. Meet other booklovers who gather at the **San Francisco Bay Area Book Festival** in November, and let your voice be heard at the Sing-it Yourself *Messiah* held in the **Davies Symphony Hall** in December.

Going places with themes automatically gives you something to talk to new group companions about and provides natural opportunities to participate together in an event. So playing group Scrabble going to a games party, joining a bird walk, all give you a reason for comfortable interaction. It is fitting and respectable for an opera lover to chat with someone new at intermission about the performance at the **San Francisco Opera,** share an opinion at a book reading group, express yourself to anyone and no one about the boat race at a summer regatta, yell for the home team at **Giants** or **49'rs** games, or laugh out loud at **Cobb's Comedy Club** surrounded by others enjoying a lighter moment of life. The more enthusiasm you have, the more opportunities you will find to meet people in places that are Cheap or Free!

Artists' Television Access
"Basic MAC and Internet for the Overwhelmed"

992 Valencia Street, San Francisco, CA 94110
(415) 824-3890   ata@atasite.org   http://www.atasite.org

How can you not respect a center that offers a 3-hour computer class that is "clear, cheap and cuts the crap." Other computer and media classes are offered in English and Spanish at this hip location for media arts.

☼ Saturdays

💰 $15

Center for the Arts Yerba Buena Gardens "Summer Stage"

701 Mission Street, San Francisco, CA 94103
(415) 978-2787   yerbamembr@aol.com   http://www.yerbabuenaarts.org

From May through October, find free lunch-time concerts featuring both traditional and experimental local dance and music artists. Grab a sandwich, find a seat in the bleachers, and enjoy the entertainment.

☼ Thursdays   ⏰ 12-1:30pm

City College of San Francisco, Older Adults Division

Mission Campus, 106 Bartlet Street, San Francisco, CA 94110
(415) 550-4415

The Older Adults Department conducts life-enriching classes for senior citizens (55+) throughout the city. Enrollment is open to new students throughout the semester and you register by just showing up. Take a computer, literature, Tai Chi, music, sewing or writing class or one of many others to be found at City College.

💰 Free

Exploratorium

3601 Lyon Street, San Francisco, CA 94123
(415) 561-0360
Activity Location: McBean Theater

Interesting new or unusual short science films are shown each weekend afternoon at this world-famous interactive science museum. Free to all paying museum visitors.

Cheap or Free

Ferry Plaza Farmers' Market
San Francisco Market Collaborative
41 Sutter Street,#1744, San Francisco, CA 94104
(415) 981-3004
Activity Location: Ferry Building at the foot of Market Street

Another great place to meet others interested in the pleasure of fresh, organic produce and products. The vendors are fast to start a conversation and soon everyone is talking. You never know which friends you might run into, and for anyone who is new to the city this is a wonderful way to begin to feel like home. You'll find another market on Tuesdays between 11am-3pm at Market and Steuart Streets.

☼ Saturdays & Sundays   ☎ Sat 8am-1pm
☎ Sibella Kraus   Sun 9am-1pm

Friends of Recreation and Parks
Golden Gate Park (McLaren Lodge), San Francisco, CA 94117
(415) 750-5105

Involve yourself with others who are interested in more than just scratching the surface of Golden Gate Park. Get off the main track with this group and learn about Strawberry Hill, Stern Grove and Lloyd Lake. The cogniscenti know there's more to the Park than JFK Drive.

☼ May-October
🎗 Free

Golden Gate Park Band "Sunday Concerts in the Park"
San Francisco, CA
(415) 831-2790
Activity Location: Music concourse band shell between the M.H. De Young Museum and the California Academy of Sciences.

Every summer Sunday people of all ages come together to listen to the 114-year old tradition of performances in the Park. What a marvelous way to enjoy the afternoon—listening to the music with other regular attendees. Bring a picnic and dine under the shade of the cypress trees.

☼ Summer Sundays   ☎ 1pm

HomeChef

3525 California Street, San Francisco, CA 94118
(415) 668-3191

If you have a desire to learn how to cook or already enjoy cooking but want to learn more, take advantage of the free hour-long lecture/demonstration classes that are offered at the HomeChef. An added bonus is the tasting at the end of each class.

Mad Magda's Russian Tea Room & Cafe

579 Hayes Street, San Francisco, CA 94102
(415) 864-7654

Tarot readings are offered everyday at this exotic, off-beat cafe. Stop by the counter and buy a numbered ticket for $13. Readings last about 15 minutes, but if it's not too busy they'll run over a bit. Getting a reading here is fun.

☀ Everyday   🕑 Wednesday-Saturday
💰 $13   until midnight

Marina Skate & Snowboard

2271 Chestnut Street, San Francisco, CA 94123
(415) 567-8400

The staff here knows every new skater needs lots of help and encouragement when they get up on wheels. Learn how to glide and turn and stop. You can't go skating if you can't STOP! Joining other beginners is a good (and safe) way to get started in a new sport.

☀ Saturdays   🕑 8:30-10am
💰 Free (and free skate use with the class)

Cheap or Free

Market Street Association "People In Plazas"

870 Market Street, Suite 456, San Francisco, CA 94102
(415) 362-2500
Activity Location: In or near plazas around Market Street

Come out and hear the Bay Area's finest musicians perform every thing from Rhythm & Blues to Retro-Rock. Give Lynn a call and she will put you on the mailing list and send you a schedule of events.

☼ Monday-Fridays (July-September)   ☎ 12-1pm
☎ Lynn Valente

Museum of the City of San Francisco

2801 Leavenworth Street, San Francisco, CA 94133
(415) 928-0289   *http://www.sfmuseum.org*
Activity Location: The Cannery

Whether you are new to the city or have been here all your life, you'll learn a lot from these talks about the city. It's a great way to learn more about San Francisco's past and meet others who love the history.

☼ Wednesday-Sunday   ☎ 10am-4pm
💰 Free

Old St. Mary's Cathedral "Noontime Concerts"

660 California Street, San Francisco, CA 94108
(415) 288-3840

The fine concerts here are predominately classical music. Go several times and you'll become part of the large contingent of regulars.

☼ Tuesdays & Thursdays   ☎ 12:30pm
💰 $3 donation

Outdoors Unlimited "Knots for Boaters"

550 Parnassus Avenue, San Francisco, CA 94122
(415) 4762078
Activity Location: University of California, San Francisco Campus (UCSF)

Here is your chance to learn how to tie your basic bowline and slip knot and meet others interested in learning boating skills. Call for their catalog or look for upcoming classes listed on the Community Bulletin Board.

💰 Free

Pier 29 Antiques & Collectibles Market

San Francisco, CA
(415) 956-5316

Activity Location: Pier 29, the Embarcadero

If you love collecting and meeting others who share this activity, then this is the place for you. With over 400 dealer spaces, you can spend as little or as much time as you want, browsing or selling. The people are friendly and love to chat about their stuff, er, valuables. A super place to go if you find yourself alone on a Sunday afternoon. Take a large carry-all bag!

☼ Sundays
☎ Carol or Gerry Barrard
💰 $10 before 9:30am; $2 after

🕐 Early bird 7-9:30am;
general 9:30am-5pm

Precita Eyes Mural Arts Center

348 Precita Avenue, San Francisco, CA 94110
(415) 285-2287

Before you go anywhere, you are informed by an introductory slide talk and tour given by a professional muralist. Then you're ready to walk and view over 70 murals in an eight-block area. This Center also offers classes and studio space for beginning and experienced artists for a small cost.

☼ Saturdays
💰 $4/general; $3/senior; $1/child/student

🕐 1:30-3:30pm

San Francisco Croquet Club

3350 Octavia Street, #5, San Francisco, CA 94123
(415) 776-4104   *http://www.ontheweb.com/usca*

Activity Location: Stern Grove, 19th Avenue and Wawona Street

SFCC is the largest, non-profit club of its kind on public turf in America, and is home of the San Francisco Open and other major tournaments. Beginning adult players are encouraged to attend a free croquet lesson or call about the Saturday morning program: "Introduction to Six-Wicket Croquet." You'll need to wear flat-soled shoes to protect the green (true), and your gatsby hat (untrue).

☼ 1st & 3rd Wednesdays/month
☎ Bob
💰 Free

🕐 1-4pm

Cheap or Free

San Francisco Design Center "Idea House San Francisco"

Two Henry Adams Street, Suite 450, San Francisco, CA 94103
(415) 490-5823
Activity Location: Galleria Building, 101 Henry Adams Street
(415) 864-1500

Idea House San Francisco is the country's first design project to showcase three stylish residences simultaneously. The first showcase is so popular that they are currently working on plans for future themes. If you're interested in design this is a great place to meet others who share your flair. Get on the mailing list for upcoming social events with these terrific folks who spotlight the project while raising money for the San Francisco Opera.

☼ Monday-Friday   ⏰ 10am-5pm
☎ Susan Hruby
💰 Free

San Francisco Flower Mart

640 Brannan Street, San Francisco, CA 94107
(415) 392-7944

If you love fresh flowers, this is the place for conversing with flower experts and learning about your favorite bloom. The Flower Mart is open only to the trade before 9am, but there are plenty of flowers to buy and enjoy during the public hours.

☼ Monday-Saturday   ⏰ 9am-3pm
💰 Free

San Francisco Lawn Bowling Club

Golden Gate Park, Bowling Green Drive, San Francisco, CA
(415) 753-9298

If you're curious about this sport, mosey over to the Park on Wednesdays and watch or join the free class. If you want to try it, you'll need flat soled shoes to protect the grass.

☼ Wednesdays   ⏰ 12pm
💰 Free

Cheap or Free

San Francisco One Dollar Statue Walks
"Sunday Statue Walk"

365 Hanover Street, Oakland, CA 944606
(510) 834-3617
Activity Location: Meet at Ferry Building, 1 Embarcadero, San Francisco

L earn more about the city through its statue art. Peter Garland, poet-historian, might be dressed in a renaissance costume to guide you through this educational and entertaining walk. Each statue represents a world of adventure, stories, history and beauty to be discovered. Also ask about the Haig Patigan Statue Walk.

☼ Sundays   🕑 1pm
☎ Peter Garland
💰 No fee, donations welcome

San Francisco Recreation and Park Department

50 Scott Street , San Francisco, CA 94117
(415) 554-9523
Activity Location: Various recreational centers

H ave you secretly wanted to learn how to Tap dance? How about learning Square, Folk or Afro-Brazilian dances? For a small fee you can join others who enjoy movement through dance. Call for a schedule of upcoming classes and events.

San Francisco School of Circus Arts

755 Frederick Street, San Francisco, CA 94117
(415) 759-8123   *http://www.sfcircus.org*
Activity Location: West Polytechnic Gymnasium

H ave you ever thought of giving juggling a try? Take advantage of this excellent chance to learn or improve your technique at the weekly "Juggle Night." All ages are welcome. Be sure to ask about the drop-in trampoline and flying trapeze classes. Whizzzz!

☼ Sundays   🕑 7-10pm
💰 $2

Cheap or Free

San Francisco Shakespeare Festival "Shakespeare in the Park"

P.O. Box 590479, San Francisco, CA 94159
(415) 422-2222
Activity Location: Golden Gate Park

All you need is something to sit on to enjoy this outdoor theater event but get there early for the best space on the grass. Whether you're coupled or alone, these Shakespeare lovers will delight you and fill your hearts with romance. These are magnificent artistic performances in a splendid setting for connecting with other theatergoers.

☼ Labor Day Weekend
☎ Kimberly

Society for the Prevention of Cruelty to Animals (SPCA)

2500 16th Street, San Francisco, CA 94103
(415) 554-3073

There is something special about people who really love their animals. You will find them in SPCA "Dog Behavior Classes" where you and your dog can learn some new techniques together. For cats who are behaviorally challenged, call Kate (415) 665-5559.

☼ Last Saturday/month   ⏰ 3-5pm
☎ Bob Gutierrez

Strybing Arboretum and Botanical Gardens

Golden Gate Park @9th Avenue at Lincoln Way, San Francisco, CA 94122
(415) 661-1316 ext.312

Activity Location: Strybing bookstore (Main Entrance); Friend Gate (North Entrance); Golden Gate Park @9th Avenue at Lincoln Way

Join botanists and regular plant lovers to explore the flora indigenous to the Bay Area and countries worldwide. The presentation of these plants is magnificent.

☼ Everyday   ⏰ Mon-Fri 1:30pm;
☎ Wendy Holmes   Weekends 10:30am & 1:30pm;
💰 Free   Wed, Fri, Sun 2pm

Swedenborgian Church
"Hour Of Peace—Gentle Piano Music"

2107 Lyon Street, San Francisco, CA 94115
(415) 346-6466   *http://www.sfswedenborgian.com*

G entle music in a serene environment. Put some peace in your hectic
world. Need we say more?

☼ 2nd Tuesday/month   ☎ 7pm
💰 Free

The Foundation for San Francisco's Architectural Heritage

2007 Franklin Street, San Francisco, CA 94109
(415) 441-3004

Activity Location: California Historical Society, 678 Mission Street,

T ake part in in this colorful walking tour that highlights the diverse
and interesting architecture, both new and historic, in the South of
Market area contiguous to Yerba Buena Gardens. The walk lasts about an
hour rain or shine. Be sure to ask about the other walks including
Victorian and Edwardian Pacific Heights which feature Victorian and
pre-World War I Mansions and magnificent family homes. These walks
last about two hours. Bring a sweater just in case the fog rolls into town.

☼ 1st Saturday/month   ☎ 10am
💰 $5/adult; $3/seniors & children

The San Francisco African-American
Historical and Cultural Society

762 Fulton Street, San Francisco, CA 94102
(415) 292-6172

Activity Location: Center for African Art and Culture

T hese splendid Thursday night poetry readings feature special guests
who read and discuss their work. Afterwards the members of the
audience are encouraged to share their work. Refreshments are served
while you meet others for conversations about poetry.

☼ 2nd Thursday/month   ☎ 7pm
☎ Eric DuPree
💰 Free

Cheap or Free

Above: Ferry Plaza Farmers' Market, Photograph by William A. Porter
Right: Golden Gate Bridge Fort Point Joggers Photo by Kerrick James. Courtesy of S.F. Conv. & Visitors Bureau

Coffee & Tea Cafés

Coffeehouses

Internet Cafés

Tea-Time

Coffee & Tea Cafés

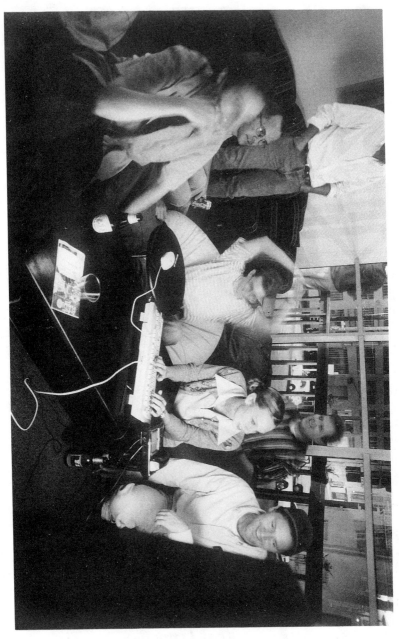

Cyber-nomads discovering the full potenital of the net
at INTERNET alfredo

Coffee & Tea Cafés

D on't know if you remember, but it used to be that when you wanted to socialize and no one had asked you out-to or over-to dinner, there was only one place to go—the clubs. Clubs are places where people can hang out together to schmooze, listen to music and maybe dance. Alcohol is a big factor in this scene—good news and bad news, depending on your point of view. One down side of the booze factor is that it puts clubs off the list for people who don't "drink" because of age or preference, and for those who are in recovery from overdrinking. Not being able to go to clubs left a lot of people without casual, saunter-on-down-and-hang-out-with-old-and-new-friends places to go.

Well, coffeehouses are back, like they were in the 60s—or better! Coffeehouses with or without entertainment, coffeehaunts within bookstores, tea houses and lovely hotel tea-afternoons. Places you can go to take a load off, refresh and renew, look over your favorite magazine with a spot of tea and have a crumpet or savory sweet. You can meet a friend to chat in the mid-afternoon, sample some delectable flavors of tea or coffee (who needs wine tasting?), and hang out any night of the week by yourself or with people you like, often with live entertainment. Read your favorite novel (from the shelves), check your email or do a research paper while you make your way through the foam of a perfectly made cappuchino at a coffee-drinkers' bookstore. You can go for an entire evening or stop by on the way home from another event. Coffee and Tea Cafes fit right into our lives.

In San Francisco there are coffeehouses in the neighborhoods like there are bars on the corners of most cities. Look around, find the ones near you, and go regularly with your daily paper. It's a good way to meet your neighbors. If you're lucky, "your" coffee or tea cafe will have something interesting, like music, poetry, open mic, games or the Internet. Not only does that add dimension to the place but it gives you an interesting way to have a discussion with the people there. (Are you sick of this theme yet? Remember, this is a Connecting book!) We've included a few of our favorite coffee and tea cafes scattered around the city, but we encourage you to hunt for ones near you offering the activities you like best.

The poetry reading scene in San Francisco is rich, as detailed in the

Coffee & Tea Cafés

Writing & Poetry Chapter. There is original work being presented in open mic forums in coffeehouses as well, such as at **Cafe Sapore, Cafe International** and **Cafe Francisco** on the weekends. If you have material to share, we suggest that you visit a few times to get a sense of the place, and then find out how to get on the line-up. Cafe International and Cafe Francisco have music and comedy too, performed by local entertainers, and Club Sapore has occasional book readings. The **Coffee Zone** in the Haight has fiction-reading on Tuesday nights and music on Wednesdays. If you want to know what you're going to hear, give them a call. If you just want a nice place to be, walk (or bus) on down and check it out.

Activities of other kinds have invaded the beaneries. Computers with rentable time where you can wander around your favorite web pages can be found at **Cyberworld** and **INTERNET alfredo**. We like the way these establishments have made the process user-friendly by providing structured help in the form of classes or informal assistance from knowledgeable users. The web has produced many sub-cultures, including users helping novice users. And where is it more fun and less intimidating to find net experts than in the cyber cafes? Also, many coffeehouses have newspapers and magazines available, soft couches and chairs on which to read them, and games for occasional players. **Muddy's Coffeehouse** has organized regular game nights where you'd better be on time to get in on the challenge.

The month of November is notable in the coffee/tea and arts alliance because the National Poetry Association sponsors the **Annual Cafe Arts Month**. More than 300 writing/music/art performance events take place in cafes all around the city. What is especially nice is the range of presentations, from audience reactive events to exhibits and performances of outstanding artists. There is something for everyone with lots of people interaction around the arts. A very special event that makes San Francisco proud.

Even if you haven't been much of a tea drinker, make your way to **Tea & Company** where there are regular classes and tea tastings in the early evening. Just the time for a picker-upper *and* you get to discover the vast tastes in tea, from sturdy morning teas to sweet toffee teas for dessert, sans calories. It's lots of fun meeting interesting people with whom you can compare tea impressions. Or you can "make the rounds" of some of the loveliest settings for afternoon tea in the country, including hotels offering opulent surroundings and gorgeous views. Having tea is a lovely thing to do, especially if you really get into it. Wear a hat, a fancy jacket, an ascot, your best earrings or a long, slender Garbo coat. Be your most elegant self and have a great time! (Or go in your casuals, whatever suits. It's OK with us.)

Whoever was responsible for the resurgence of the coffee and tea cafes (remember they were big in the San Francisco 60s)—we are GRATEFUL. (Yes, we're shouting.) Going out for coffee is again a major venue for being with people we like and we are doing it in record numbers. It's definitely cool.

A note for people who are *serious* about non-alcoholic socializing: This is the chapter that inspired all of the Connecting books. Ruth wanted to know if casual, drop-in socializing ended if a person decided to stop drinking alcohol. You'll notice that most of the listings in this book are non-drinking activities—places where serious non-drinkers will be comfortable. It is very important to know that there *are* places where alcohol is not served and you can go hang out there and enjoy yourself when you're in the mood to be with people. It is also important to be with friends on a regular basis who enjoy the activities you love. Here are a couple of suggestions for developing a new social life:

Be prepared. Take steps to develop your network of friends who also enjoy a diversity of non-alcoholic socializing activities. Where do you find them? Ask people in your new circle of non-drinking friends what they do for fun and join them doing it. Look into renewing contact with old chums that you remember as healthy and active. Get together with current friends and invite friends of friends to meet each other for a juice and soda brunch. Check out your favorite activities in this book and get to know some of the participants. Ask them to go for a movie or coffee. Having about four or five people ("regulars") to go places with really helps in going out to meet other new people—maybe to a sober dance, to Muddy's to play Scrabble, to the art journey on First Thursdays or to jump around Greek Folk dancing at Fort Mason.

Have an activity that repeats on a regular basis, like the Sunday breakfast ride across the Golden Gate Bridge, a class in the Internet, a meditation or yoga group or a class in something you've always wanted to learn. Having regular non-drinking social activity keeps you from feeling stale and bored and reminds you of how good you feel being active and involved and present!

Coffee & Tea Cafés

Café life in Haight-Ashbury. Photo by Kerrick James.
Courtesy of S.F. Conv. & Visitors Bureau

Coffeehouses

Café Francisco

2160 Powell Street, San Francisco, CA 94133
(415) 397-2602

Many regulars frequent this charming and friendly North Beach spot, perfect for a cup of coffee or a light meal throughout the day. They host music on Friday and Saturday nights with occasional comedy and poetry open mic events.

☀ Everyday

🕐 Closes 9pm Thurs-Sat;
Closes 8pm Sun-Wed

Café International

508 Haight Street, San Francisco, CA 94117
(415) 552-7390

A great location to enjoy a light snack and a coffee drink. Readers, musicians and an eclectic range of performers are part of the package if you make your way to the cafe on most Friday nights around 9pm. Prepare your material and take part in the open mic that follows.

☀ Fridays

🕐 Closes 11pm

Caffé Sapore

790 Lombard Street, San Francisco, CA 94133
(415) 4741-222

A nice neighborhood spot that features poetry and book readings. Events are ongoing but are subject to poets' and authors' schedules, so call ahead for programs.

☀ Everyday

🕐 Closes 9pm

Castro Country Club

4058 18th Street, San Francisco, CA 94114
(415) 552-6102

This clean and sober social club is a fine alternative to bars. Come and chat over coffee with people who you know have clear eyes and dry brains.

☀ Everyday

🕐 Sun.-Thur. till 11pm
Fri. & Sat. till 12am

Coffee & Tea Cafés

National Poetry Association
Annual San Francisco Cafe Arts Month

934 Brannan Street, 2nd Floor, San Francisco, CA 94103
(415) 673-3080   http://www.slip.net/~gamuse

C offee and tea drinkers have enjoyed this exciting annual event for over five years. More than 300 art exhibits, poetry readings and musical performances will be sponsored by neighborhood cafes and businesses. These include: Golden Cup Awards (coffee tasting); performance collaboration between writers, poets and visual artists; interactive Romance Events between artists and the audience; and regular Cafe Crawls, featuring the best coffee you've ever had. Call for a calendar and check-out the local papers for more details.

☼ All of November

☎ Johnny Davis

The Club Coffeehouse

920 Valencia Street, San Francisco, CA 94110
(415) 821-7112

T his popular neighborhood coffeehouse features the work of local artists. The crowd is friendly and you can feel comfortable going alone. Check the dessert menu while enjoying your coffee, tea or soft drink. Very fine!

☼ Everyday   ⏰ Closes at midnight

The Coffee Zone

1409 Haight Street, San Francisco, CA 94117
(415) 863-2443

I f you stop by a few times, you'll begin to recognize the regulars who frequent the Zone. Scheduled fiction open mic on Tuesdays, music open mic on Wednesdays and a featured reader on Saturdays. Check in around 7:30pm to see what's happening. The program will vary depending on who shows up to perform.

☼ Everyday   ⏰ Closes 11pm

Internet Cafes

Cyberworld

528 Folsom Street, San Francisco, CA 94105
(415) 278-9669   cworldcafe@aol.com   http://www.cyberworldsf.com

Grab a cup of coffee, relax on one of the comfortable couches at Cyberworld, and play your favorite computer game. Come here to have a meal, attend a lunchtime educational session or enjoy an evening party. Check it out for breakfast, lunch and dinner and take in a panoramic view of the Bay Bridge.

☼ Mon-Fri;   ⏰ 9am-6pm;
Sat & Sun   10am-6pm

INTERNET alfredo

790-A Brannan Street, San Francisco CA 94103
(415) 437-3140   al@ina.com   http://www.ina.com

If computers are your thing, you'll want to visit this exciting 24-hour Cyberlounge where you are guaranteed to meet others who share your interest. The computers on site are for rent and classes are offered. It's easy to have a chat and learn something new from one of the regulars. Alfredo also boasts espresso drinks "served to perfection" in the cyberlounge where they frequently host parties.

☼ Everyday   ⏰ 24-hours

Tea-Time

Fairmont Hotel

150 Mason Street, San Francisco, CA 94108
(415) 772-5000

Step back in time and indulge yourself in the luxury of the Fairmont Hotel. The fine service, delectable goodies and ornate decor all add to the experience of elegance. Having tea, once considered a high-brow excursion, now is enjoyed by all as an afternoon time-out tradition. Go alone or with others, but go.

☼ 7 Days; Mon-Sat   ⏰ 3-6pm;
Sunday   1-6pm

Coffee & Tea Cafés

Lovejoy's Antiques & Tea Room

1195 Church Street @24th, San Francisco, CA 94114
(415) 648-5895

An authentic English tea room where you can go alone or bring a friend. Enjoy the fragrance, antique decor, delicious teas, pastries and traditional English tea room "fayre." Lovejoy's is the perfect reason for an excursion to Noe Valley.

☼ Closed Mondays　　　　　　　☎ Until 7pm
☎ Clint

Mad Magda's Russian Tea Room & Café

579 Hayes Street, San Francisco, CA 94102
(415) 864-7654

Tarot card readings are offered every day at this exotic, off-beat cafe. Buy your ticket for $13 and enjoy hearing about your life's direction through time-old symbols and signs. It lasts about 15 minutes, and when it's not busy they run over a bit. Fun for a night out or a respite during the day.

☼ Everyday　　　　　　　　　　☎ Wed-Sat until midnight

Palace Hotel

2 New Montgomery Street, San Francisco, CA 94105
(415) 392-8600

Treat yourself to an afternoon at the Garden Court at the Palace Hotel. Men and women alike love to sit surrounded by the lavish decor and be regally treated by the excellent service. A great daytime date place, too!

☼ Wednesday-Sunday　　　　　　☎ 2-4pm

Ritz-Carlton, San Francisco

600 Stockton Street, San Francisco, CA 94108
(415) 296-7465 ext.44

Spending time at the Ritz-Carlton is like taking a short, luxurious trip. The elegant setting with piano music, fine service and high tea is truly a treat.

☼ Everyday　　　　　　　　　　☎ 2:30-4:30pm

Tal-y-Tara Tea & Polo Shoppe

6439 California Street, San Francisco, CA 94121
(415) 751-9275

This charming combination equestrian shop and English Tearoom is the place to meet fellow horse lovers, have a bite to eat and enjoy friendly conversation.

Tea & Company

2207 Fillmore Street, San Francisco, CA 94115
(415) 929-8327

A cozy spot that is a favorite with regulars as well as tea drinkers just passing by. The owners, experts in teas and tea accessories, will be able to suggest one that best suits your mood. There are informational handouts and tastings between 11am-12pm and 5:30-7pm when you can enjoy your tea with interesting conversation.

☼ Everyday

🕮 Closes Mon-Thurs 10pm; Fri & Sat 11pm; Sun 10:30pm

"When you get tired of walking around in San Francisco you can always lean against it."–Unknown

"If you're alive, you can't be bored in San Francisco. If you're not alive, San Francisco will bring you to life."
–William Saroyan

Community Service

Animals • Arts • Civic Activities
Environmental Issues • Meals • Medical/AIDS
Neighborhood Organizations • Teaching/Tutoring
People to People Services • Political Activities

Community Service

Gulf Of The Farallones National Marine Sancuary and the Farrallones Marine Sanuary Assocation - SEALS volunteers survey the situation during a training class. Photo by Jan Rolleto

Volunteers with Habitat for Humanity
mix mortar for home repair and construction.

Community Service

What is it about giving our resources and time that lifts our spirits? You always hear people saying that *they* got more from "helping out" than the people who received the help. Maybe it's just because being fully engaged with others takes your mind off yourself. When we are voluntarily lending what we have to uplift those who could use a hand right now, it occurs to us at some level that we all have times of strength and times of need—that the human condition is about the ebb and flow of trouble and triumph, and we all take our turns along that wavy line. It *feels* right to reach out and share your current resources when you're in a position of strength. It also gives perspective to have real contact with the world that extends beyond your personal needs and have a working connection with some living, breathing part of your community.

Beyond the opportunity to expand yourself is the real bonus of finding other people involved in community service who believe in those values, people who *make* time in their busy lives to care about others and don't just talk about it. They don't just look good—they *are* good. When you find people who are busy putting their hands where their mouths are, so to speak, you can see what they really care about and the values they hold. They can see yours, too.

It's amazing to discover the diversity of activities around San Francisco where you can donate your time and energy. Tutor/teach an adult learner how to read (**Bay Area Literacy Program**), protect the Bay from environmental abuse (**BayKeeper**), or help feed the homeless (**St. Anthony Foundation**). Are you good with a hammer? Pound some nails in remodeled houses for young, eager families with **Habitat for Humanity**. Get your hands dirty at a weekly "weeding party" with fellows from the **California Native Plant Society**. Monitor harbor seals (**The Farallones Marine Sanctuary Association**) or the autumn flight of 19 species of birds of prey (**Golden Gate Raptor Observatory**). You can get to know your neighbors through the many neighborhood organizations (like the **North Beach Neighbors**) located throughout the city to make the streets where you live feel more like home. There are numerous significant cultural institutions that depend on volunteer efforts such as the **San Francisco Symphony and Opera**. Plus there are many, many opportunities to provide nurturance, strength and hope to people who

Community Service

are sick or disabled in hospitals or at home.

We've heard people say that they are afraid to volunteer their time because they have so little of it and are worried that they will get pressed into more service than they can manage. We think that the opposite is true: one of the best things about volunteering is the control you *do* have over what and how you give your time. Most organizations understand the heavy time demands you have and appreciate what time you can give, but it's important to be as clear as possible about *your* situation so they can develop clear expectations. You should be free to commit a lot of time or very little time without guilt, which, of course, means you can wade in slowly or jump in head first and really do a job.

Another concern some have is that they ought to have special skills to be able to help—which is true sometimes and not true other times. If you call and explain what you have to offer, the group can determine if there is a way you can be useful; then you can decide if you wish to participate.

And, as always, a third concern you may have is that you will not know anybody there. Believe us: when there is an important job to do—a wall to spackle and paint, a child to be loved into reading—people get to know each other through the job and feel like buddies in no time.

San Francisco has many quality organizations and programs that need your help and would wholeheartedly welcome your participation. And for you—don't underestimate the significance of volunteering as a means of improving your life. If you are new to San Francisco or just looking for a new group of active people, if you're feeling out-of-balance and overworked, try volunteering. Do a little or do a lot and don't be surprised if it changes how you feel about yourself and brings new and interesting people into your world.

Community Service

Animals

Farallones Marine Sanctuary Association: SEALS

P.O. Box 29386, The Presidio, San Francisco, CA 94129
(415) 561-6625   http://www.nos.noaa.gov/nmsp/gfnms

Does recording data on harbor seals in places like Bolinas Lagoon or Tomales Bay interest you? If so, the SEALS (Sanctuary Education Awareness and Long-term Stewardship) volunteer program is for you. A marine or science background is not required to qualify. You must be at least 18 years old, attend the extensive training (30 hours of classroom and field studies), and be available for one weekend shift a month for a year.

☎ Leslie Grella

Golden Gate Raptor Observatory @GGNat'l. Rec. Area

Bldg. 201, Upper Fort Mason, San Francisco, CA 94123
(415) 331-0739

Track and monitor the autumn flight of 19 species of birds of prey. Volunteers will need to commit one day every two weeks from August through December, along with some weekend training in July. Recruitment and orientation meetings happen annually in April. Be part of this extraordinary opportunity.

Marine Mammal Center

Pier 39 at Fisherman's Wharf, San Francisco, CA 94965
(415) 979-4357

How would you like to be an instructor/guide who teaches groups about marine mammals and marine conservation? That's just one of the many interesting volunteer opportunities available.

Marine Science Institute

500 Discovery Parkway, Redwood City, CA 94063
(415) 364-2760

This quality organization requires bending our location rule. Spend your time caring for and learning about fish, invertebrates, plankton and hydrology (the science of water properties).

☎ Karen Grimmer

Community Service

Pets Unlimited Veterinary Hospital and Shelter

2343 Fillmore Street, San Francisco, CA 94115
(415) 563-6700

This cat-only shelter allows you to feed, groom or socialize with cats and kittens or take part in a program that brings cats to senior centers. Half-price shots for both cats and dogs are available in the clinic every Thursday night where, by the way, a lot of discussion about pets is happening too.

☎ Lisa Hockins

San Francisco Society for the Prevention of Cruelty to Animals (SPCA)

2500 16th Street, San Francisco, CA 94103
(415) 554-3000

If you can work 3 hours a week for at least 6 months or be a foster parent (usually 3-4 weeks) to an injured or very young animal, you are needed. Other opportunities include being an adoption counselor, dog walker, socializer or a teacher-volunteer that visits classrooms with animals. Don't forget to ask about volunteer opportunities at the annual "Animal Wingding."

☎ Volunteer Coordinator

San Francisco Zoological Society

1 Zoo Road, San Francisco, CA 94132
(415) 753-7172

The Zoo needs people who are enthusiastic, dependable and have a sincere interest in animals. Many levels of commitment are available. If you would enjoy helping to observe animals, prepare diets or lead tours, give a call for more information.

☎ Cara Celestine

Arts

Business Volunteers for the Arts

465 California Street, 9th Floor, San Francisco, CA 94104
(415) 352-8832

As part of the Business Assistance Program you can share your professional skills and expertise with nonprofit arts organizations. Professionals are needed who can commit an "average of 12 hours/month over a 4-6 month project duration." Training is provided. BVA is affiliated with the San Francisco Chamber of Commerce. Here's a way to make a significant contribution to the arts.

☎ Cathy Booth

KQED: Public Broadcasting Volunteer

2601 Mariposa Street, San Francisco, CA 94110
(415) 553-2153   volunteer@KQED.org

Be part of the TV & Radio Pledge Festivals, provide tours of KQED to school groups and adult organizations, or assist in the office. Many other volunteer opportunities are available during daytime and evening hours and on weekdays or weekends.

☎ Felicia Keenan

San Francisco Architectural Heritage

2007 Franklin Street, San Francisco, CA 94109
(415) 441-3000
Activity Location: Haas-Lilienthal House

Become a docent by taking a short course on the architectural and historical developments of the city and learn about the role played by the Haas and Lilienthal families. Docent tours take place on Wednesday and Sunday afternoons.

☎ Stacia Fink

Community Service

San Francisco Opera Guild Volunteer Program

301 Van Ness Avenue, San Francisco, CA 94102
(415) 565-6433

There are so many important jobs to be done to make an opera happen, and volunteers are a vital part of it all. They work in the Opera Shop, give tours of Davies Hall, the Opera House and the Herbst Theater, donate computer proficiency in the administrative office or do crocheting and beading in the Costume Shop. Day and evening hours are available for convenience of volunteers. Think of the music lovers you'll meet!

☀ Monday-Wednesday   🕐 9am-3:30pm
☎ Myra Shapiro

San Francisco Symphony Volunteer Council

Davies Symphony Hall at Grove & Van Ness Streets, San Francisco, CA 94102
(415) 552-8000 ext.500

Provide service at concerts, be staff at Repeat Performance (the symphony's thrift shop) or work as an office volunteer. You could also visit classrooms through the Concerts For Kids program as a docent presenting audiovisual material to prepare students for a concert they will attend. A flexible time commitment is available, with day and evening hours to fit your schedule.

☀ Monday-Friday   🕐 9am-5pm

Civic Activities

Friends of the San Francisco Public Library

Main Library at Civic Center, San Francisco, CA 94102
(415) 557-4256

Do we love our new library! Be a part of this exciting library program by staffing the Welcome Desk, being a Book Buddy who reads to children in local hospitals, or by collecting, sorting and selling books at the annual "Big Book Sale" at the Herbst Pavilion at Fort Mason Center. Call to be involved.

☎ Patricia Coyle

Rotary Club of San Francisco

55 New Montgomery Street, San Francisco, CA 94105
(415) 546-0644

Activity Location: Kensington Park Hotel, 3rd Floor, 450 Post Street

Established in 1908, the Rotary Club is a preeminent international service organization with local branches for business professionals interested in promoting community service. Joining the club requires a commitment: members are expected to attend meetings, serve on committees and contribute their professional experience. You will be rewarded by knowing you have provided needed community services and by having a chance to interact with civic-minded professionals.

☼ Tuesdays   ☎ 12-1:30pm
💰 Membership dues plus luncheon fees

San Francisco's Computer Museum

P.O. Box 420914, San Francisco, CA 94142
(415) 703-8362   erich@fog.com   http://www.fog.com

An exciting opportunity for those of you interested in seeing the Computer Museum become a reality. Your help is needed in this two-year development program. Web experience a plus but there are many opportunities in other areas, including fund-raising, public relations and office support. Those of you with a strong back can help move the antique computers.

☎ Eric Schienke

Volunteer Center of San Francisco

1160 Battery Street, Suite 70, San Francisco, CA 94111
(415) 982-8999

The Volunteer Center is a clearinghouse for nonprofit organizations, city agencies, civic groups and volunteers. If you want to volunteer, the center can provide information on worthy organizations in need of your support.

☎ Chuck Green

Community Service

Environmental Issues

Bay Area Ridge Trail Council
26 O'Farrell Street, 4th Floor, San Francisco, CA 94104
(415) 391-9300

Y ou can get active with this group in completing a 400-mile, multi-use, ridgeline trail surrounding the Bay. Two hundred miles have been finished at this point. Volunteers are always needed and there is a variety of opportunities available to suit your particular interests. If you can't volunteer your time, you could support the organization through your membership.

🐷 $35/year membership; $15 students

BayKeeper
Building A, Fort Mason, San Francisco, CA 94123
(415) 567-4401   *baykeeper@aol.com*   *(800) KEEPBAY (Info Line)*

G et involved and help protect our delta rivers and bay, fisheries and wildlife, from environmental abuse. Volunteer your time in such areas as monitoring and investigating sites, educating the public and organizing events.

☎ Matt Fottler

California Native Plant Society, Yerba Buena Chapter
(415) 731-3028
Activity Location: Various locations in San Francisco

G et some exercise and help restore native plants in the Twin Peaks, Bayview, Tank Hill and Mt. Davidson districts. Dig in at work parties ("weeding-parties") that take place weekly. Call for a schedule of their Habitat Restoration Program.

☼ Thursdays   ⏰ 1-4pm
☎ Jake Sigg

Community Service

Clean Water Action

944 Market Street, #600, San Francisco, CA 94102
(415) 362-3040   cwasf@cleanwater.org   http://www.essential.org/cwa

Join this outreach staff and work at a grassroots level to prevent water pollution and protect lakes, rivers, wetlands and estuaries.

☎ Jason Mitchell

Earth Save Bay Area Action Group

P.O. Box 591047, San Francisco, CA 94159
(415) 765-7665

This volunteer-run group organizes meetings, dinners and potlucks with the goal of educating people about the benefits of moving toward a plant-based diet. For up-to-date information on their next event, call the information number and meet others who work to protect the earth.

☼ 4th Monday/month   🕐 6:30pm

Friends of Recreation and Parks

McLaren Lodge, Golden Gate Park, Fell & Stanyan Sts., San Francisco, CA 94117
(415) 750-7442

An excellent organization that assists the Recreation and Park Depart ment to improve parks city-wide. Volunteers can help with membership, public relations, special events, office support or be park guides.

Friends of the Urban Forest

512 2nd Street, San Francisco, CA 94107
(415) 543-5000

Give a hand to help clean the environment by planting trees because "trees act as the lungs of the city, filtering particulates, absorbing carbon dioxide and releasing oxygen." They also make the city prettier. Join others in planting and maintaining trees or organize a planting in your neighborhood. It's easier than you may think.

Community Service

Planet Drum Foundation, Green City Volunteer Network

P.O. Box 31251, San Francisco, CA 94131
(415) 285-6556   planetdrum@igc.apc.org

Planet Drum matches volunteers (free over-the-phone referral service) with more than 425 Bay Area environmental groups that need help. Call for a copy of "Green City Calendar," a guide to ecological seminars and events.

Meals

Meals On Wheels of San Francisco

1375 Fairfax Avenue, San Francisco, CA 94124
(415) 920-1111

Volunteers are needed to deliver meals, provide companionship or run errands for a senior once a week. This is a fundamental service in our community and is greatly appreciated by recipients.

☎ Amy Kirk

Project Open Hand

2720 17th Street, San Francisco, CA 94110
(800) 551-6325   info@openhand.org

Be a volunteer and help provide meals, groceries and nutrition counseling to people living with symptomatic HIV and AIDS. Call for upcoming orientation dates.

☎ Marilyn Picariello

St. Anthony Foundation

121 Golden Gate Avenue, San Francisco, CA 94102
(415) 241-2600
Activity Location: St. Anthony's Dining Room, 45 Jones Street

Help this quality organization devoted to helping the homeless and persons living in poverty. Volunteers are needed to help serve the daily meal. Work in the service line, deliver trays to seniors, disabled people and families with children or help keep the dining room clean.

☼ Everyday   🖾 9:30am-1pm
☎ Donna Harville

The San Francisco Food Bank

333 Illinois Street, San Francisco, CA 94107
(415) 282-1900

Volunteers come together to help with warehouse food distribution, fund-raising, food drives, special events, clerical tasks, promotion and other duties.

Medical/AIDS

AIDS Emergency Fund

1540 Market Street, Suite 320, San Francisco, CA 94102
(415) 558-6999

An all-volunteer organization that raises funds to pay housing and medical bills for low-income people. A wide range of volunteer opportunities are available.

California Pacific Medical Center: Hospice Program

3360 Geary Street, San Francisco, CA 94118
(415) 750-6800 ext.21701

You can be a volunteer who provides care and support to people with HIV/AIDS, cancer and other life-threatening illnesses. You could also assist in a non-direct patient capacity. Call for an orientation schedule.

☎ Pat Bregant

The Family Link

317 Castro Street, San Francisco, CA 94114
(415) 703-9050   *http://www.slip.net/~famlink*

Become part of the "family" that provides guest housing for families visiting people with AIDS. You can transport guests to and from the airports and hospitals, maintain the house, prepare meals or help with the endless amount of paperwork. A fine organization that will welcome your help wholeheartedly.

☎ Ruth Hall

Community Service

Names Project Visitor Center
2362-A Market Street, San Francisco, CA 94114
(415) 863-1966

D onate sewing machines, fabrics or your sewing expertise to panel-makers or make a panel yourself to be included in the AIDS Names Project Quilt, the world's largest community art project.

☎ Matt Riutta

San Francisco Public Library, Friends for Life
Main Library Civic Center, San Francisco, CA 94102
(415) 557-4351

D eliver library books, audio and video tapes to homebound persons with HIV and AIDS.

☎ Karen Strauss

St. Lukes Hospital Auxiliary
3555 Cesar Chavez Street (Army), San Francisco, CA 94110
(415) 641-6538

A variety of volunteer opportunities are available in the dietary and business services, and at the information desk, gift shop, emergency room and clinics. This is one of many hospitals who welcome volunteers—try one close to you.

☎ Lucinda Morlin

Neighborhood Organizations

Italian-American Community Service Agency
678 Green Street (3rd floor of Casa Fugazi), San Francisco, CA 94108
(415) 362-6423

A community service agency that serves a specific segment of the population. You can get involved doing interpreting and translating, case management, food relief or assisting in administrative tasks. You'll pick up interesting bits of Italian culture and history along the way.

☎ Jessica Cohen

North Beach Neighbors

Box 330115, San Francisco, CA 94133
(415) 771-5250

Activity Location: San Remo Hotel Restaurant, 2237 Mason Street, San Francisco.
(415) 673-9090

N orth Beach Neighbors is an example of one of *many* local neigh
borhood organizations that are supported by community members.
Monthly meetings, open to all, include discussions about community
development and preservation. Events calendars are provided to members. Look in your neighborhood for a local group. You'll meet your
active neighbors and improve your community.
☎ Ella Mae Lew   🕐 7pm
💰 $15/year membership; $20 household

People to People Service

Center for Elderly Suicide Prevention & Grief Related Services

3330 Geary Boulevard, San Francisco, CA 94118
(415) 750-5355

B y volunteering on the 24-hour Friendship Line, you can be there
for someone who feels forgotten. Volunteers participate in 20 hours
of geriatric specific training and a 16-hour suicide intervention workshop. The center also needs persons interested in helping with events,
marketing and graphics.

Habitat For Humanity, San Francisco

4319 Geary Boulevard, San Francisco, CA 94118
(415) 750-4780   habsf@hooked.net

A nationally famous group organizes and instructs housebuilding
crews who turn buildings into homes for people with low incomes.
You can be experienced or a novice and still be very useful here. Plus
you'll enjoy wielding hammers and saws with this nice group.
☎ Nana Parks McCarthy

Community Service

James S. Brady Therapeutic Riding Program for the Disabled
6439 California Street, San Francisco, CA 94121
(415) 751-9275
Activity Location: Fort Miley

If you have experience working with horses and want to help the disabled, this program needs you. Volunteers attend classes to fulfill certification requirements. Call to learn more about the benefits of Therapeutic Riding and how you can get involved.

☎ Melba Meakin

Retired and Senior Volunteer Program
1125 Quintara Street, San Francisco, CA 94116
(415) 731-3335

If you are over 55, you qualify to be a member of this group. Many varied opportunities are available, such as child care, counseling, friendly visiting, gardening, mentoring youth, serving on committees and teaching and tutoring. You will receive training, support and, along with other contributors, recognition as a RSVP volunteer.

San Francisco Court Appointed Special Advocate Program
250 Sansome Street, Suite 203, San Francisco, CA 94104
(415) 398-8001

The Courts seek volunteers to become officers of the Juvenile Dependency Court and advocates for abused and neglected children. You can really help a child in this Program.

Political Activities

Amnesty International USA
500 Sansome Street, Suite 615, San Francisco, CA 94111
(415) 291-9233   aiusasf@igc.apc.org http://www.amnesty-usa.org

Group that discusses human rights issues and takes action on political projects. They hold letter writing meetings and events that feature a speaker and discussion. For the local group closest to you, contact the Western Region Office listed above.

Community Service

Republican Party of San Francisco

World Trade Center, Suite 336, San Francisco, CA 94111
(415) 837-0100

Y̶ou can join the political party of your choice and actively help your candidates to be elected.

☎ Cyrus Johnson

San Francisco Democratic Party

100 Van Ness Avenue, 25th Floor, San Francisco, CA 94102
(415) 626-1161

Y̶ou can join the political party of your choice and actively help your candidates be elected. Or you can choose a candidate and independently work for him/her.

Teaching/Tutoring

Institute of International Education

41 Sutter Street, Suite 510, San Francisco, CA 94104
(415) 362-6520

I̶IE is a nationwide organization established to promote international education. Its primary focus in the Bay Area is the coordination of the Fulbright Program for foreign exchange students. Volunteers can host a dinner for foreign scholars or assist in fund-raising.

☎ Carl Zachrisson

San Francisco Bay Area Book Council Read Aloud Day

123 Townsend Street, Suite 260, San Francisco, CA 94107
(415) 908-2833   sfbook@best.com   http://www.sfbook.org

T̶his is an opportunity, for even the most severely time-challenged person, to do some good. Read aloud to school children once a year and play a role in this excellent Bay Area literacy campaign that highlights the importance of adults reading to children.

Community Service

San Francisco Public Library Literacy Program

Civic Center, San Francisco, CA 94102
(415) 557-4388

Do you know how embarrassing it is not to be able to read? As a Project Read tutor, you will use all your relationship skills as you meet regularly with an adult learner who wants to improve his or her reading and writing. Tutors must be at least 20 years of age and have a high school diploma or equivalent.

San Francisco School Volunteers

65 Battery Street, San Francisco, CA 94111
(415) 274-0250

A city program that recruits, trains and links business and community volunteers with students in over 100 public schools. Research shows that mentoring really makes a difference.

St. John's Tutoring Center

1661 15th Street, San Francisco, CA 94103
(415) 864-5205

The Center provides tutoring throughout the school year for 35 young people, ages 8 to 18, twice weekly from 3-6pm. Give your time, knowledge and friendship and reap the rewards of watching young minds grow.

☎ Ethel Newlin

Dance

*Ballet • Ballroom • Classes • Country-Western
Dinner Dance • Folk • Irish • Latin
Movement Miscellany • Square • Tap*

Dance

Hustle Dance Club members Bobby Concepcion and Lana Malinka
and others enjoying the dance

D ancing, the universal delight of moving to music, has become for many a performance nightmare instead of the right of spontaneous expression. As the melting pot of many cultures, we seem to have no claim to our *own* traditional dances. Somehow, we've evolved to where we no longer teach our children to dance and no longer enjoy dancing in a community setting. Instead, in our society, it is thought that dancing is done only by the graceful, the knowers-of-the-steps, the people who get chosen by partners. "No, I don't dance," is the common refrain at many joyous dancing affairs. That probably means, "I don't dance well," or well enough to be seen dancing. To those who feel that way, we suggest that you ask yourself: Do you really want to miss this wonderful activity just because people you don't know (usually) don't like how you do it? The people you *do* know and who matter to you care only that you are joining them to have fun!

Men and women have danced alone and together since the Very Beginning, because, performance aside, it is so much fun. It is also a first-rate opportunity to have contact with someone you want to get to know better. Probably the best way to get rid of the performance issue is to engage in low-risk dancing events where instruction is provided and where everybody wants to help beginners. Often these dancing events do not require you to bring a partner. Some are not even partner dances.

Not only is dancing great fun and interactive, it is also easy to *find*. Networks of dancers abound in the area. There is folk dancing some-where every night of the week with a rich community of dancers who make up the core group. Try the group that meets at **Fort Mason** on Mondays for Greek Folk Dancing. Give Israeli Folk Dancing a whirl at the **Jewish Community Center of San Francisco** on Tuesdays. For a mix of International Folk Dances, stop by the **Mandala Dance Group** (Thursdays) that meets at **St. Paul's Presbyterian Church** at 43rd Avenue and Judah Street—a popular meeting location for other Folk Dancing, English Country and Contradance and Square Dancing groups.

There are *all kinds* of dances for you to learn and become proficient in, from Irish Ceili (**United Irish Cultural Center**) and English Contradance (**Bay Area Country Dance Society**), to our very own distinctly Californian dance, the West Coast Swing (**The Next Genera-tion Swing Dance Club**). Be daring ladies and discover the art of

Dance

Belly Dancing to a Middle Eastern beat at **Amina's Studio**. More traditional dance classes are offered by the **San Francisco Recreation and Park Department**, where you can find excellent low-cost lessons in a comfortable atmosphere.

Then there are the kinds of dances you've always known about and maybe wished you were really good at, like the Tango. Good news! A variety of Ballroom dances are taught throughout the area, enjoyed by an enthusiastic following who welcome newcomers. All types of wonderful Ballroom classes are taught at the **Metronome Ballroom** which also offers dance parties with informal group lessons preceding the dance. At the **Mark Hopkins Inter-Continental Hotel "Top of the Mark,"** Cynthia Glinka, a lively dancer/instructor, hosts a weekly dance beginning with a lesson. By the way, starting the evening with a complimentary group dance lesson can be a great ice breaker. By the time the dance begins, you've all spent time dancing, learning, talking and laughing together—greatly reducing the uncomfortable feeling of being at a dance alone or not having people to dance with whose twirl ability is similar to your own.

We welcome the current Ballroom revival as an exciting sign that people are going out dancing again. And not for singles only! Dancing is a great way for couples to add spark to their relationship. While you're both trying to master that sexy Tango twist, there isn't much time to worry about whose turn it is to pick up the dry cleaning or do the grocery shopping. Of course you'll have to work out who gets to lead....

How about Square Dancing? One group for beginners who want to learn is the **Bachelors 'n' Bachelorettes Square Dance Club**, which encourages singles and couples to attend its classes and events. If you go, the regulars will teach and encourage you, gently make room for you, and you, after a million mistakes, will learn. Then *you* will be the regular! And Polka! Just as there are ballrooms for Fox-trot, so there are ballrooms for Polka which often include instructions. The **Polish Club**, a friendly and lively place, is open to anyone who wants to learn Polish Folk Dance. People dancing Polkas are known to smile a lot!

Going on a dancing tour is a fabulous way to have a night on the town whether you go single or have a partner. Let's face it: nightclubs can be lonely places. When you go with a group, you walk in connected to other people who you can dance and talk with without feeling awkward. Latin dance lovers can Salsa and Mamba at the 'hottest' Latin and Caribbean clubs by taking a ride on **The Mexican Bus.** Another fine nightclub tour company is **Three Babes and a Bus** whose members boogie the night away at clubs featuring Top 40s tunes.

Dancing is probably happening in *your* neighborhood more than one night a week for beginners and advanced dancers. There is dancing for kids, young adults, adults and older adults, in same-age and mixed-age groups. Places to dance can be cheap and informal or elegant and expensive. Churches and synagogues sponsor regular dances, as well as schools, singles' groups and restaurants/clubs. Dancing is everywhere—and has a universal appeal. Loving dancing is our birthright.

People are very sensitive about being pushed to go dancing so we want to refrain from this offensive behavior. But if you should just want to look around, the best places to check are those where structured instruction is offered. People are eager to teach you if you show interest, partly because the more people enjoying the activity, the more fun the whole group has. You will be valued more for your earnest effort and enthusiasm than for your dance expertise or demeanor with "attitude." And since partners don't drop out of the sky for any but the gorgeous (And how many of *them* are there?), you might ask someone for one dance to help you learn. Most people are happy to help an eager beginner. On the whole, women are more likely to engage freely in dancing than men, and commonly decry the lack of men partners. So single men wishing to meet women, consider polishing up your dancing skills!

Dance party at the Metronome Ballroom

 # Walk Thru'

Greek Folk Dancing

To find Greek Folk Dancing on Monday nights, you only have to follow the lyrical strains of sweet Greek folk music coming through the window at Fort Mason's Building C. It's hard to resist dancing your way up the stairs but do, because it's more fun if you know the steps!

Inside, you'll find a small to medium group of mixed-age dancers that meet every week for instruction and a variety of dances. No matter how experienced the dancers are, what is noticeable about them is the expression on their faces—attentive, but full of enjoyment. Most participants are regulars coming from all over the city, but people from out-of-town come for these beautiful dances as well.

The instructor, Anna, and the group are welcoming, inviting you to join them and learn. Since many are hand-holding line dances, you'll have an expert on either side to gently guide you through it. It's wise to be on time for instruction, especially if you are new to folk dance. Although many of the steps are simple and repetitive, they can get quite tricky as the music speeds up. No matter how easy the dance, it's a thrill to put together the steps and move your body in conjunction with the line to that wonderful music. You'll be sorry to see the evening end!

Ballet

Academy of Ballet

2121 Market Street, San Francisco, CA 94114
(415) 552-1166

An adult program that emphasizes toning, stretching, strengthening and relaxing the body through the use of classical ballet. This is an excellent way to exercise, while you participate in a beautiful art form. Classes of varied levels are available, as well as a separate class for men.

☼ Monday-Friday   🕯 Evenings
💰 About $9/class

Brady Street Dance Centre

60 Brady Street, San Francisco, CA 94103
(415) 558-9355

From the adult beginner to the advanced professional dancer, the centre offers classes that are right for your ability level. You can feel the positive "buzz" from the teachers and staff who truly love their jobs. Give it a try—ballet is not just for prima ballerinas.

☼ Sunday-Saturday
💰 About $9/class

ENCORE

455 Franklin Street, San Francisco, CA 94102
(415) 553-4634

Encore members are a sophisticated group of professionals who are interested in supporting the San Francisco Ballet. They sponsor many events throughout the season including pre-performance celebrations, cocktail receptions and the immensely successful neighborhood membership socializers which are a great place to meet fellow ballet aficionados.

💰 $60/year membership; $95 couple

Dance

Ballroom

Commodore Sloat School
50 Darien Way, San Francisco
(415) 661-2746

Learn from Bart and Judy Lewis, dance instructors and enthusiasts, the basics of social Ballroom dance including the Rumba, Samba, Cha Cha, Tango, Waltz, Fox Trot, Swing, Mambo and more. The classes are held in six-week sessions. Call for upcoming dates.

☏ Bart & Judy Lewis
💰 $50

Cynthia Glinka Roll up the Carpet Dance Productions
P.O. Box 194762, San Francisco, CA 94119
(415) 485-5500
Activity Location: Mark Hopkins Inter-Continental Hotel, Number One Nob Hill
(415) 616-6916

Put on your dancing shoes and join Cynthia Glinka every week as she teaches your favorites including Swing, Fox Trot, Charleston and Latin as well as the dances of the 90's. An extra bonus is the incredible view from this outstanding landmark. Go ahead: she can teach anyone how to dance in just one hour. Besides, you'll have such a good time meeting others you'll forget that you have two left feet! After the class stay to enjoy great vocals and dancing music from Lavay Smith & the Red Hot Skillet Lickers.

☀ Wednesdays   ⏰ 7:30pm
💰 Free dance lesson; $6 after 8:30pm

Metronome Ballroom
1830 17th Street, San Francisco, CA 94103
(415) 252-9000   *metronom@dnai.com*

Group classes, private lesson, and dance parties featuring Ballroom, Latin and Swing dancing are held in this San Francisco treasure. Friday is Newcomer's and Argentine Tango Night, Saturday is West Coast Swing and Jitterburg Night and Sunday is Ballroom, Swing and Latin Night. Wow. Call for a calendar.

💰 $10/lesson & party; $8/party; $6/students

Renaissance Ballroom

285 Ellis Street, San Francisco, CA 94102
(415) 474-0920

An excellent place to learn to do the Fox Trot, Swing, Tango, Rumba, Cha Cha, Waltz and other social dances. Get started and soon you'll be "hitting the floor" with confidence.

Classes

City Dancers of San Francisco

2201 Lawton Street, San Francisco, CA 94122
(415) 387-0380
Activity Location: Sunset Park Recreation Center

Put on your dancing shoes and join the City Dancers at their weekly lessons and afternoon dance. This is an enjoyable way to learn Ballroom, Modern and Latin dancing. The beginning lesson is from 1-1:30pm, followed by the intermediate lesson at 1:30-2pm. After the lessons the general dance begins. We have been told by group members that this is their favorite way to spend a Sunday afternoon!

☼ Sundays   🕐 12:30-5pm
💰 $4

Drama, Dance & Music Division, SF Recreation & Park Dept.

50 Scott Street, San Francisco, CA 94117
(415) 554-9523
Activity Location: Harvey Milk Recreational Arts Building

Take advantage of the exciting classes offered including Tap Dance, Mexican Folk Dance, Square Dancing, Jazz, Ballet, Capoeira, and adult Fitness & Exercise. Very very reasonably priced for such fun.

💰 $3-$8/class

Dance

YMCA - Embarcadero

169 Steuart Street, San Francisco, CA 94105
(415) 957-9622 ext.413

Why not stay downtown after work and take a dance class? Ballet, Salsa, Belly Dance and Swing and others are offered here, very reasonably. Call for a catalog to see when you can begin.

💰 About $30/series of four classes

Country - Western

The Rawhide

280 7th Street, San Francisco, CA 94103
(415) 621-1197

Learn to Line Dance and Two-Step Waltz in this predominately gay but straight-friendly club. We love the western theme and large dance floor. The dance lessons are open to all with admission.

☼ Monday-Friday   🕐 7:30pm
💰 $2

Country and Western Line Dancing

(415) 365-2815
Activity Location: United Irish Cultural Center, 2700 45th Avenue
(415) 661-2700

Line Dancing is all the rage and this is a group that knows why! Beginners should come between 7-8:15pm to learn the basic steps, with Intermediate dancing from 8:15-10pm. All ages of dancers attend and you don't need a partner.

☼ Tuesdays (except August)   🕐 7-10pm
☎ John & Elizabeth Mulhall

Dinner Dance

Italian-American Social Club of San Francisco

25 Russia Avenue, San Francisco, CA 94112
(415) 585-8059

Another hidden SF tradition and a fabulous way to have fun, relax, eat a great meal and dance to live music. Reservations are required and everyone is welcome. Call for upcoming dates and times.

☼ 4th Friday/month (except Dec)　　🕑 7:30pm
💰 $19/for non-members

Verdi Club

2424 Mariposa Street, San Francisco, CA 94110
(415) 861-9199

This wonderful eating and dancing club has been around since 1916. Enjoy a delicious meal, wine, dance to a four-piece band and meet new people. Everyone is welcome but make a reservation.

💰 $19/for non-members

Folk

Cafe Lahat at the Jewish Community Center of SF

3200 California Street (at Presidio), San Francisco, CA 94118
(415) 346-6040

You don't have to be Jewish to love Israeli dancing! You can learn the steps and join hundreds of other Bay Area dancers who love it as well. All ages and beginners are welcome. No partner is necessary. Refreshments are included.

☼ Tuesdays　　🕑 7:30-10:30pm
💰 $5

Dance

Greek Folk Dancing

(510) 339-8357
Activity Location: Fort Mason, Building C, Buchanan & Marina Blvd.
(415) 441-3400

Learn the Misirlou and fundamentals of many popular Greek Folk dances with this lively ongoing group. The instruction is excellent and you can also learn by watching. After that, you won't be able to keep still. For more information, call Anna, the event coordinator and instructor—and say "hi" for us.

☼ Mondays   🕐 8-10pm
🕿 Anna Efstathiou
💰 $7/class

Mandala Dance Group

Activity Location: St. Paul's Presbyterian Church,
43rd Avenue & Judah Street, (415) 566-7838

If you're interested in International Folk dance, stop by this weekly event, watch for a while, and then move on in! You won't be sorry—it's a lot of fun. Call St. Paul's to confirm dates and times.

☼ Thursdays   🕐 7:30pm

Slavonic Cultural Center

60 Onondaga Street, San Francisco, CA 94112
(415) 584-8859

Traditional Croatian Folk dancing and singing groups meet weekly here. Dates and times change periodically so be sure to call ahead. Get on the mailing list and enjoy interesting events, including the Poklada celebration that features professional Slavonian musicians and dancers plus plenty of delicious ethnic food.

The Polish Club

3040 - 22nd Street, San Francisco, CA 94110
(415) 550-9252

A friendly and welcoming group that hosts dances for anyone with the desire to learn Polish Folk dance. Dances are held throughout the year for your pleasure.

☼ Tuesdays & Thursdays   🕐 7:30pm

Irish

Irish Country Dance with Larry Lynch

(415) 952-9989

Activity Location: Fort Mason Center, Building C
Buchanan Street & Marina Blvd. (415) 441-3400

Learn Irish social dancing sets for adults in a non-competitive, non-performance setting. No partners necessary. Don't miss the potluck dance party on the last Wednesday of the month (8-10:30pm) with live music, dancing and socializing. You don't have to be a student to attend. Call Larry for more details.

☀ Wednesdays   ☎ 8-9:30pm
☎ Larry Lynch
💰 $5/lesson; $45/series of nine classes

Shannon Arms

915 Taraval Street, San Francisco, CA 94116
(415) 665-1223

We're so glad that we discovered this quiet pub that comes alive for a "seisiun" (Irish music playing) every first Thursday. The evening begins with a dancing lesson where you can learn the fundamentals of set dancing. Soon everyone is involved! Beginners are welcome and encouraged to participate. By the end of the night you'll be having so much fun, your skill level won't matter.

☀ 1st Thursday/month   ☎ 8pm
💰 Free

United Irish Cultural Center

2700 45th Avenue, San Francisco, CA 94116
(415) 661-2700

Live Irish music here! Excellent instruction for beginners (6-7pm) who then kick up their heels in open dancing for everybody. A lively and friendly group to dance with and enjoy.

☀ 2nd Sunday/month   ☎ 6-10pm
☎ Frank Lynch
💰 $5

Dance

Latin

Mission Cultural Center for Latino Arts

2868 Mission Street, San Francisco, CA 94110
(415) 821-1155

An excellent place to experience Colombian Folk and Brazilian dances. It's fun to participate in these colorful dances that get your feet moving as well as your spirits. Don't worry about knowing all the moves because the class has dancers of all levels. Call for a calendar and ask about the other dance, theater and art classes that are offered .

🌣 Free-$8

Sol Y Luna

475 Sacramento Street at Battery, San Francisco, CA 94111
(415) 296-8191   *http://www.blasto.com*

Whether you are a beginner or an expert wishing to brush up on your moves, Salsa lessons will get you dancing. Stop by for a lesson Monday night and be ready to move to the music on Wednesday through Saturday nights from 10pm-2am.

☼ Mondays   ⏰ 8-9pm

The Mexican Bus

(415) 546-3747
Activity Location: Meet the bus at Chevys Mexican Restaurant,
150 - 4th Street (415) 543-8060

Board the "mambo cabaret on wheels" and go club-hopping to local Latin and Caribbean clubs. The cost includes your transportation and cover admission. A great way to meet people and explore new clubs without doing it all alone. You must be 21 and reservations are required.

☼ Fridays & Saturdays   ⏰ 9:45pm-2am
🌣 $30

Movement Miscellany

Amina's Studio: Middle Eastern Dancing & Drumming

829 Elizabeth Street, San Francisco, CA 94114
(415) 282-7910   aminajune@aol.com

I f you've ever wanted to learn how to belly dance, here is your chance. Your instructor, Amina, has worked in Middle Eastern nightclubs and is a member of the Belly Dance Hall of Fame. Soon you'll be dancing to live music. Drumming classes are offered as well. The Giza Club meets at the studio every 2nd Sunday/month from 3-6pm for lectures, videos/ slides and book readings. Everyone is welcome.

☎ Amina

Bay Area Country Dance Society (BACDS)

115 Eugenia Avenue, San Francisco, CA 94110
(415) 282-7374   http://www.well.com/user/cwj/bacds/
Activity Location: St. Paul's Presbyterian Church
43rd Avenue & Judah (415) 566-9309

M any English Country and Contradances are going on in the area and this is one terrific example. If you haven't seen Contradancing, it is gorgeous! Take a look for yourself. Calendar available.

☼ 1st & 3rd Saturday/month & 4th Friday/month
⏰ 7:30pm lesson; 8pm dancing

Beth Abrams' Dance Workshops

123 Gates Street, San Francisco, CA 94220
(415) 282-6177
Activity Location: San Francisco Dance Center, 4th Floor
50 Oak Street (415) 863-3040

B eth brings more than 21 years of dancing experience to her classes. She combines movement from different disciplines including Jazz, Yoga and Ballet. Teens and adults of all ages, levels and body types are encouraged to attend. Check with Beth about the other classes she teaches throughout the city.

☎ Beth Abrams
💰 About $9/class

Dance

Hustle Dance Club

P.O. Box 945, Brisbane, CA 95004
(415) 467-8830   *http://www.rahul.net/dhesi/hustle/wtd/html*
Activity Location: Metronome Blockparty. 300 De Haro Street (415) 252-9000
You can also buy your tickets at the Metronome Ballroom (1830 17th Street).

Get up with this fun and lively group dedicated to disco dancing every night of the week with events scheduled throughout the Bay Area. They meet in San Francisco on the 2nd Friday of the month. Club president, Raul, gives beginning (7:30-8:15pm) and intermediate (8:15-9:00pm) Hustle lessons before the dance party (9pm-12am). Go ahead and "do the Hustle!"

☼ 2nd Friday/month
☏ Raul Ante
💰 $15/year membership; $20 couples

Royal Scottish Country Dance Society

25 Vista Verde Court, San Francisco, CA 94131
(415) 333-9372
Activity Location: Millberry Fitness Center, 500 Parnassus Avenue
(415) 476-1115

RSCDS sponsors classes and monthly social dances, a formal Valentine's Ball, special events, workshops, and publishes a bi-monthly newsletter. No partners needed to attend classes or parties and you don't have to be Scottish. Taking a class is a great way to get started in the group and membership is not required to participate.

💰 About $5/class

San Francisco Waltzing Society

(510) 284-1003

Don't miss the formal "Fall Ball" with its 18-piece orchestra and elegant flair. The dress code for the event is ballgowns for women and white tie (preferably) for men. Smaller dances are held periodically. If you want to "brush up" on your moves, Waltz lessons are offered on a ongoing basis through the Society.

☏ Gail Enright
💰 About $25/lesson

Three Babes and a Bus Nightclub Tours

(415) 552-2582

Activity Location: New Joe's Restaurant, 347 Geary Street (415) 397-9999

Not for women only—this is the perfect way to explore the night club scene! Board the bus and you're off for an evening of experiencing some of San Francisco's hottest dance clubs. If you don't know them, these folks do! The price includes your transportation and cover admission charges. You must be 21 and reservations are required.

☼ Saturdays   ☎ 9:30pm-1:30am
💰 $30

Square

Bachelors 'n' Bachelorettes Square Dance Club

Activity Location: Ebenezer Lutheran Church, 678 Portola Dr., (415)681-5400

A great place for beginners who want to Square Dance. The first three classes are free. Singles as well as couples are encouraged to attend. These dancers do it well.

☼ Fridays   ☎ 7pm lesson;
☎ Jim Wylie   dancing 7:30-9pm
💰 $2.50

Caper Cutter Square Dance Group

(415) 566-6179

Activity Location: St. Paul's Presbyterian Church, 43rd Avenue & Judah Street
(415) 566-9309

This group is rather advanced and the majority of members have established partners. If you have Square Dancing experience, give them a call or stop by and observe.

☼ Mondays   ☎ 8pm

Dance

Swing

Cafe Du Nord

2170 Market Street, San Francisco, CA 94114
(415) 861-5016

A great way to get warmed up and feel less intimidated about dancing is to take a group lesson. You can do this on Tuesdays at 9pm (Salsa) and Sundays at 8pm (Swing). Lively dances take place after the lessons.

🔊 $3

The Next Generation Swing Dance Club

236 West Portal Avenue, Suite 329, San Francisco, CA 94127
(415) 979-4456
Activity Location: The Irish Cultural Center, 2700 45th Ave. (415) 661-2700

A fabulous venue to dance California's very own West Coast Swing. You can fill your calendar with many things to do with this dance organization that sponsors a monthly "Club Night Out," social events, workshops, classes and regular "Welcome Dinners" for new members.

☎ Karen Zimmermann
🔊 $25/year membership

Tap

Tap Dance Center

(415) 621-8277

Tap classes are offered in a professional tap dancer's studio. Adult beginners interested in discovering their natural ability to tap dance are welcome. Shoes are provided free. Serious students only should apply because the group is tightly bonded and perform together.

YMCA - Buchanan Branch

1530 Buchanan Street, San Francisco, CA 94115
(415) 931-9622

The Y's can be depended on to offer everything, including this ongoing, beginning to intermediate level, tap class. Get your dancing shoes out and shuffle on down to Buchanan Street!

☼ Mondays   🕐 6:30-7:30pm

Discussion Groups

*About San Francisco • Art & Architecture
Books • Contemporary Issues • Cultural Groups
History & International Affairs • Miscellany
Nature & Travel • Spiritual*

Discussion Groups

"A Girl a Guy a Landscape: Novel on the Wall," installation opening.
Installation by Burning Books at
The San Francicso Center for the Book.

San Francisco is a place where all types of people live together respecting each other's opinions and perspectives. Within the city limits you can find compadres who share your degree of conservatism or liberalism, as well as those whose different ideas will expand your point of view. San Franciscans are more than merely tolerant. They embrace the differences that are created by the diverse ethnic backgrounds, sexual preferences and creative dreams of its residents.

How did San Francisco get to be such a free thinking city? We believe it started with the pioneers of the late 19th Century who made their way to California to escape the traditional mores of the East. The frontier town was a wild place with the freedom to say, do and live without too much scrutiny.

The migration has continued to this day. The city has been home to the Beatniks, Hippies and currently the Technogeniuses, whose novel ideas and visions have dramatically influenced all of our lives. Many of us find it important to have places to hash things out with a group of thoughtful people, and where we can also meet new people with fresh ideas. Sharing and debating opinions is a great time and we all need to exercise the mentally active part of ourselves. Besides, we need to use it so we don't lose it!

So where can you go for great discussions? One place many people go to talk is bars. If you're a comfortable drinker, that may work for you, although you also may wish to have discussions on a more serious (and sober) playing field. Of course if you are not much of a drinker, bars just don't feel like the right place.

Believe it or not, discussion groups are found in neighborhoods all over the city. Take **Great Books Groups**, for example. You can join them to discuss the finest books in the Western World in a place pretty close to your house because they meet in many local areas. The **Free Library** also has interesting lectures/discussions on fine literature, both classical and modern, at your closest branch. (We wonder if we take the Free Library for granted and don't utilize and value the excellent programs it routinely provides—maybe because it *is* free?)

For a short bus/cable car ride downtown, many bookstores host presentations and discussions with authors of every kind of book. They also have music events and games and beer tastings and who-knows-

Discussion Groups

what-else. It's free. Yes, for nothing but your bus money and a good cup of coffee if you like. Many enjoy these evenings enough to be regulars at their favorite reading haunt.

If you're a history buff, take a walking tour with **City Guides** and have lively discussions about San Francisco's architectural, economic and cultural past. These walks are attended by many locals as well as out-of-towners, so don't overlook an opportunity to connect with other like-minded people who might become your walking companions. The **California Historical Society** sponsors a Thursday evening program that includes a wine and cheese reception and an interesting live program that investigates the rich historical past of California. Making conversation at events like these is easy because everyone is simultaneously sharing the experience.

The **Hotel Rex San Francisco**, with its magnificently decorated Salon, provides a rich thought-provoking environment. Numerous art and literary clubs meet there for stimulating discussions, film screenings, poetry readings and other "don't miss" interactive events. **The San Francisco Literary Society** hosts a fantastic series of programs featuring writers, poets and dramatists, buffet dinners and open discussions to conclude each stimulating evening.

San Francisco is rich in cultural organizations offering outstanding monthly programs where you can experience the world without ever leaving the city. Why not discover French wines through **Alliance Francaise**, Italian cinema with the **Amici Dell' Italia Foundation**, or an authentic Japanese tea gathering with the **Urasenke Foundation**? You could be a "citizen diplomat" and host international visitors through the **International Diplomacy Council**. The Council holds more than 30 events a year, giving you an in-depth opportunity to meet others who are also intrigued by international affairs.

Who is going to be in these groups? Intimidating people? Maybe. People who know a lot about the subject, or at least know more than you (or *think* they do) and therefore make you feel stupid? Maybe.

There certainly *are* people like that in nice places who, for their own reasons, need to behave in patronizing ways. You can let them be the gatekeepers to the world you want to explore *or* you can decide that you'll be in charge of where you go and what you learn and discuss, thank you very much, and if they're so distressed that you don't know "anything," *they* can leave. This, of course, does not mean that you want

Discussion Groups

to go barging about, dominating the time with beginners' questions. But we know you wouldn't do that. You'd watch for a while, get a feel for the place and the group norms, and venture in with some consideration for your own newness. And when you're ready, you will put in your two cents and begin to be part of the group—probably a valued member at that.

Whom will you meet? You certainly will meet people who are interested in things, who want to learn, who want to bat ideas around to further their own thinking. They are likely to be people who want to have their ideas on the table for your reaction, too. You'll find that they are not interested in spending their lives watching TV, preferring to be in an active rather than passive mode. After all, they got *there* didn't they? And they probably enjoy interaction with people, which is why they are out there connecting—the way you are!

For the Resisters ("I'd like to try a new group but..."): We suggest that you assume for the moment that you *will* find a spot by checking out the many groups in San Francisco, and that you *will* discover a venue where people are talking about just the things that interest you. To venture out, you may need to decide that it is ok NOT to say anything if you don't feel like it. But do remember that you don't have to *know* anything about a subject to want to learn about it or ask questions. Once you've started, you may find that a world opens up to you.

On the other hand, if you go, you might find out that you *don't* enjoy the subject, even though you thought you might. Having gone to check it out means you concluded this after a fair chance.

If you *never* feel in the right mood to risk a new group, let us encourage you to GO anyway and check one out because

where you are

what you are doing

and what you are talking about

can change your life.

Walk Thru'

Helen Thomas signing books after an insightful discussion at The Commonwealth Club of California

The Commonwealth Club of California

Founded in 1903, The Commonwealth Club of California has become one of the largest and most prestigious public affairs speaking forums in the U.S. Throughout the year there are more than 500 interesting and provocative programs covering a wide spectrum of regional, national and international topics. Past speakers have included Secretary of State, Madeline Albright; investigative journalist and segment producer for 60 Minutes, Lowell Bergman; and Luba Brezhnev, the niece of General Secretary of the former Soviet Union, Leonid Brezhnev. You do not have to be a member to participate in events, but joining offers the benefit of special discounts on admissions.

The Club attracts a professional, educated group that discusses social and political issues at luncheons held in downtown hotels or in the evenings at the organization. Get there early to find and meet friends, have pre-meeting conversations about the topic, and socialize. The "Let's Talk about It" Monday night discussion series is a less formal way in which to meet people and be a part of the stimulating discussions.

One member said about her evenings at The Commonwealth Club, "I have never left an event without feeling excitement about what I have just learned, and a hunger to learn more."

Discussion Groups

About San Francisco

Board of Supervisors

War Memorial, 401 Van Ness Avenue, San Francisco, CA 94102
(415) 554-5184

K eep abreast of current issues in local government and meet others who are also interested in having a voice in civic affairs. All meetings are open to the public.

☼ Wednesdays   ⏰ 1pm

San Francisco Planning and Urban Research Assn. (SPUR)

312 Sutter Street, #500, San Francisco, CA 94108
(415) 781-8726   spur@well.com   http://www.spur.org

A n outstanding organization that sponsors over 150 public forums held throughout the year that address issues such as "Pedestrian Places," "Earthquake Insurance," "Waterfront Land Use" and the creation of the "Fillmore Jazz District." Call for the latest calendar of discussion topics.

💰 Free-$3/non-members

San Francisco Police Commission

Hall Of Justice, 850 Bryant Street, 5th Floor, San Francisco, CA 94103
(415) 553-1667

I ssues regarding police policy and policy change are discussed. Public comments are welcome at all of the weekly meetings.

☼ Wednesdays   ⏰ 5:30pm

San Francisco Recreation and Park Commission

McLaren Lodge, 501 Stanyan Street, San Francisco, CA 94117
(415) 831-2750

P lay a civic role by knowing what policy decisions are being made or considered within our park system. All meetings are open to the public and participation is encouraged.

☼ 3rd Thursday/month   ⏰ 2pm

Discussion Groups

Art & Architecture

American Institute of Architects: SF

Hallidie Building, 130 Sutter Street, Suite 600, San Francisco, CA 94104
(415) 362-7397   AIASF130@aol.com

This active group of architects/enthusiasts meet monthly for a host of informative sessions, including discussions, seminars, workshops, exhibitions, site visits and dinners. Held in various interesting locations around the city.

💰 $77/year associate

California College of Arts and Crafts

450 Irwin Street, San Francisco, CA 94107
(415) 703-9520   http://www.ccac-art.edu

Excellent public programs, including monthly lectures ("Gutenberg to the Golden Age of the Poster"), discussions, exhibitions, symposia, artist receptions and much more. Very well-attended events.

💰 Free-inexpensive

City Arts and Lectures, Inc.

1415 Green Street, San Francisco, CA 94109
(415) 563-2463

Activity Location: Herbst Theater, 401 Van Ness Avenue, (415) 392-4400

A variety of presentations with well-known writers and poets (John Updike, Joan Didion, Maya Angelou), celebrities (Rosemary Clooney, Lauren Bacall, Lily Tomlin), journalists, photographers, sports figures and other prominent guests from diverse fields. You might be willing to pay a fortune to hear Maya Angelou in person—but through City Arts and Lectures, high quality programs are available to all.

💰 About $20

City Guides

Main Library Civic Center, San Francisco, CA 94102

(415) 557-4266   *http://www.hooked.net/users/jhum*

J oin these guided city walks for lively discussions about San Francisco's architecture. Find out why the Palace Hotel was truly a structural feat in 1909. Observe the once-controversial 30's fresco murals depicting life as "Firebelle" Lillie Coit must have experienced. Or discuss the "Painted Ladies," including the world famous postcard row. Let's take full advantage of what is in our own backyard.

San Francisco Museum of Modern Art (SFMOMA) "Art Sandwiched In"

151 3rd Street, San Francisco, CA 94103

(415) 357-4125   *http://sfmoma.org*

S FMOMA offers outstanding lectures, catered luncheons and evening programs such as "Booktalk," a public forum that unites authors with artists, critics and historians. The popular annual "Design Lecture Series" presents a different topic each year in several installations. You do not have to be a member to attend these high quality events (but it wouldn't hurt).

West Coast Live — San Francisco's Radio Show to the World

915 Cole Street, San Francisco, CA 94117
(415) 664-9500

Activity Location: Cowell Theater, Fort Mason Center, Buchanan & Marina Blvd.
(415) 441-3400

B e part of the energetic live studio audience to see first-hand the production of this informative, two-hour live radio show featuring celebrities, varied discussions and musical performers. Reservations are required. Tune in to 91.7FM to listen.

☼ Saturdays   ☎ 10am-12pm
💰 About $12

Discussion Groups

Books

Borders Books & Music

400 Post Street, San Francisco, CA 94102
(415) 399-1633   *http://www.borders.com*

The Tranquility and Insight Reading Group addresses such ethereal topics as God and spiritual issues, reading related books for varied perspectives for discussion. Call to confirm the current topic and reading material.

☼ 1st & 3rd Wednesday/month   ⏰ 7pm
🥤 Cost of reading material

Great Books

(415) 241-9252

Activity Location:Presidio Branch Library, 3150 Sacramento Street,(415) 292-2155

Join this group, currently reading the fifth series of the Adult Great Books program, and see why the "classics" are just that—universal and classic. A lively discussion with regular members.

☼ 4th Tuesday/month   ⏰ 7pm
☎ Steven Matosich
🥤 Cost of reading material

Great Books Council

35 Fairmont Drive, Daly City, CA 94015
(415) 285-8409

One book a month is discussed by this group, selecting from both classic and modern readings. Call for information on other group locations.

☼ 3rd Sunday/month   ⏰ 8pm
☎ Duke Edwards
🥤 Cost of reading material

Discussion Groups

Hotel Rex San Francisco

562 Sutter Street, San Francisco, CA 94102
(415) 433-4434   *http://www.joiedevivre-sf.com*

D on't miss the art and literary events held in the hotel's salon. Decorated with antique furnishings, portraits and magnificent carpets, this is the perfect thought provoking environment. Call to get on the mailing list for upcoming readings, discussions, film screenings and other rich interactive events.

Mystery Readers International, SF City Chapter

P.O. Box 8116, Berkeley, CA 94707
(510) 339-2800

D iscuss British and American mysteries. Regular attendance is necessary to maintain the quality of discussion that this small, informal group of readers enjoys. Also ask about the Mystery Readers Journal, an excellent resource for book groups and mystery fans. Each issue contains reviews, articles, a calendar of events and other mystery-related information.

☎ Janet A. Rudolph
💰 $24/year subscription

San Francisco Literary Society

1 Weatherly Drive, Suite 402, Mill Valley, CA 94941
(415) 381-9091

Activity Location: Northern Trust Bank, Conf. Rm., 580 California, Suite 1800
(415) 765-4400

T he Literary Society offers an excellent way to keep your reading up-to-date and share your ideas about literature. On Thursdays, this lively group enjoys a buffet, a variety of interesting speakers (writers, poets and dramatists) and an engaging open discussion. Be sure to ask about the upbeat Literary Soirées at the Hotel Rex.

☼ Scheduled Thursdays   ⏰ 7pm
☎ Peter Robinson
💰 $225/year membership; $400/year family

Discussion Groups

San Francisco Public Library

100 Larkin Street, San Francisco, CA 94102
(415) 557-4400   *http://sfpl.lib.ca.us*

Library branches throughout the city offer a monthly calendar of excellent literary programs and events. Past programs have included dramatic readings from great literature, slide and lecture presentations featuring Californian historians, exhibitions and more. When you see the calendar of events, you'll be amazed at the variety of programs.

Solar Light Books

2068 Union Street, San Francisco, CA 94123
(415) 567-6082   solarlight@aol.com   http://www.san-fran.com/solarlight

This informal women's reading group is one of many taking place all over the city—maybe right next door to you. If you are interested, call or stop by to find out about the current topic of discussion.

☼ 1st Tuesday/month   ⏰ 7:30pm

Tse Chen Ling, Center for Tibetan Buddhist Studies "Book of the Month"

4 Joost Avenue, San Francisco, CA 94131
(415) 339-8002   *tclcenter@aol.com*

A book group that reads and discusses a new title every month focusing on Tibetan and Buddhist culture, history and politics.

☼ 3rd Friday/month   ⏰ 7pm
💰 Cost of reading material

Western Addition Branch Library "Fiction Reading"

1550 Scott Street, San Francisco, CA 94115
(415) 292-2160

A discussion group for fiction lovers that reads a new book each month. Newcomers are always welcome but are asked to call ahead to find out what book will be the focus of discussion. The majority of books being read can be borrowed from the library, so the cost of this activity is minimal.

☼ 1st Wednesday/month   ⏰ 7:30pm
☎ Joan

Contemporary Issues

Commonwealth Club of California "Public Affairs Forum"

595 Market Street, San Francisco, CA 94105
(415) 597-6700   cwc@sirius.com   http://www.sfgate.com/~common

Throughout the year there are more than 500 interesting and provocative programs offered that cover a wide spectrum of regional, national and international topics. Non-members are encouraged to attend these excellent events and learn more about the organization. Check into the Monday Night Discussion Series.

🐚 $110/yr membership; $90/yr (65+ or -29 yrs.)

Pacific Research Institute

755 Sansome Street, Suite 450, San Francisco, CA 94111
(415) 989-0833   http://www.ideas.org

This group holds provocative and timely public policy forums on issues such as education, health care and civil rights. Get involved and voice your opinion on important issues of common concern. This is an enjoyable event that is usually presented in a luncheon or dinner format.

☎ Cindy Sparks
🐚 About $20

Parents' Place

3272 California Street, San Francisco, CA 94118
(415) 563-1041   http://www.jfcs.org

Workshops offered for mothers, fathers and caretakers who want to be better informed about child development and parenting skills. Discussions and workshops are hosted at Parents Place.

🐚 About $15/workshop

Discussion Groups

San Francisco Chamber of Commerce

465 California Street, 9th Floor, San Francisco, CA 94104
(415) 392-4520 ksivesind@sfchamber.com http://www.sfchamber.com

The Chamber gives you many opportunities to participate with a broad diversity of business professionals and take programs to develop your business acumen. Membership privileges include "Business after Hours" networking events and various quarterly forums. Terrific information, discussions and networking around SF's business environment.

☎ Kristin Sivesind

Saybrook Society

450 Pacific Avenue, 3rd Floor, San Francisco, CA 94133
(415) 433-9200 rhesseling@iac.apc.org. http://www.saybrook.org
Activity Location: The Rollo May Center, 4th Floor

Try this meeting ground if you're interested in exploring how business, law, education, health and the arts intersect from psychological, political, philosophical and spiritual perspectives. A diverse group which shares varied viewpoints ensuring evenings of conversation and learning.

💰 Free-moderate

Cultural Groups

African-American Historical Society, Fulton Street Center

762 Fulton Street, San Francisco, CA 94102
(415) 292-6172
Activity Location: 708 Montgomery Street

The center hosts many interesting literary, musical, theatrical and educational programs throughout the year, including an active calendar for February's Black History Month. Call for upcoming events and ask about their Saturday walking tour that explores the "black presence in 19th Century San Francisco."

☀ Saturdays   🕐 10am
💰 $25/year membership

Alliance Francaise

1345 Bush Street, San Francisco, CA 94109
(415) 775-7755   afsf@afsf.com   http://www.afsf.com

For you Francophiles, there are countless activities offered monthly that you will love—including lectures, wine tastings, Club Gastronomique, Cine Club and conversation and grammar classes. This is your chance to learn about the many facets of France and French life with others who share your interest.

🔔 Most events free to members

Amici Dell' Italia Foundation

353 Sacramento Street, Suite 600, San Francisco, CA 94111
(415) 837-0235

An exciting series of events about Italian culture that span art to technology, ballet, music, cinema and food. Scheduled throughout the year.

🔔 $30/year membership; $20 seniors; $15 students

Anglophiles

(415) 292-0716

An informal monthly group interested in English, Scottish and Irish literature and history. They meet at various coffee and desert houses around the city and are open to new members.

☎ Margaret Jenna

Chinese Cultural Foundation "Chinese Heritage Walk"

750 Kearny Street, San Francisco, CA 94108
(415) 986-1822

Activity Location: Walk begins at the center

The center offers a variety of educational and cultural programs that include lectures, workshops, art exhibitions, dance and musical performances. A special attraction are the docent-conducted walks that offer an insider's perspective into life in Chinatown.

☀ Saturdays & Sundays   🕑 2pm
🔔 $15/adult; $5/under 18

Discussion Groups

Friends of Vieilles Maisons Francaises, Inc.

566 Mountain Home Road, Woodside, CA 94062
(415) 851-7196

These Francophiles and Francophones work to restore and preserve Chateaus and other historic buildings in France. They are an open and welcoming group. The Northern California Chapter sponsors interesting lectures, slide shows (Versailles), discussions, open houses, dinners and fund-raising events.

☎ Marie-France de Sibert
💰 $75/year membership

Goethe Institute

530 Bush Street, 2nd Floor, San Francisco, CA 94108
(415) 391-0370   gisfprog@sirius.com   http://www.eline.com/Goethe/

Excellent monthly lectures and discussions, exhibitions and films about German culture. The institute's language department offers evening classes for all levels. Many of the events are free and open to the public.

Istituto Italiano di Cultura

425 Bush Street, San Francisco, CA 94108
(415) 788-7142   istituto@sfiic.org   http://www. sfiic.org

The institute sponsors free lectures and discussions, films, exhibitions, poetry readings and musical programs exploring the different facets of Italian culture. You do not have to be Italian to attend or be on the mailing list.

Japan Society of Northern California

312 Sutter Street, Suite 401, San Francisco, CA 94108
(415) 986-4383   jsnc@us-japan.org   http://www.us-japan.org/jsnc

Meet with other members and participate in an international cultural exchange through lectures and discussions, exhibitions, receptions and other events. Non-members are welcome. Look into their Japanese language classes.

💰 $40/year membership; $15 students

Discussion Groups

Jewish Community Center of San Francisco

3200 California Street, San Francisco, CA 94118
(415) 346-6040

A center that sponsors monthly programs, including lectures and discussions, classes and other varied cultural activities, including Israeli Folk Dancing. Call for a catalog that outlines the adult programs and activities. Non-members are encouraged to attend and people who are not Jewish are welcome.

New College of California Weekend Workshop Series

766 Valencia Street, San Francisco, CA 94110
(415) 241-1302 ext.427   *http://www.newcollege.edu*

I f you want to learn more about Irish culture and history but don't have time during the work week, the Weekend Workshop Series is great for you. Through the New College Irish Studies Program you will explore and learn through discussions and lectures. You may find a group of new friends who love Ireland as well.
🐍 About $50

Urasenke Foundation

2444 Larkin Street, San Francisco, CA 94109
(415) 474-3259

T he sacred art of tea and tea rituals are explored and shared at these wonderful tea gatherings. They are limited to 15 people to allow plenty of time for questions and answers. Other lectures on tea arts and classes in Kaiseki cooking are offered. Non-members are encouraged to attend but reservations are required.
☼ 3rd Friday/month   🕐 6pm
🐍 $12/person; $25/year membership

Discussion Groups

History & International Affairs

California Historical Society

678 Mission Street, San Francisco, CA 94105
(415) 357-1848 ext.13 *info@calhis.org*

It's not just historians who will appreciate these wonderful programs highlighting California's rich historical past and the people who shaped the state. Past programs have included Sara Holmes Boutelle's slide-illustrated lecture about California architect Julia Morgan, and historian-storyteller Robert Ryall Miller's evening of tales about such folks as a maritime officer who jumped ship and founded the pueblo of Yerba Buena. A great way to hook up with other history buffs.

☼ Thursdays 🕐 5:30pm reception; 6pm program
💲 Free unless otherwise noted

City Guides

Main Library Civic Center, San Francisco, CA 94102
(415) 557-4266 *http://www.hooked.net/users/jhum*

Join other history buffs on these wonderful walking tours to discuss how San Francisco became an instant city during the Gold Rush days. Learn about the controversy that accompanied the creation of the fabled "Path of Gold" from the foot of Market to Lotta's Fountain and more. Free!

International Diplomacy Council

312 Sutter Street, Suite 402, San Francisco, CA 94108
(415) 986-1388 *idc@slip.net*

Become a "citizen diplomat" and meet (or host) international visitors who are leaders in their professions and represent vast social, economic and cultural backgrounds. There are over 30 IDC events a year to attend, including lectures, receptions and discussion programs.

☎ Jessica Nelson
💲 $25-$99/year membership

World Affairs Council of Northern California

312 Sutter Street, Suite 200, San Francisco, CA 94108
(415) 982-2541   *http://www.wacsf.org*

W orld Affairs offers about 250 programs a year to promote education and knowledge about international affairs. They sponsor
lecture forums, conferences, seminars, a speaker series, and discussion
and study groups—perfect for active and curious minds.

⭐ $55/year membership; $25 student

Miscellany

"After Hours" at Good Vibrations

1210 Valencia, San Francisco, CA
(415) 974-8980   *goodvibe@well.com*   *http://www.goodvibes.com*

F irst of all, Good Vibrations is the most woman-friendly sex empor-
ium to be found anywhere. The programs are conducted with good
taste and are clearly described in their literature so you know what to
expect. Past programs included a book signing by the authors of *Erotic
Fairy Tales,* when everyone was invited to read their favorite *Tale* as part
of the "Erotic Reading Circles". Talk to them in advance if you're
skittish.

Mensa

110 Garden Avenue, San Rafael, CA 94903
(415) 289-7080   *sfrmtest@aol.com*

T his highly intelligent group meets for luncheons, dinners, meetings,
great books discussions, bike riding and other social intellectual and
social events. Admission test required to join.

☎ Valerie Taylor
⭐ $45/year membership

Discussion Groups

Nature & Travel

Golden Gate National Recreation Area

Building 201, Fort Mason, San Francisco, CA 94123
(415) 556-0560   http://www.nps.gov/goga

From guided walks and discussions about raptors on Hawk Hill to exploring the role of early aviation at Crissy Field, the center informs about all aspects of local natural activities. If you become a member you'll receive a quarterly newsletter that serves as a calendar of upcoming events. You won't believe how much there is going on to interest you!

🐚 $25

Rand McNally

595 Market Street, San Francisco, CA 94105
(415) 777-3131

You may already know about these terrific ongoing travel lectures. These exciting programs are filled with interesting information and are usually accompanied by a slide presentation. Examples of past programs include "Road Trip USA," "Cheap Airfare Strategies" and "Family Camping." The discussions are informal, so feel free to ask questions. Meet others who love to travel while getting ideas for your own adventures from a premier travel organization.

📅 5:30-6:30pm
🐚 Free

San Francisco Natural History Series

(415) 554-9604   http://www.wco.com/~dale/randall.html
Activity Location: Randall Museum, 199 Museum Way, (415) 554-9600

Take part in the monthly presentations and events which include lectures, slide shows and field trips—all moderated by expert naturalists .

☼ 4th Thursday/month   📅 7:15-9:45pm

Spiritual

Sacred Space

776 Haight Street, San Francisco, CA 94117
(415) 431-0878

If you've been looking for opportunities to discuss major arcana, decks and divination, attend the "Tarot and Tea Parties" held periodically at the Space. They also host an interfaith group on the last Friday of the month that discusses interesting issues such as "Who do you think you are?" and "Spirit and the ego." Check with them to see what's coming up.

💰 Donation

Sivananda Yoga Vedanta Center

1200 Arguello Boulevard, San Francisco, CA 94122
(415) 681-2731   swsita@ix.netcom.com   http://www.sivananda.org/

Take part and share time with yogis and friends who practice different levels of Yoga on a regular basis. This supportive group shares a vegetarian dinner followed by lectures, discussions or films.

☼ Fridays   📅 7pm
💰 About $12

Discussion Groups

The Commonwealth Club of California

Especially
For Women

Business/Career • Especially For Moms
Getaways • Music Groups • Political Groups
Reading Groups • Service • Social Groups
Sports • Writing

Especially for Women

Members of the Golden West Women Flyfishers on an angling outing.

Especially for Women

To have a healthy social life, it is important to have same sex friends: people of your own gender with whom you can hang out, go to the movies, play pick-up golf, discuss political issues, take long walks, lunch on sushi or just have a coffee and shop on Union Street. This chapter is to give women some ideas about where to find women who can be *new* friends and who can join them in doing new activities.

Our observation is that, in general, when women get together they spend the majority of the time talking about their relationships rather than being active and involved in play. While men can spend an entire day playing or watching sports without uttering one word about their personal lives or significant other, as soon as two women get together they are analyzing their family tree.

We wish that women would play more. We'd like them to take their minds off serious things more often and goof-off, be silly, laugh and just have fun for its own sake. Similarly, we'd like to see more women involved together in ongoing group activities like sailing, choral singing or book discussion clubs. Whatever you choose, we think it's crucial to have a network of same-sex friends in your life, women who also love to hear that oar cut through the bay. Don't get us wrong. There is nothing more important than having a friend's shoulder to cry on when bad times roll around. But having fun is not a crime—it's a necessity, one you have to make happen by planning and showing up in the right places, *your* places!

Fortunately, there are many terrific places to find active women having a great time in San Francisco. Here are some that we've tried and/ or love—just a sample of spots where you can enjoy special events.

Starting with a cultural group that is *much* fun: "**Donne Italiane che Vivono in America**," (**DIVA**) is a wonderful group of women who meet once a month for Italian cultural activities. Recent programs have included a dinner and lecture event on how to rent a villa in Tuscany, a wine tasting and an exploration of Majolica (Italian Ceramics). You don't have to be of Italian heritage nor speak the language to attend. Just bring your love and passion for Italy. Diane has attended all of the group's events, finds them first rate and loves that they are social outings where you'll relax, have a glass of wine and not worry about impressing anyone.

Especially for Women

For those who love being active, the **Golden West Women Fly-fishers** is an avid group that meets monthly to plan fishing trips, share fishing adventure stories, and learn new techniques. With more than 130 women of all ages, backgrounds and angling proficiency, it's the right place for fisherwomen to make some new fishing buddies. Have you ever ogled the in-line skaters with envy? **Roller Divas** would love for you to join them for in-line skating in Golden Gate Park. Why skate alone when you can skate with a friendly and energetic group of women? If you're afraid because you've never skated before, take a free Saturday morning class offered by **Marina Skate and Snowboard** to learn the basics. Go for it, girl!

Would you rather be making music? How about playing a musical instrument with the **Community Women's Orchestra** or singing with the **San Francisco Sweet Adelines**, a women's barbershop harmony chorus. If you play an instrument or can carry a tune, why not be part of an orchestra or learn four-part harmony with these groups who are looking for members to make music come alive?

Don't underestimate doing volunteer work as a way to meet interesting and enjoyable women. San Francisco is overflowing with volunteer opportunities where you can do good as well as build friendships. We know that you are busy and that your time is a scarce commodity. Most organizations are sensitive to the time restrictions that their volunteers face and are flexible to accommodate their hectic schedules. Check the Community Service chapter for a list of organizations that would welcome you wholeheartedly, and where you can connect with other women who value "giving back" the way you do.

San Francisco is certainly a user-friendly city for women to pursue careers and network with other like-minded women around work. San Francisco has the highest average salaries for women in the country and a significant number of successful women business owners. Independent professional women will find an abundance of women's business support groups that provide career benefits as well as enjoyable networking opportunities. The **San Francisco Chamber of Commerce** sponsors bimonthly **"Women in Business Roundtable"** networking breakfasts. These events often attract large groups of professionals because of their excellent programs featuring speakers specifically of interest to business-women. We have met many entrepreneurial women through these events, including various members of the **Association for Women in Communications,** the **Women's Philharmonic, American Association of University Women,** and **SF NOW.**

The **San Francisco Business and Professional Women,** founded in 1916 in San Francisco, has grown into an international organization for the professional and personal development of women in business. If you take part in one of the interesting networking and discussion events, you'll find that just because these organizations focus on business related activities does not mean that they are not fun and sociable at the same time.

Enjoyable networking is what the **Executive Women's Golf League** is all about. EWGL is an association of women from diverse work environments who share business info and support while playing some exciting golf in the San Francisco area. You can learn how to play in one of their clinics or improve your golf game and develop your business at the same time.

For the woman who dreams of having her own business or needs help/financial support to sustain her business, the **San Francisco Renaissance Entrepreneurship Center** (415-541-8580) is an excellent resource.

Perhaps you've decided to exchange the "career track" for the "mommy track." We've talked with women who feel disconnected after quitting their day jobs to do the important job of staying home and raising children. There is no need to feel isolated and estranged from other women because your world has changed. There are all types of groups, friends and events that can keep you linked to the activities you love.

Formerly Employed Mothers at the Leading Edge (F.E.M.A.L.E.) is a group of women who get together bimonthly for "Mom's Night Out" activities. If you have twins, the **San Francisco Mothers of Twins Club** is a supportive group where you can discuss the issues of raising twins and pool your collective knowledge and resources. For women who are feeling the strains of managing life as a single parent, the **Children's Council of San Francisco** (415-243-0111) is a source for subsidized child care and counseling.

The good news is that there are too many terrific women's organizations and resources in the city for us to name them all. They would fill a

Especially for Women

book of their own. We suggest that you conduct your own search of groups and organizations that fit your needs. You could start by checking the business white pages in the telephone directory under "**Women**" for information about groups and organizations that sound interesting. Ask your friends and acquaintances and people you meet at the organizations from this book what they do after hours for fun and networking. Keep a notebook of the places you hear about and try. When you can't find an activity group you want, consider starting it yourself!

Especially for Women

Business/Career

Association for Women in Communications

120 Village Square, Suite 143, Orinda, CA 94563
(415) 403-4816   *http://www.wicisf.org*

An organization that offers professional women a resource system where they can network and access a job bank. Participating in organizations like AWIC is a good way to find support and build friendships with other women from your particular industry.

☎ Starla Navis

Metropolitan Club

640 Sutter Street, San Francisco, CA 94102
(415) 673-0600

This private club for women provides educational and social activities as well as an excellent athletic program and facility. A fine venue for professional women.

☎ Kim Cross-Membership

San Francisco Business and Professional Women (SFBPW)

P.O. Box 191385, San Francisco, CA 94119
(415) 241-1589   *Sfbpw@aol.com*

Founded in San Francisco in 1916, this well-established group has grown into an international organization that supports the professional and personal development of woman in business. Benefits of membership include business contacts, informative programs, support and friendship. A really helpful group, and they have fun too.

💰 $75/year membership

Especially for Women

San Francisco Chamber of Commerce
"Women in Business Roundtable"

465 California Street, San Francisco, CA 94104

(415) 352-8850   kshields@sfchamber.com   http://www.sfchamber.com

Attend these popular bimonthly networking breakfasts and you'll be treated to speakers of particular interest to professional women and women business owners. These events are well attended and often attract a sizable and diverse group. You don't have to be a member to attend but you may want to join after you go.

☎ Kelly Shields   ⏰ 7:30-9am
💰 $20/non-members

Especially For Moms

F.E.M.A.L.E.- Formerly Employed Mothers at the Leading Edge
(415) 731-5326

Activity Location: Kaiser Hospital, 4131 Geary Boulevard, San Francisco
(415)202-2000

These formerly employed women know that raising kids is harder than most jobs outside the home. Discussions, play group, babysitting co-op and "Mom's Night Out" are some of the neat activities these gals enjoy.

☀ 1st & 3rd Wednesdays/month   ⏰ 7:30-9:30pm
☎ Joanne Hayward

San Francisco City College
Child Development and Family Studies Department
1860 Hayes Street, Room 139, San Francisco, CA 94117
(415) 561-1922

Activity Location: Various locations throughout the city

Non-credit classes are held during the fall and spring semesters for persons interested in child development issues. Past classes have included: "Parents and Infants," "Child Observation, 15 Months To Kindergarten" and "Intergenerational Parenting." An excellent way to learn more about your children while being exposed to the latest child development theories.

Especially for Women

The San Francisco Mothers of Twins Club

3760 Fillmore Street, San Francisco, CA 94123
(415) 775-3865

Activity Location: UCSF, Ambulatory Care Center, 400 Parnassus, Room A455

Join this supportive group of mothers who share the joys and problems of raising twins, and who are eager to pool their knowledge with lively discussions.

☼ 2nd Wednesday/month   🕐 7:30-9pm
☎ Leanne Parsons
💲 $25/year membership

Getaways

Call of the Wild

2519 Cedar Street, Berkeley, CA 94708
(510) 849-9292   trips@callwild.com   http://www.callwild.com

From organized Bay Area day hikes to exploring Alaska's Denali National Park to landing on Mount McKinley's "Ruth Glacier" by bush plane, this company caters to adventurous women. Experienced leadership, tents, group equipment, a pre-trip class and great food is just a sampling of what has gone into making COTW's trips special for over 20 years. Sounds fabulous!

☎ Carole Latimer

Merlyn's Journeys

P.O. Box 277, Altaville, CA 95221   (800) 509-9330   (209) 736-9330
merlyns@goldrush.com   http://www.merlynsjourneys.com

If you are feeling the need to get away from it all, maybe you should take part in one of Merlyn's "adventures for city-weary women." These are three-day getaways to places rich in natural beauty where you can hike, soak in hot tubs, ski or just relax. Trip itineraries depend upon the season and delicious home cooked meals are always included. Just thinking about it drains away tension!

Especially for Women

Music Groups

Community Women's Orchestra

P.O. Box 30924, Oakland, CA 94604
(510) 428-1350
Activity Location: San Francisco & Oakland

If playing an instrument is your passion, you can join this interesting group of women who have a common desire to make music and have fun. CWO is an amateur orchestra where no one is turned away because of skill level. However, a commitment to attend rehearsals is required.

The San Francisco Sweet Adelines

25 Lake Street, San Francisco, CA 94118
(415) 665-7960

The Sweet Adelines are a women's barbershop harmony chorus. They are looking for women to join them who love to sing and think singing four-part harmony is one of life's greatest pleasures. (Ruth is a believer.) Listen to them and see what you think. No formal training is needed.

☼ Thursdays   ⏰ 7pm

The Women's Philharmonic

44 Page Street, Suite 604D, San Francisco, CA 94102
(415) 437-0123   *womensphil@aol.com*
Activity Location: All concerts held at Herbst Theater, 401 Van Ness Avenue
San Francisco, (415) 621-6600

Attend these concerts and help support women musicians and composers. If you become a member, you'll be entitled to participate in pre-concert and post-concert salons, music reading sessions and more. This is a superb musical group.

Political Group

Pacific Heights Republican Women's Club

1940 Broadway, San Francisco, CA 94109
(415) 929-1940   (415) 780-0000

Activity Location: Fort Mason Officer's Club, Buchanan Street & Marina Blvd.
San Francisco, (415) 441-7700

This group of professional women work to support the Republican party and its platforms. Guests are welcome to join their monthly meetings which often feature a program and supper. This is a good place to find/make friends with whom you can discuss your politics and be active. Space is limited, so call to confirm your attendance.

☼ 3rd Wednesday/month   ☎ 5:45pm

☎ Terry Clausen

💲 $15/supper; no charge for meetings

Reading Group

Solar Light Books

2068 Union Street, San Francisco, CA 94123
(415) 567-6082   solarlight@aol.com

This is an informal women's reading group that reads a really good book a month. Call or stop by to find out what they are currently discussing and you may wish to join. Don't forget to say hello to the bookstore cat for us. (That's the kind of place this is.)

☼ 1st Tuesday/month   ☎ 7:30pm

Especially for Women

Service

American Association of University Women (AAUW)
9 Grijalva Drive, San Francisco, CA 94132
(415) 391-4050

A AUW has been helping women realize the dream of achieving higher education for over 112 years. They work to effect change by promoting gender-fair classrooms and influencing public policy regarding education. Membership is open to all women with a bachelor's or higher college degree, or who are currently enrolled degree students. Long-time friends have developed out of activity with this hard working group.

☏ Sara Weaver

Friends of San Francisco Commission on the Status of Women
25 Van Ness Avenue, Room 130, San Francisco, CA 94102
(415) 252-4653   103164.1416@compuserve.com
Activity Location: 25 Van Ness Avenue, Suite 70

S upport the advancement of the "status of women" by helping to shape legislation designed to improve the quality of women's lives. Stopping domestic violence, sexual harassment and job discrimination are only a few of the issues championed. They will be very glad to have your help. Call to confirm the month of the meeting.

☼ Meets quarterly   ☎ 5:30pm
☏ Mary Anne O'Shea, President

League of Women Voters of San Francisco
114 Sansome Street, Suite 513, San Francisco, CA 94194
(415) 989-8683   sfvoter@slip.net

T his outstanding nonpartisan political organization encourages participation of citizens in the political process. You've probably seen them helping to (wo)man the polls on election day. But, very importantly, they work to describe and explain major public policy issues to the general public. They research, write, produce and distribute over 35,000 free nonpartisan voters guides for each election. If you're interested in understanding issues and promoting democracy, you couldn't be part of a better group.

Especially for Women

SF NOW- National Organization of Women

3543 18th Street, San Francisco, CA 94110
(415) 586-18880

The San Francisco NOW chapter is entirely staffed by volunteers. You can assist this diverse group in their continued work in areas of reproductive rights, lesbian rights, affirmative actions, violence against women, economic justice and women's health issues. If not NOW, when?

The Junior League of San Francisco

2226A Fillmore Street, San Francisco, CA 94115
(415) 775-4100

An altruistic group of women dedicated to supporting families and preventing domestic violence. All active members are required to show their support by doing acts of good work. An orientation is offered periodically for prospective members.

Women's Heritage Museum

870 Market Street, Suite 547, San Francisco, CA 94102
(415) 433-3026

A wonderful museum dedicated to preserving and highlighting women's role in history. You can support them through membership or volunteer to help with exhibits and displays, public programs, research, fund-raising and much more.

Social Groups

DIVA - "Donne Italiane che Vivono in America"

182 22nd Avenue, San Francisco, CA 94121
(415) 668-4535

You don't have to be of Italian heritage to join this wonderful social club that meets once a month to participate in Italian cultural events. Just bring your love and passion for Italy. Recent events have included a dinner and lecture on how to rent a villa in Tuscany, a wine tasting and a pizza and film night. (Look for more information about DIVAS in a Walk Thru on page 240.)

☎ Caterina Rando

Especially for Women

Stogettes
270 Funston Avenue, San Francisco, CA 94118
(415) 751-9680

Join this trend-setting group of women who share an interest in discovering SF's hottest restaurants and clubs. Monthly theme events are scheduled. Some are cigar-related but the theme topic varies to accommodate non-smokers. What a great way to get out about town!

☎ Barbara Nadig

Sports

Executive Women's Golf League
4681 Albany Circle, #419, San Jose, CA 95129
(408) 296-4706

EWGL is a national career-oriented organization with more than 200 professional women members in the local chapter. This is an opportunity to improve your golf game and make professional contacts at the same time. Isn't it time women expanded our business-golf game networking afternoons?

☎ Judy

Golden West Women Flyfishers
2342 9th Avenue, San Francisco, CA 94116
(415) 661-7638

Have fun flyfishing with over 130 women of all ages, backgrounds and angling proficiency. Informal monthly club meetings are great fun for sharing fishing adventure stories, learning new techniques and conducting club business.

☼ 2nd Tuesday/month ☎ 6pm
☎ Irmke
💰 $25/year membership

Especially for Women

Hoy's Sports, Impala Racing Team

1632 Haight Street, San Francisco, CA 94117
(415) 252-5370   (510) 531-5471

I mpala runners are competitive women racers who work out and compete regularly during the season. The diverse group (ages 20 to 60+) has different divisions to accommodate a runner's age.

☎ Sue Johnston

Roller Divas

410 North Civic Drive, #301, Walnut Creek, Ca 94596
(415) 771-3326   http://www.hooked.net/~sk8away/rdhom.htm
Activity Location: SF Park Branch Library, 1833 Page Street (415) 666-7155

D ivas include skaters (including beginners) of all ages and back grounds for speedskating, roller hockey and in-line skating. Monthly meetings are informal with snacks, guest speakers and info about events. A not-for-profit group that provides a supportive network for women in sports.

☼ 3rd Wednesdays   ⏰ 7-9pm
☎ Kelly McCown

San Francisco Recreation and Park Department "Volleyball"

800 Stanyan Street, San Francisco, CA 94117
(415) 753-7032
Activity Location: Kezar Pavillion

I f you want to have fun while you exercise, try women's volleyball! It's played inside on Monday nights from 7-9:30pm from September to June, and on Tuesday nights from June to September. Leagues play from October to December. Beginners and intermediate players encouraged.

☎ Jim Jackson
💰 $2

Virago Self-Defense

P.O. Box 210767, San Francisco, CA 94121
(415) 752-8542   viragosd@sirius.com

L earn more about this progressive training program designed for the empowerment of women and girls through classes in martial arts education. An exciting way to build confidence, improve fitness and protect yourself.

Especially for Women

Women's Motorcycle Contingent

P.O. Box 14781, San Francisco, CA 94114
(415) 395-8318

Activity Location: San Francisco Eagle, 398 12th Street
(415) 626-0880

All women riders are encouraged to attend the weekly meeting held in the back bar area. Who said women can't handle a "real bike?"

☼ Wednesdays   ☎ 7-8pm

Women's Mountain Bike and Tea Society (Wombats)

P.O. Box 757, Fairfax, CA 94978
(415) 459-0980   *http://www.wombats.org*

A fun group of women of all ages and backgrounds who share a love of bike riding and the great outdoors. Call about the exciting Thursday night rides in San Francisco and other outdoor Bay Area activities.

Writing

Women in Creative Process

5835 College Avenue, Suite A, Oakland, CA 94618
(510) 528-1872

Join this professionally-facilitated monthly group where you'll receive support and feedback from other women who are also involved in writing.

☎ Marie Farrington

Women's Writing Classes

(415) 337-7207   *writeclass@aol.com*
Activity Location: San Francisco and East Bay

These classes and workshops will help you hone your writing skills and provide a friendly, supportive place to share your writing. They include the use of dreams and photos for creative exploration. All levels and styles are welcome. Choose from a 12-week series, one-day workshops or three-hour write/read workshops.

☎ Linda Elkin or Anne McDonald

Film

Classes • Film Festivals • Film Programs
Foreign Films • Miscellany • Travel Films

Film

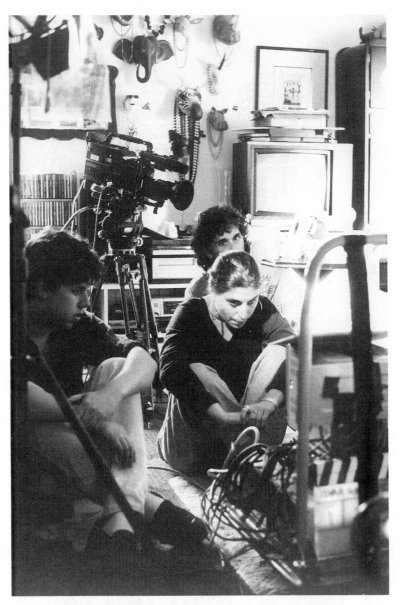

The making of the *Project Open Hand* public service
announcement, in a Bay Area Video Coalition's (BAVC)
Professional Video Production Class

Film

San Francisco has always been a film town. Scores of eclectic theaters feature mainstream movies *and* all manner of independents. But despite the fact that movie-going is a major social activity, unless you're 13 going to an afternoon matinee, you're unlikely to make new friends at a regular movie house.

Since this book is about connecting with people who share your interests, the following film activities have been included here because they provide interaction experiences, like post-film discussions or lecture/discussions by the film producer. We've also included film events where conversation is very likely to happen, such as at presentations of unusual films followed by receptions for the audience. In these situations, the type of movie tells you something about the interests of the people attending, especially if you see them regularly at movies of the same style.

Film buffs who love the big studio releases also appreciate fine independent films, and San Fran's small, budget film producers are successfully creating quality releases in greater numbers. These once cinematic fringe B-movies have challenged their shady past and are moving swiftly towards mainstream sophistication. At recent Oscar ceremonies, the word "independent" has been said so many times you might think independent films were taking over. The good news is that the Bay Area is privy to a complete menu of all types of films on a regular basis. The major repertory film theaters, **The Castro**, **Red Vic** and **Roxie**, have full cinema schedules which include special events around independent films. For informal viewing, the charismatic **Casting Couch Micro Theatre** has replaced the standard uncomfortable theater seats with couches, love seats and armchairs, creating a social atmosphere, living room style, for movie watching.

Film festivals attract people who enjoy discussions about what they have experienced. You can carry on long conversations before and after film viewing during the **San Francisco International Film Festival**. While there, you'll meet card-carrying members of the **San Francisco Film Society**, a group of ardent film lovers devoted to and appreciative of the craft. We've been told by members that the discounts on tickets throughout the year, plus invitations to sneak previews, special screenings and receptions are a great way to be involved in the film commu-

Film

nity. Although San Francisco is proud that the International Film Festival is the oldest of its kind in the country, we are proud also to host other excellent quality film festivals, like the **American Indian Film Festival**, the **Jewish Film Festival** and the **International Lesbian and Gay Film Festival**.

Film festivals are not always about serious art. For a truly unusual evening, join the lively group that gets together for the **Brainwash Drive-In Movie Festival** on the July Fourth weekend. They begin with a tailgate party before viewing independent films from the perspective of a newly arrived space alien who is hoping to understand life on earth by attending a drive-in film festival. Shelby Toland, the events founder, has reassured us that at the end of the festival the attendees are not chasing Hale-Bopp.

Do you enjoy foreign films? **Alliance Francaise** and **Instituto Italiano di Cultura** have ongoing Tuesday night showings. How about travel films? Join the **Golden Gate Geographic Society** and see magnificent geographical documentaries. The program is hosted by the people who photographed the films and lived them.

Have you thought about working as an "extra?" Yes, *you*! You don't have to be gorgeous, but you do have to submit photos and meet certain requirements. If you qualify, you'll have a chance to work with struggling actors, make a few bucks, eat a catered lunch and maybe get to play the role of human landscape. Being on a set is a good way to get an insider's perspective into how films are made.

Perhaps you want to get involved in making your own films. The **Artists' Television Access** offers affordable classes in video production, editing, imaging and documentary making. In addition, the **Bay Area Video Coalition** sponsors more than 200 workshops and seminars that promote the use of video technologies and provide hands-on technical learning, with state-of-the-art equipment. The **Film Arts Foundation** offers about 170 practical and high-quality seminars and workshops and if you're a member, you have access to production and post-production equipment at a reasonable cost. The Foundation also sponsors frequent film screenings for us, the general public.

For the shyest of shy interactors, going to film events is one of the easiest things to try. Going to the movies is easy, and going to a discussion group about a movie is pretty easy too. If you are nervous about joining the discussion, you can go home after the movie or just listen. At first, it might be hard to go alone—but try it. Once you get used to it, it's kind of neat because you can go on the spur of the moment, even when you're supposed to be doing your bills or weekly laundry. Also, you don't have to find someone who is in the same mood you're in to see what you feel like seeing. It's a luxury to go alone—and once you're there, you might be more inclined to take a risk, chat with the person next to you and eventually be a "regular" in the discussion group. You'll make a place for yourself in the community of people who love films.

Film

Classes

Artists' Television Access (ATA)

992 Valencia Street, San Francisco, CA 94110
(415) 824-3890   ata@atasite.org   http://www.atasite.org

ATA is a good resource for those interested in shooting films and having a venue to exhibit their work. They offer affordable classes in video production, editing, imaging and documentary-making for filmmakers of all levels. Computers are available for design and editing for a reasonable rental fee. Screenings and other creative events that feature independent works are offered to the public.

☼ Monday-Saturday   🕐 10am-10pm

Bay Area Video Coalition

2727 Mariposa Street, San Francisco, CA 94110
(415) 861-3282   videonet@aol.com   http://www.bavc.com

Throughout the year BAVC offers more than 200 workshops and seminars that promote the use of video technologies and hands-on technical learning. Take part in their "introduction" meetings where members meet and share ideas with other film enthusiasts.

💰 $45/year membership

Film Arts Foundation

346 9th Street, 2nd Floor, San Francisco, CA 94103
(415) 552-8760   filmarts@best.com   http://www.filmarts.org

Join this enthusiastic group of people interested in making independent films and videos. FAF is an excellent source for filmmakers and film lovers at every experience level. Over 160 seminars and workshops are held throughout the year as well as monthly screenings and guest lectures. Production and post-production equipment is available to members.

💰 $45/year membership

Film

San Francisco Art Institute

800 Chestnut, San Francisco, CA 94133
(415) 749-4554   yap@sfai.edu

A fine-art filmmaking class that deserves attention by anyone interested in film production. Students create their own films, combining theoretical and practical approaches, using Super 8 cameras. The institute's Extension Education Program includes this exciting class, film screenings and discussions by contemporary filmmakers.

☼ Saturdays

The Studio "Creative Workshop For Screenwriters"

582 Market Street, Suite 2008, San Francisco, CA 94104
(415) 789-7399   sasent@sirius.com   http://www.sirius.com/~sasent

Whether you're interested in writing screenplays as a professional or a talented amateur, you'll find classes at the Studio that are practical and useful. They include: "Screenwriting 101," "Selling Your Script," and "Creating Characters," all presented in a productive environment where people with similar aspirations assist each other.

☎ Sam Scribner
💰 About $150/three-session class

Film Festivals

American Indian Film Institute Festival

333 Valencia Street, San Francisco, CA 94103
(415) 554-0525   aifisf@aol.com
Activity Location: Palace of Fine Arts, Kabuki Theater, and Los Gatos Cinema

Held in the fall, this is the oldest and most recognized international film festival devoted to Native Americans. There are some wonderful films shown here. Call to confirm dates, screening times and locations.

Brainwash Movie Festival "Drive-in Film Festival"

P.O. Box 881914, San Francisco, CA 94188
(415) 273-1545   *http://www.wenet.net/~squidink/brainwash/htm*

Have fun with this group of film watchers who take the perspective of a fictitious space alien who has just arrived on earth to attend a drive-in film festival with hopes of understanding life on earth. Many interesting independent short films are selected to assist him...her...it (?). May 1st is the final day to submit a film for the festival with a $10 entry fee. You really don't want to miss this.

☼ July 4th
☎ Shelby Toland

Frameline "International Lesbian and Gay Film Festival"

346 9th Street, 2nd Floor, San Francisco, CA 94103
(415) 703-8650   *frameline@aol.com*   *http://www.frameline.org*

The International Lesbian and Gay Film Festival is the oldest and most well-known gay film festival. It continues to play a pivotal role in influencing how gays and lesbians are portrayed in the media. Beyond breaking stereotypes and providing an insider's perspective, this festival is fun and different because of the varied made-for-television programs, documentaries, shorts, as well as many wonderful films. Straight audiences are encouraged to attend.

San Francisco International Asian-American Film Festival

346 9th Street, San Francisco, CA 94103
(415) 863-0814   *naata@sirius.com*   *http://www.sirius.com/naaata/festival*
Activity Location: Kabuki Theater and Pacific Film Archive (Berkeley)

Held in the spring, this high quality film festival spotlights Asians and Asian-Americans in film and video. The films are colorful, majestic and action-oriented. Check dates, screening times and locations. Sponsored by the National Asian-American Telecommunication Association.

Film

San Francisco Film Society
"San Francisco International Film Festival"

1521 Eddy Street, San Francisco, CA 94115
(415-929-5000   sfiff@sfiff.org   http://www.sfiff.org
Activity Location:Festival-Kabuki and Castro Theaters, Pacific Film Archive
(Berkeley)

The San Francisco Film Society produces the oldest film festival in the United States with some of the best independent films being produced. The SF Film Society includes a group of devoted supporters and ardent film lovers who enjoy many privileges through membership ($55/year). They receive advance mailing of the annual Film Festival program, discounts on tickets and free admission to preview screenings throughout the year.

☀ Festival every spring; SFFS meets all year

San Francisco Jewish Film Festival

346 9th Street, 2nd Floor, San Francisco, CA 94710
(510) 548-0556   jewishfilm@aol.com   http://www.sfjff.org

This summer film festival promotes the secular awareness of the Jewish culture and emphasizes peace in the Middle East. The films are informative, entertaining, compelling and culturally rich. Call to confirm the dates and ask to be on the mailing list if you wish to be privy to the special events that accompany the festival.

Film Programs

Center for the Arts Yerba Buena Gardens "Screening Room"

701 Mission Street, San Francisco, CA 94103
(415) 978-2700   yerbamembr@aol.com   http://www.yerbabuenaarts.org

If you haven't discovered the 90-seat plush screening room on the second floor of the main art gallery at the Yerba Buena Center, you've been missing out. Past screenings have included non-fiction art films, documentaries and experimental works that accompany the current art exhibitions. On Thursday nights S.F. Cinematheque screens avant-garde, historical and experimental works.

🐌 $5/general; $3 students

Exploratorium

3601 Lyon Street, San Francisco, CA 94123
(415) 561-0360   ronh@exploratorium.edu http://www.exploratorium.edu
Activity Location: McBean Theater

New or unusual short films, free to museum visitors with admission, are shown each weekend afternoon. On Wednesdays the museum is open late, with occasional programs in the evenings.

Red Vic

1727 Haight Street, San Francisco, CA 94117
(415) 668-3994   http://www.redvicmoviehouse.com

This collectively-owned repertory theater focuses on screening independent releases of classic and contemporary cult films.

☎ Dennis Conroy
💰 About $6

Roxie

3117 16th Street, San Francisco, CA 94103
(415) 863-1087   http://www.roxie.com

The Roxie is known for showing the best new alternative films in the city. Call for a schedule of upcoming films and prepare to be impressed.

💰 About $6

S. F. Cinematheque

480 Potrero Avenue, San Francisco, CA 94110
(415) 558-8129

Enjoy screenings of avant-garde, historical and experimental works at the Center for the Arts on Thursdays and at the S.F. Art Institute on Sundays (except in July and August).

☀ Thursdays & Sundays   🎬 7:30pm
💰 $6/general; $3 members, students & seniors

Film

The Casting Couch Micro Cinema

950 Battery Street, San Francisco, CA
(415) 986-7001

At the Casting Couch, standard movie theatre seats have been replaced with couches, love seats and armchairs, instantly creating a relaxed and more social environment for movie watching. Only independent films are shown. These fresh, sometimes off-beat films often stimulate reactions from viewers making conversation easy. Have a snack in the new cafe and, while you're there, consider discussing the film with someone who looks interesting.

☎ Edgar Marroquin
💰 $8.50

The Castro

429 Castro Street, San Francisco, CA 94114
(415) 621-6120   *http://www.thecastro.com*

The Castro is known for its Wurlitzer organ and provocative film selection. This outstanding and unique theater hosts countless film festivals, classic showings and documentaries from local independent filmmakers throughout the year. You'll want to take in a great flick in this special space as often as you can.

💰 About $6.50

Venue 9

252 9th Street, San Francisco, CA 94103
(415) 626-2169   *ftloose@best.com*   *http://www.ftloose.org*

Get on the mailing list of this multi-use performance space that features independent and experimental films and videos as well as theater productions, comedy and musical performances. These events are interestingly different and reasonably priced.

💰 About $5-$10

Foreign Films

Alliance Francaise "Ciné-Club"

1345 Bush Street, San Francisco, CA 94109
(415) 775-7755   afsf@afsf.com   http://www.afsf.com

Don't miss these beautiful, sometimes tender and romantic, universally human, superb movies. The videos/films are in French with English subtitles. The mailing list informs you of upcoming films.

☼ Tuesdays   ⏰ 7pm
💰 Free/members; $5/non-member

Ciné Accion

346 9th Street, 2nd Floor, San Francisco, CA 94103
(415) 553-8135   cineaccion@aol.com

Ciné Accion was created to encourage the production, distribution and understanding of independent Latino cinema. Try the regularly sponsored screenings, as well as special events, including the work of Latin American women filmmakers, Latin American animation and the annual Festival Cine Latino.

💰 $35/year membership

Goethe Institute

530 Bush Street, 2nd Floor , San Francisco, CA 94108
(415) 391-0370   gisfprog@sirius.com   http://www.eline.com/Goethe/

Films on video are available in English and German with subtitles. Call for a calendar of events and also ask about "Berlin and Beyond," the annual festival of German-speaking films.

☼ Most Tuesdays & Thursdays   ⏰ 6:30pm
💰 Free

Istituto Italiano di Cultura

425 Bush Street, #301, San Francisco, CA 94108
(415) 788-7142   istituto@sfiic.org   http://www.sfiic.org

Many great Italian films are shown free of charge. "Sta scherzando!" No, we're not kidding, and the films have subtitles so that everyone can enjoy these excellent films.

☼ Tuesdays   ⏰ 6:30pm
💰 Free

Film

Miscellany

ASIFA-San Francisco "Animated Films"
P.O. Box 14516, San Francisco, CA 94114
(415) 386-1004

Remember how much fun it was to watch Saturday morning cartoons? Granted it's been a long time...but you're never too old to enjoy animation! Join this group of animators, fans and students at one of their monthly film showings and screenings, sneak previews and interesting programs. Find out how current animation technologies are changing the craft.

💰 $18/year membership

Bea Bonneau Casting
84 - 1st Street, San Francisco, CA 94105
(415) 346-2278

The days are long and the pay isn't great but working as an extra on films can be an exciting way to meet others and have fun. Plus you'll find out about films from behind the scenes.

The Cinema Club
Hotel Rex, 562 Sutter Street, San Francisco
(415) 433-4434

Ed Dornbach, the Ambassador of Film, makes these ongoing lectures, discussions and screenings truly "don't miss" events. The group meets monthly but the dates vary. Call to receive the events calendar and soon you'll be enjoying all the drama.

☎ Ed Dornbach   ⏰ 6:30pm
💰 $5

Travel Films

Golden Gate Geographic Society "Travel Film Series"

1290 Bayshore Highway, Burlingame, CA 94010
(415) 347-3636
Activity Location: San Francisco Herbst Theater or Scottish Rite Memorial Theater

What really makes this film series outstanding is that the programs (90 minute color travel films) are narrated live by the film producers. Ask about the Saturday morning program held at the Herbst Theater (Van Ness Avenue & McAllister Street) and the Saturday matinee program held at the Scottish Rite Memorial Theater (19th Avenue at Sloat Boulevard).

🐌 About $8/program

Japan Information Center

50 Fremont Street, Suite 2200, San Francisco, CA 94105
(415) 777-3533 ext.464

Learn more about the Japanese culture by watching these interesting, informative and beautifully scenic films.

☼ First three Wednesdays/month   🕐 12-1pm
🐌 Free

Film

Films Arts Foundation (FAF) Filmmakers Symposium

Games, Sports & Outdoors

Biking • Boating • Climbing
Environmental Sporting Activities • Flyfishing
Golf • Hiking, Backpacking & Snow Camping
Indoor Games • Inline Hockey & Skating
Miscellany • Motorcycles • Running
Sailing & Windsurfing • Swimming • Tennis

Rock Rendezvous Members Max Moehs, Lisa Newcomb
and Inez Drixelius with Nancy Schaefer atop
Matterhorn Peak in the Eastern Sierras of California

Golden Gate Park Skaters Photo by Mark Downey.
Courtesy of S.F. Conv. & Visitors Bureau

Games, Sports & Outdoors

San Francisco beckons to those who thrive on opportunities to enjoy a spectacular natural environment. This includes hikers, bikers, climbers, swimmers, runners, skiers, kite flyers, golfers, sailors, lawn bowlers, motorcyclists, rowers, snowshoers, windsurfers, and advocates of every conceivable contraption that one can mount, strap on, glide on, ride or float through the natural wonders of California. One advantage of partaking in these activities is that you will stay trim and lower your stress level. Another advantage is that you will not meet any couch potatoes there. The people you *will* find care enough about themselves to get moving while learning and having fun at the same time. Those kinds of people are fun to spend time with, don't you think? They'll think that about you too!

In the world of outdoor pleasures, we all have our favorites. For some, a night spent alone in the wilderness is a magical experience. Others love riding a bike down an unfamiliar road listening only to the sound of tires on the pavement and voices of wildlife. Still others go for the challenge of climbing a mountain with only ropes and muscle. To find a solo adventure that's right for you or if you just want to find a few outdoor comrades, read on!

You will be astounded at the great diversity of activities to be found all around the Bay Area where you can play at something, whether a physical sport or game of mental strategy. Most of them are low cost or free. And they take place on many days of the week and at many times of day. If you want to go out for *it*, *it's* out there for *you*.

Here is a sample of activities for you to consider:

HIKING: You can hike short or you can hike long. You can hike in the city or you can hike on mountain tops. You can be as skilled as major *HikerMan/Woman* or you can be an ordinary business person who just likes to just walk around and look at things. Try **San Francisco Urban Hiking**, a group that meets and hikes in areas that are easy to get to by foot or public transportation. You will meet a wide diversity of people there who know about different areas of nature, architecture and geography. That doesn't mean you have to be knowledgeable yourself; after all, they need people to listen. Or you could join the **Sierra Club** for wilderness outings and backpacking with people who love exploring and protecting the wild places of the earth. Or help the **Bay Area Ridge Trail**

Games, Sports & Outdoors

Council complete the last 200 hundred miles of the multi-use ridgeline trail surrounding the bay. Choose your favorite: it's up to you.

SAILING: Sail for a fresh breeze in your hair and a silky smooth ride through the waves. If you've been longing to find a way to get out on the bay, sailing is available to anyone with the willingness to learn. **Sailing Education Adventures** is a community-based organization that provides sailing education and promotes conservation of the bay. The **South Beach Yacht Club** is home to the **Bay Area Association of Disabled Sailors**, open to able-bodied and disabled persons who want to start tacking. If it's racing that turns you on, boat owners and interested crew can call the **Yacht Racing Association** for a free racing calendar that lists more than 300 boating activities throughout the year.

For the Windsurfers, try Lake Merced for a beginning or moderate sail. You can rent your equipment and take a lesson from **San Francisco Windsurfing**. Advanced surfers might move out to the Crissy Field location—but watch yourself. The water is cold, the tides unpredictable, and you'll be traveling in heavy shipping lanes. Those big guys can't stop for you.

GOLF: If you've ever thought of golfing, the time is now, the place is here. The area courses are spectacular! Fairways are lined with Cypress Trees nestled on cliffs overlooking the Pacific Ocean meeting the Golden Gate Bridge. For the beginner, the **Mission Bay Golf School** offers free introductory lessons on weekend mornings. They also sport an excellent driving range for all the practice you need. Now it's time to tee off on one of the gorgeous public courses right in the city, including **Lincoln Park**, the **Presidio** and **Harding Park**.

TENNIS: Finding a tennis partner is no problem if you join the **Golden Gate Tennis Club**, active since 1901. They sponsor social events and a series of tournaments including the historic San Francisco City Championship and the San Francisco Resident's Tournament which invites participation from the public. First you might want to take several free tennis lessons at a local park, such as the **Moscone Recreation Center**.

GAMES AND MISCELLANY: People come from all over to play darts at one of many games sponsored by the **San Francisco Dart Association**. The Scrabble Club meets weekly at a downtown location and beginners are welcome. We hear they have some pretty serious players and a fine time socializing as well. If chess is your game, you can find a pick-up game at the **Mechanics' Institute Library & Chess Room**. There are regular tournaments, and the director teaches a free weekly class for beginners and intermediate players. Classes are given by the **San Francisco Go Club** on Thursday nights for anyone interested in this fascinating and ancient game. And every Wednesday you're invited to stop by **Muddy's Coffeehouse** to play card and board games. Couldn't ask for more, could you? Yes, San Francisco is for gamers!

You can fly a kite at Marina Green, shoot an arrow at Golden Gate Park (47th Avenue near Fulton Street), bike ride with the **Parnassus Bike Club**, or be part of a game night for adults with **RECESS for Grown-Ups**, ride a cycle with the **San Francisco Motorcycle Club**, and swim at the **Dolphin Swim and Boat Club**.

And more.
All around here.
All with groups who are delighted to have new members, or with people who come together for a day or two to participate in a new thing.
You can go with a friend, or you can go alone and make friends.
It's up to you.

Walk Thru'

Golden Gate Sport & Social Club Soccer Champs "Team Riley" enjoying a moment of winning and camaraderie

The Golden Gate Sport & Social Club

The Golden Gate Sport and Social Club is perfect for serious players who also enjoy the social aspect of sports. There are coed and same-sex teams that play all types of sports over a 10-week season that fill up on a first come, first served basis. Call for the newsletter, choose your sport and let the club know about your interests. Your name will be posted on the board and as soon as there are enough people to constitute a team, you will be notified. Tossing a hoop or spiking a ball together is a great way to get to know at least ten new active people. After the games, you can join your fellow teammates at the "sponsor bar" where you can catch up with a mix of players from many teams to share a discounted food special for league players.

Membership is not required to play on the leagues or to enjoy the social events, which include a monthly party and three huge Halloween, New Year's Day and St. Patrick's day bashes. It's also not necessary to join to be part of the adventure trips, such as whitewater rafting, backpacking, mountain biking and rock climbing. However, members do receive special discounts on all activities and have the chance to meet many of the more than 4000 people involved in each league session.

So get moving!

Games, Sports & Outdoors

Biking

Parnassus Bike Club

131 Parker Avenue, San Francisco, CA 94118
(415) 292-6555

The club offers road and mountain bike rides around the Bay Area. Road rides are usually on Saturday and mountain bike rides are on Sunday. They are solid rides (30 to 40 miles) and are noncompetitive, enjoyable and a great way to encourage yourself to get in better biking shape with new bike riding friends.

☎ Chris Lane
💰 $10/year membership

(ROMP) Responsible Organized Mountain Pedalers

P.O. Box 1723, Campbell, CA 95009
(408) 777-9904   romp-owner@cycling.org
http://www-leland.stanford.edu/~scoop/romp/

Join this mountain cycling advocacy and social group by participating in their activities and rides around the Bay Area. Take part in trail building, participate in volunteer patrols or just go riding. Their web site is a good source of information about their activities and includes other biking sites to search.

☎ Bob Kain
💰 $20/year membership

San Francisco Bicycle Coalition

1095 Market Street, Suite 215, San Francisco, CA 94103
(415) 431-2453

This group's goal is to help the environment and the safety of bike riders by making the roads safer and more conducive to cycling. Monthly activities include bike rides, action groups and several events during the year that are purely social.

☎ Joe Carroll
💰 $25/year membership

Games, Sports & Outdoors

Boating

Bay Area Sea Kayakers

229 Courtright Road, San Rafael, CA 94901
(415) 457-6094   *http://www.bask.org*
Activity Location: UCSF, 505 Parnassus Ave., Health Science West Building, #310

This active group has formed a cooperative network for sharing trips, workshops and a vast variety of sea kayaking activities. All skill levels are welcome to attend their evenings which include a social hour and guest speaker. You can see the city from sea level on the Bay. It's glorious.

☼ Last Wednesday/month   🕑 6:30-9:30pm
☎ Penny Wells
💰 $25/year membership; $15 seniors & students

California Floaters Society (CFS)

171 Clarck Street, San Rafael, CA 94901
(415) 435-7936   *coyleapt@microweb.com*   *http://www.cfsonline.org*

CFS is for networking paddle craft and river enthusiasts of all types and skill levels. Society members paddle rafts, canoes, hard-shell and inflatable kayaks, river boards and miscellaneous flotsam and jetsam. The group is strictly recreational and noncommercial while embracing a philosophy of preservation and protection of river life. They meet bimonthly to plan trips, host workshops, swap stories and have fun.

☼ Bimonthly meetings
☎ Peter Coyle
💰 $20/year membership; $25/year family

Dolphin Swim and Boat Club

502 Jefferson Street, San Francisco, CA 94109
(415) 441-9329

An outdoor club that rows on the Bay and also at Lake Merced. If you want to participate in rowing, this is a great place to start. Other club activities include handball, running and swimming. To join or learn more about them, attend a monthly meeting.

☼ 3rd Wednesday/month   🕑 6:30pm
💰 $6.50/day use; Membership: $240 first 6 mo., then $30/mo.

Games, Sports & Outdoors

South End Rowing Club

500 Jefferson Street, San Francisco, CA 94109
(415) 776-7372

All levels of men and women rowers take part in this active environment. Rowing instruction is offered with membership at no extra cost. You can also join them for swimming, handball and running activities or work out in the gym. Get in shape while you enjoy people who like to play. The facilities are open to the public on certain days.

💰 $6/day use; Membership: $100 initiation fee;
$165 for 6 months, then $325/year

UCSF Rowing Club

(415) 675-9744
Activity Location: Lake Merced, 1 Harding Road

This is a very good place to learn to row. Lessons are available for $45 and last approximately two hours. The club owns eight singles and a double scull and members have full access to all boats at anytime of the day.

💰 $180/year membership

Climbing

Mission Cliffs

2295 Harrison Street, San Francisco, CA 94110
(415) 550-0515   http://www.mission-cliffs.com

This indoor climbing facility features a 50-foot high lead wall, 14,000 square feet of climbing terrain and much more. If you want to learn how to climb, get in shape for your next climb or are just curious, stop by and take a look around. First Friday of the month is "Women's Day."

💰 $14/day use plus cost of class and equipment;
Membership: $100 initiation, then $50/month

Games, Sports & Outdoors

Rock Rendezvous

(510) 549-9236   *inezdrex@uclink.berkeley.edu*
http://www.rockclimb.org/rr.html

This informal group meets once a month at a different member's home to talk about climbing, plan trips, share stories and slides and find climbing partners within the group. Whether you climb sport, alpine, traditional, boulder or ice, you will connect with others who share your specialty. They do not provide instruction or equipment, so if you've never climbed before, get some training before taking any risks.

☼ 1st Tuesday/month
💰 $15/year membership; $7 after mid-year

Environmental Sporting Activities

Bay Area Ridge Trail Council

26 O'Farrell Street, San Francisco, CA 94104
(415) 391-9300   *ridgetrail@aol.com*

Join this group in completing a 400-mile, multi-use, ridgeline trail surrounding the Bay. Two hundred miles have been finished by now. Hikers, mountain bicyclists and equestrians are invited to join an experienced outing leader on the trail to learn more. Call for further information about upcoming outings and volunteering.

💰 $35/year membership; $15 students

Greenbelt Alliance

116 New Montgomery Street, Suite 640, San Francisco, CA 94105
(415) 255-3233   http://www.greenbelt.org/gba

Help the alliance protect the region's "Greenbelt" space and enhance the entire city. This group also sponsors many outings to interest the serious hiker, biker and walker.

💰 Free

Games, Sports & Outdoors

Sierra Club

85 Second Street, San Francisco, CA 94105
(415) 977-5653   information@sierraclub.org   http://www.sierraclub.org

A well-known national group dedicated to exploring, enjoying and protecting the wild places of the Earth. They sponsor hundreds of regional and local wilderness outings and tours for those who love hiking, backpacking and trekking. Many of these trips are combined with projects to support the natural environment. If you love nature, take a good look at their catalog or website.

Flyfishing

Golden Gate Angling and Casting Club

c/o McLaren Lodge, Golden Gate Park, San Francisco, CA 94117
(415) 386-2630

Activity Location: McLaren Angler's Lodge: Take John F. Kennedy Drive and look for signs of casting pools across from Buffalo Paddock.

E njoy these hidden gems, the casting pools and Angler's Lodge, that were both constructed in 1938. Membership is open to all. Most club activities are planned for weekends.

🐷 $24/year membership; $12 after 6/30; $10 initiation fee

Lincoln Silver Flyfishing

846 Vallejo Street, San Francisco, CA 94133
(415) 393-8070   northfork@rocketmail.com

L earn casting and fly-tying skills in private, personalized and inexpensive lessons. They even make house calls!

☎ Lincoln Silver

Games, Sports & Outdoors

Golf

Harding Park Golf Course

99 Harding Road, San Francisco, CA 94132
(415) 664-4690
Activity Location: Off Skyline Blvd. by Lake Merced

Come and fill out a foursome on this 18-hole public golf course bordering beautiful Lake Merced.

🐚 $26 Mondays-Fridays;
$3 Saturdays & Sundays

Lincoln Park Golf Course

Corner of 34th Avenue & Clement Street,
San Francisco, CA 94121
(415) 221-9911

This public 18-hole course is one of the prettiest you'll ever play, with scenes of ocean-side cliffs and long fairways lined with lush Cypress trees.

☎ Tom McCray
🐚 $23 Mondays-Fridays;$27 Sat & Sun

Lincoln Park Photo by Kerrick James,
Courtesy S.F. Conv. & Visitors Bureau

Mission Bay Golf School

1200 6th Street, San Francisco, CA 94107
(415) 431-7888

Golf lessons help you to develop good swing habits whether you're an old hand or a beginner. You can take a free introductory lesson on Saturday at 8am or Sunday at 10am. Classes are limited to eight persons and reservations are requested. After the class, plan on staying to practice your shots at the driving range.

Presidio Golf Course

300 Finley Road, San Francisco, CA 94129
(415) 561-4653

This challenging golf course is now open to the public after being part of the Presidio military base for more than 100 years.

🐚 $35 Mon.-Thurs.; $45 Fri.; $55 Weekends

Games, Sports & Outdoors

Hiking, Backpacking & Snow Camping

SF Urban Hikers

375 Vernon Street, San Francisco, CA 94132
(415) 469-8960   Infodiva@bigfoot.com

Want to explore the city on foot in an organized way? Started by a native San Franciscan and city dweller, this club is growing in popularity. Hikes are held once a month on Sundays and meeting places vary. Many participants don't have cars, so the hiking routes are easy to get to by foot or public transportation. Ask about the "infamous hillside stride route."

☎ Bessie Barnes

Snow-Campers and Mountaineers (SnoNet)

(415) 931-2057   Mark_Chin@cc.chiron.com   http://www.well.com/user/akka/snonet/index.htm
Activity Location: UCSF, Millberry Union Conference Center, 500 Parnassus Ave., (415) 476-2035

An informal group that meets monthly and maintains a phone and email network of people who enjoy snowcamping, cross country skiing and climbing peaks "just for the pleasure of skiing back down!" The best way to get involved is to send an email or attend a meeting.

☼ 2nd Wednesday/month (winter & spring)   ⏰ 7pm
☎ Mark Chin

UCSF Hiking and Backpacking Club

500 Parnassus, San Francisco, CA 94143
(415) 476-2035   Mary_McDonald.mps@quick.mail.ucsf.edu
Activity Location: UCSF, Millberry Union

Hey— all you enthusiastic people who would like to search out new destinations for hiking and backpacking adventures—this is your group. You do not have to be affiliated with UCSF to participate with this cooperative network. Get yourself on the list for the bimonthly newsletter and calendar, and we'll see you on the trail.

☼ 1st Wednesday/month   ⏰ 7pm
☎ Mary McDonald

Games, Sports & Outdoors

Indoor Games

Army Street Bingo

1740 Cesar Chavez Street, San Francisco, CA 94124
(415) 550-8570

H ave fun for two good causes. The earlier Sunday bingo game raises funds for Renaissance Parents of Success and the later game raises funds for Sojourner Truth Foster Family Service. Bingo is also played here on other days and at various times. Volunteers are always needed.

☼ Sundays   🕐 12:30pm & 6:45pm

Bernal Heights Branch of SF Public Library "Scrabble Night"

500 Cortland Avenue, San Francisco, CA 94110
(415) 695-5160

T est your word power! Join this sociable group of Scrabble players who are welcoming and friendly.

☼ Wednesdays   🕐 7:30pm
💰 Free

Bridge Club of San Francisco

777 Jones Street, San Francisco, CA 94109
(415) 776-6949

Y ou can sign up for lessons at every skill level of rubber bridge in an unintimidating environment. Then you'll be ready to try your hand at a game with others during regular club hours.

☼ Everyday   🕐 12-6pm;
   Tuesdays, Wednesdays & Fridays   7:30pm-Midnight
☎ Augie Hunt

California Bridge Club

1748 Clay Street, San Francisco, CA 94109
(415) 239-9776

C ome and join this friendly group of men and women playing duplicate bridge on Tuesdays at 7:15pm and open stratified on Saturdays at 1pm. Lessons for beginners and intermediate players are offered in eight-week sessions.

☎ Cathy

Chalkers Billiard Club

101 Spear Street, San Francisco, CA 94105
(415) 512-0450

Whether you already play billiards or want to learn, this is a fine social place to enjoy the game. For beginners, a four-week program is offered that will teach you the basics. Then you're on your own!

☀ Tuesdays   ⏰ 6-7pm
☎ Billy Aguero
💰 $50/four classes

Great Entertainer

975 Bryant Street, San Francisco, CA 94103
(415) 861-8833

Overall, a great place to shoot pool and socialize. Ladies are welcome!

☀ 11-2am everyday

Japan Bowl

1790 Post, San Francisco, CA 94115
(415) 921-6200

Different leagues play here and are always open to new bowlers. Stop by to sign up and find a group that fits your level of play.

Mechanics' Institute Library and Chess Room

57 Post Street, Suite 401, San Francisco, CA 94104
(415) 421-1768

The Chess Club is a great place to find a pick-up game, practice your moves and compete in regular tournaments. The director teaches a free weekly class for beginners and intermediate players. Membership offers access to the library. Orientations for new members are held every Wednesday at noon.

☀ Everyday   ⏰ 11am-10:50pm
💰 $60/year membership

Games, Sports & Outdoors

Muddy's Coffeehouse

1304 Valencia, San Francisco, CA 94110
(415) 679-3680

People who love card and board games meet new challengers. A great evening for fun and relaxation. No experience needed.

☼ Wednesdays　　　　　　　⏰ 7:30pm
🕯 Free

San Francisco Dart Association

1300 Irving Street, #1, San Francisco, CA 94122
(415) 668-5334

If you want to know how to get involved in league darts or find out where the weekly tournaments are taking place, call Harry. You can ask him about league membership, a pub list (an extensive listing of all the places darts are being played) and the latest on dart equipment. Also look into the Golden Gate Darting Association at 415-665-1435.

☎ Harry Trout

San Francisco Go Club

2949 Balboa, San Francisco, CA 94121
(415) 386-9565

Membership is open to all who want to learn to play this incredible complex game. The club is open daily from 12pm to 8pm. A beginning lesson is taught on Thursday evenings.

☼ Thursdays　　　　　　　⏰ 6:30pm

Scrabble Club of San Francisco

(415) 467-9464

Activity Location: Carl's Jr Restaurant, 4 Embarcadero Center (415) 391-7780

This is a great group you might never have found. All levels of skilled Scrabble players here. Beginners are welcome but they won't be beginners for long.

☼ Tuesdays　　　　　　　⏰ 6-10pm

Games, Sports & Outdoors

Inline Hockey & Skating

Inline Hockey

Activity Location: Pacelli Gym, 145 Lake Merced Blvd., Daly City
(415) 991-8001

O pen to all adults looking for a pick-up game of roller hockey. It's fast, but that adds to the excitement. Coed teams available.

☼ Mondays & Tuesdays   ☎ 10pm-midnight
💰 $5

Bladium Inline Hockey Stadium

1050 - 3rd Street, San Francisco, CA 94107
(415) 442-5060

B eginners can take part in a starter league which is half instruction and half actual game play. Advanced players are required to be members to play. If you've always wanted to try your hand (foot?) at a puck sport, this is a good place to test it out.

💰 $35/year membership

Marina Skate And Snowboard

2271 Chestnut Street, San Francisco, CA 94123
(415) 567-8400

T his terrific place offers free inline skate lessons every Saturday morning. The skate rental is also free with the lesson. Now there's nothing to stop you from giving this graceful sport a try. (And you'll tone up your legs something fierce!)

☼ Saturdays   ☎ 8-10am
💰 Free

Midnight Rollers "Friday Night Skate"

Activity Location: Ferry Building on the Embarcadero, (415) 752-1967

W eather permitting, this energetic group numbering anywhere from 200 to 500 skaters joins together for a 12-mile loop through the city. You'll find that evening skating is enchanting.

☼ Fridays   ☎ 8pm
☏ David Miles

Games, Sports & Outdoors

Nuvo Rollerblades "Monday Night Skate"

3108 Fillmore Street, San Francisco, CA 94123
(415) 771-6886

A weeknight evening communal skate meets at this popular skating store for an 11-mile glide through the city.

☀ Mondays   ☎ 8pm

Speedskating & Recreational Skating

Activity Location: Golden Gate Park   (415) 752-1967

JFK Drive is closed to all auto traffic and the street becomes a multi-use athletic playground. For you skaters who want to improve your technique, head over for a free informal skate clinic with David Miles at JFK Drive and 6th Avenue around 11am.

☀ Sundays   ☎ 11am-6pm
☎ David Miles

Miscellany

Archery

Activity Location: Golden Gate Park. Enter the park on 47th Ave. & Fulton.

This is not a formal club—rather a spot in the park reserved for public shooting. Archers must supply targets, bows and arrows. Bales are provided at a location opposite 47th Avenue near Fulton Street. Weekends are the best time to meet others interested in this sport.

Games, Sports & Outdoors

Bamboo Reef Enterprises, Inc.

584 - 4th Street, San Francisco, CA 94107
(415) 362-6694   http://www.citysearch.com/sfo/bambooreef

This organization will have you exploring the depths with local scuba divers in no time. Bamboo Reef conducts training sessions in a pool in San Francisco on the weekends, and, for full certification, open water sessions in Monterey. An advanced scuba class offers new challenges and unique adventures to the seasoned diver. Ask about the Channel Islands trip aboard the Vision and the Monterey trip aboard the PacStar.

☎ Karen Zammitti

Golden Gate Park Stables

P.O. Box 22401, San Francisco, CA 94122
(415) 668-7360
Activity Location: John F. Kennedy Drive at 36th Avenue

All you need is a reservation to join these excellent riding lessons and programs. Beginners are encouraged to attend as well as intermediate and advanced riders. Guided trail rides for groups of one to eight riders are also available.

Golden Gate Sport and Social Club

1766 Union Street, San Francisco, CA 94123
(415) 921-1233

This combination sport and social club has opportunities from coed volleyball and ballroom dancing to outdoor soccer and nightclub parties. Every season more than 4,000 people take part in coed athletic leagues. After the games, a sponsor bar offers food discounts to socializing league players.

☎ Brian Schwartz
💰 $35/yr membership

Halberstadt Fencers' Club

621 South Van Ness Avenue, San Francisco, CA 94110
(415) 863-3838

Halberstadt offers instruction for beginning and advanced fencers, and sponsors competitive training and events. A sport used by actors and others who want to improve their physical skill and grace (thrust-and-parry).

Games, Sports & Outdoors

Kite Flying
Activity Location: The Marina Green

We didn't find an organized group of kite flyers in the city but on windy weekend days, pull your kite out of the closet and run down to the Marina Green where kite enthusiasts can be found flying their "birds." You'll recognize them—they look like the Blue Angels flying in formation.

Outdoors Unlimited
550 Parnassus, near 3rd Avenue under USCF Library, San Francisco, CA 94143
(415) 476-2078   http://www.outdoors.ucsf.edu/ou

Both an excellent information resource for many local outdoor sports and adventures *and* an activity center where volunteers teach classes and organize outings. There are no dues or membership fees and everyone is welcome. Dropping in on a Wednesday night work party is a great way to get involved and find an outing that appeals to you.

☼ Wednesdays   ⏰ 6-9pm

Pacific Road and Gun Club
520 John Muir Drive, San Francisco, CA 94132
(415) 239-9750

This club has classes available for $15 and $16 including shells. The weapon is provided free of charge and you do not have to be a member to participate in the classes.

💰 $100/year membership, plus $6.25/month dues

Recreation and Park Athletic Office "Softball"
Golden Gate Park, San Francisco, CA 94117
(415) 753-7023
Activity Location: Various parks throughout the city

If you want to play on a softball team (women, men, or coed), the season starts in March. Call the softball headquarters to get your name, playing level and desired position added to the list. By the way, other sports are offered to the public through this office.

Games, Sports & Outdoors

San Francisco Croquet Club

3350 Octavia Street, #5, San Francisco, CA 94123
(415) 776-4104   http://www.ontheweb.com/usca
Activity Location: Stern Grove, 19th Avenue & Wawona Street

S FCC is the largest non-profit croquet club of its kind on public turf in America. It's home of the San Francisco Open and other major tournaments. Beginning adult players are encouraged to attend a free croquet lesson or call about the Saturday morning program "Introduction to Six-Wicket Croquet." You'll need to wear flat-soled shoes to protect the green.

☼ 1st & 3rd Wednesday/month   ⌚ 1-4pm

San Francisco Lawn Bowling Club

Activity Location: Golden Gate Park, Bowling Green Drive, San Francisco, CA
(415) 753-9298

I f you're curious about this sport, try the free class at noon on Wednesdays. Call for details, and wear your flat soled shoes. When you're an official player, you'll wear all white for the games.

☼ Wednesdays   ⌚ 12pm
💰 Free

San Francisco Vikings Soccer Club

3208 Irving Street, San Francisco, CA 94122
(415) 753-3111

T his 70-plus year old club is proud to provide soccer for all levels, age groups and genders. This is a fast-paced sport and loved by its devotees.

Motorcycles

Bay Area Motorcycle Training

P.O. Box 14195, San Francisco, CA 94114
(415) 285-8827

L earn to ride in a safe, unintimidating environment where the motorcycles and helmets are provided. Learn basic maneuvers or, for the more advanced rider, improve your swerving, braking and cornering techniques. Call for a schedule.

Games, Sports & Outdoors

Montgomery Street M.C.

(415) 332-8800

Activity Location: New Pisa Restaurant, 550 Green Street (415) 989-2289

This group of experienced riders meet every second Thursday for a lunch meeting to plan rides and sometimes hear a guest speaker. Group is open to all who are enthusiastic about motorcycles.

☼ 2nd Thursday/month   🕰 12pm

NORCAL Motorsports

(415) 885-3363

A serious but enthusiastic group of riders who travel mostly on Japanese and BMW bikes. Four rides a year are required.

☎ Chuck

San Francisco Motorcycle Club

2194 Folsom Street @18th, San Francisco, CA 94110
(415) 863-1930

Established in 1904, this is America's second oldest motorcycle club. They ride all types of bikes and are relaxed and friendly. The best way to get involved is to stop by on a Thursday night where visitors are most welcome.

☼ Thursdays   🕰 8pm

Running

Enviro-Sports

P.O. Box 1040, Stinson Beach, CA 94970
(415) 868-1829   envirosp.well.com   http://sfbayrun.com/envirosports

Enviro-Sports is a nonprofit running club that sponsors the "Enviroventure Series," and supports trail maintenance and habitat restoration to preserve wilderness and parklands. Past series events have included the "Big Sur Trail Marathon," "Napa Wine Country Classic Marathon," "Orcas Island Swim," and "Yosemite Cloud's Rest Hike." We've heard that these events are outstanding but challenging runs.

☎ Dave Horning

Games, Sports & Outdoors

Golden Gate Triathlon Club

P.O. Box 591745, San Francisco, CA 94159
(415) 434-4482   markw@sirius.com http://www.hulaman.com/ggtc.html
Activity Location: Golden Gate Park, Kezar Stadium

An athletic group of people who swim, run and bike as well as meet for other social events. You don't have to swim in the "Escape from Alcatraz" event to qualify for membership! Just enjoy organized workouts in and around San Francisco.

💰 $45/year membership; $15/month track dues

Hoy's Sports

1632 Haight Street, San Francisco, CA 94117
(415) 252-5370
Activity Location: Kezar Stadium

This is an outstanding men's racing team. (See Chapter 16 for women's.) If you want to make a commitment to racing, give them a call.

☎ John Murtagh

San Francisco East Bay Hashes

415) 334-4274

This group of runners enjoys socializing and having a great time as well as running activities. Call for the time and location of their next run date and run along with this strong-legged bunch.

☀ Mondays

Sailing & Windsurfing

Bay Area Association of Disabled Sailors

P.O. Box 193730, San Francisco, CA 94119
(415) 281-0212
Activity Location: South Beach Yacht Club, Pier 40   (415) 495-2295

The club is opened to all able-bodied and disabled persons interested in sailing. An excellent venue to learn how to sail inexpensively and be taught by people who care.

☀ 3rd Saturday/month   ⏰ 10am
💰 $24/year membership

Games, Sports & Outdoors

Crissy Field

Activity Location: Crissy Field, Presidio

Crissy Field is an advanced boardsailing area with dangerous conditions. The water is cold and there can be unpredictable tides and fog, not to mention the heavy shipping and boating traffic. (We're *not* recommending it.) Nevertheless, this is an exciting place to meet or watch other windsurfers during April to August.

City Front Sailboards Lessons

2936 Lyon Street, San Francisco, CA 94123
(415) 929-7873

They look so pretty out on the Bay—but have you tried to stay up on a board? It takes skill, but it's exhilarating! They'll teach you here. The windsurfing season runs approximately from April to the end of August on the Bay. We'll look for you with the red sail!

Golden Gate Yacht Club

San Francisco Marina Smallcraft Harbor, San Francisco, CA 94123
(415) 346-2628

The GG Yacht Club is a private club that has both power and sail boat enthusiasts. There are different categories of membership with different stipulations to qualify (e.g., boat owning, crew, etc.). Recently they've opened an "Affiliate" category for persons under 35 that is limited to 100 people. Are there better places in the world to sail? Not many.

☎ D. Drayer

Outdoors Unlimited Knots for Boaters

550 Parnassus Avenue, San Francisco, CA 94122
(415) 476-2078
Activity Location: University of California San Francisco Campus

Ever had a boat slip off its mooring? If you have, you'll be running to this class. Learn the basic essential knots for ocean voyages to river adventures and meet others who want to develop good boating habits. Give OU center a call and obtain their latest catalog or check their bulletin board.

💰 Free

Games, Sports & Outdoors

Sailing Education Adventures (SEA)

Fort Mason Center, Building E, San Francisco, CA 94124
(415) 775-8779

SEA is a community-based organization that provides sailing education and promotes conservation and care of the Bay marine environment. All instruction is performed by experienced volunteers. In addition to classes, members also enjoy group sailing events, lectures, picnics and many other social gatherings. Reasonably priced, it opens the door for anyone who loves sailing to get involved.

💰 $35/year membership

San Francisco Windsurfing

(415) 753-3235
Activity Location: Lake Merced, Harding Road off Skyline Blvd.

A lovely place to surf, this is an excellent spot to take classes or rent equipment without the hassle of owning your own board.

☎ Jeff Craft

South Beach Yacht Club

Pier 40, San Francisco, CA 94107
(415) 495-2295

Overlooking the South Beach Harbor Marina, the club is an attractive and comfortable place for enjoying social events, year-round racing and organized cruises. Sailboat and power boaters are both welcome to join and boat ownership is not a requirement.

Spinnaker Sailing - San Francisco

Pier 40, South Beach Harbor, San Francisco, CA 94107
(415) 543-7333   spinnsail@aol.com   http://www.baysail.com/spinnaker

Don't you love seeing those colorful spinnaker sails on the Bay on a breezy day? Put up yours! If you want to learn to sail or already sail, if you own a boat or just like to crew, this club is for you. Different "learn to sail packages" and membership categories are available.

☎ Drew Harper

Games, Sports & Outdoors

St. Francis Yacht Club

San Francisco Marina Smallcraft Harbor, San Francisco, CA 94123
(415) 563-6363

St. Francis Yacht Club is located directly next to the Golden Gate Yacht Club and includes both power and sail boat enthusiasts. It is a private club, but does offer different categories of membership with different stipulations to qualify (boat owning, crew etc.). If you are a serious boater and want to make a long-term commitment, look into this prestigious club.

☎ Ardene Anderson

Yacht Racing Association of San Francisco Bay

Fort Mason Center, Buchanan & Marina Blvd., San Francisco, CA 94123
(415) 771-9500   http://www.yra.org

Some sailors just love to race. Others love to watch. Whichever it is, this is the premier source for boat racing as well as other water related activities. Did you know there are over 300 sailboat races a year on the Bay? It's a cutting edge experience.

🔔 Free calendar

Swimming

Dolphin Swim and Boat Club

502 Jefferson Street, San Francisco, CA 94109
(415) 441-9329

Join this group of hearty Bay swimmers for a plunge. (You'll be hearty too when you swim in that water!) Other club activities include rowing, handball and running. To join, attend a monthly meeting. The public can swim five days a week through the Dolphin and South End Rowing Club's alternating non-member policy.

☼ 3rd Wednesday/month   🕑 6:30pm
🔔 $6.50 day use; membership: $240 first six months then $30/month

Games, Sports & Outdoors

USF Koret Health and Recreation Center

2130 Fulton Street, San Francisco, CA 94117
(415) 422-6820

S wimming instruction and water aerobic classes are offered in this excellent indoor multi-use pool. Membership is not required to attend classes but there is a small fee. For full use of the club, membership is necessary.

YMCA - Presidio

Lincoln and Funston Streets, San Francisco, CA 94129
(415) 447-9622

N estled in a beautiful setting within the old Presidio, this newly remolded facility is a wonderful place to swim, get swimming instruction and enjoy other athletic activities.

🕯 $99 initiation fee; $32/month limited use

Tennis

After Work Tennis Club (AWTC)

1219 10th Street, San Francisco, CA 94122
(415) 661-2536
Activity Location: Golden Gate Park Tennis Courts

T his fun, low-key, social and athletic group meets weekly between May and September and hosts other events throughout the year. Call for more information.

☎ Dave

Golden Gate Tennis

(415) 804-8209
Activity Location: GG Park Tennis Courts opposite the Conservatory of Flowers off JFK Drive (415) 753-7001

G ive a call to learn more about the group and private clinics that are offered for all levels of players.

☎ JoJo Zalameda, Associate Tennis Pro
🕯 About $16/group lesson

Games, Sports & Outdoors

Golden Gate Tennis Club
P.O. Box 591237, San Francisco, CA 94159
(415) 436-0862
Activity Location: G G Park opposite the Conservatory of Flowers off JFK Dr.

This superb tennis club in Golden Gate Park has been open to anyone interested in playing tennis since 1901. Members take part in social events and a series of tournaments, including the historic San Francisco City Championship and the San Francisco Residents' tournament. Did you know that these challenges are open to qualifying amateurs? They're great fun to watch.

☎ Louis Rasky
💰 $35/yr membership, $30 seniors; $12 juniors

Golden Gate Tennis Courts
(415) 753-7001
Activity Location: G G Park opposite the Conservatory of Flowers off JFK Dr.

Call to reserve one of the 21 courts opposite the Conservatory of Flowers on the weekends. Lessons for children and adults are available.

💰 $6 or less

Moscone Recreation Center
Chestnut and Buchanan Streets, San Francisco, CA 94123
(415) 292-2006

Spruce up your game and develop a dynamite backhand. Your partners will be amazed! These lessons are free.

☀ Tuesdays & Thursdays   🕐 6:30pm

Tuesday Night Tennis
(415) 668-2037
Activity Location: Golden Gate Park or Mission Dolores Park

Tuesday nights throughout the year this group of diverse skill levels play doubles and singles. During the summer season, they play at the courts in Golden Gate Park. Winter season is played under the court lights of Mission Dolores Park.

☀ Tuesdays   🕐 6:30-8pm
☎ George Harrow Tuesdays

Gay & Lesbian

Activism • Business/Career
Continuing Education • Dancing & Music
History • Hobbies • Social • Spiritual
Sports & Games

Gay and Lesbian

San Francisco FrontRunners relay team at an
international FrontRunners meet

San Francisco FrontRunners all decked out for the
Christmas Relays at Lake Merced

Gay and Lesbian

The organized activities included in this book are open to everyone, unless specified as being for a certain population. In San Francisco, more than in most places, interest-based organizations *are* open to all people, regardless of their sexual preference. When it comes to sharing an interest, sexuality does not seem to be important to participants in the groups.

Although we believe that most people enjoy being active in the community at large, and want to have the choice to do so, at times they want to find others in their own reference group with whom to share common activities. Thus we have included four chapters for specific groups, including Singles, Seniors, Women and Gays and Lesbians. Sometimes the activities and events focus on content directly related to the group (e.g., gay activism). Other times they are places where people can just enjoy themselves (eg., camping, tennis) with others who identify themselves in this way. Some groups have more narrow membership (eg., lesbians only, gay people of a certain age), but many are open to all gays and lesbians and some welcome straight participants.

The Bay Area is rich with gay and lesbian activity groups. This chapter gives only an outline of the variety of organizations you can find. Once on your way, each contact will open doors to new ones. To keep in touch with what's happening moment to moment, the *San Francisco Bay Times* is without a doubt the best source for groups and organizations for the gay community and for upcoming events. Pick up thistwice-a-month paper at any major bookstore including **A Different Light** (489 Castro Street) and **City Lights Bookstore** (261 Columbus Avenue). The *sBay Times* is a great resource and an excellent read.

Sports and games groups are abundant for gay and lesbian players. **Different Strokes** is a golf club where you can practice and improve your game as well as socialize. Every Monday, Wednesday and Friday morning at 7:30 a.m., golfers play the back nine at Harding Golf Course. With phenomenal views of the ocean, it's a fantastic way to start the day—and a challenging course too. The **Gay & Lesbian Tennis Foundation** offers activities for players of all abilities. It sponsors singles and doubles tournaments and clinics for a variety of tennis games. There are many beginning tennis players among the members, so don't be dissuaded if you are new to the sport. Advanced players will find their own as well.

Gay and Lesbian

For you out-of-doors types, Marc Pierce organizes both the **High Eagle Canoeing** and **High Eagle Flyfishing** groups. He is an enthusiastic and overall nice person who will encourage you to sign up for one of many amazing trips, including the two-day group paddles on the Russian, Eel, Stanislaus and American rivers. These canoeing events sound like "don't miss" experiences to us. Trout enthusiasts, why not don your waders and explore California's scenic back county rivers and streams. These trips usually involve camping, which adds to the overall outdoor experience. Men as well as women are encouraged to participate in these sporty outdoor adventures.

Skiing. "Now we're talking," says Diane, an inveterate skier. **SAGA North** is a year-round ski club that offers winter ski trips to such magnificent destinations as Aspen for the infamous Aspen Gay Ski Week; Vail; Jackson Hole; and monthly ski trips to Lake Tahoe. During the summer, the group is involved in river rafting, water skiing, biking, hiking, potluck suppers and much more. Members say that ski clubs are some of the best places to meet people, *and*, in the process, ski some outstanding terrain.

Running. **SF Frontrunners** is a major running, walking and social club that is a staple at the **Bay to Breakers**. Diane caught up with the Frontrunners at the Hayes Street Hill as she covered the parade by scooter. They reached the finish line in the same amount of time as she did on the scooter. All right!

Great games galore! On Wednesday nights at **Muddy's Coffeehouse**, people meet to play cards and board games, including Hearts, Spades and Scrabble. No experience is needed and everyone is welcome to join the fun. If you haven't played games since you were *much younger*, check out what you've been missing. If you're skittish about competing, go with the attitude that the fun is in the playing, not the winning, and give it a try. (You could end up owning all of Pacific Avenue and shellacking everyone at the table...Ooops!) No matter what the outcome, you'll find that Muddy's is an all-round great get-together place with real good coffee.

Let's segue' now to activities that are music-related. The **Queer Jazz Club** meets in a member's home for a monthly potluck social, and plays music chosen at the previous event. This is an informal, friendly, mixed-gender club that is open to anyone who loves jazz. **The Rawhide** is a well-known spot in San Francisco that offers Country-Western dancing.

If you want to learn Line Dances and the Two-Step Waltz, this is the place to go for lessons. The dance floor is large so you'll have plenty of space to move around without worrying about bumping into someone. No partner is needed and people are totally into the footwork. There's really nothing stopping you from *mossing on down*. For Ballroom dance lovers, several major ballrooms, including the **Metronome**, offer same-sex dance lessons and parties.

A variety of other groups focus on specific interests. Gay intellectuals and visionaries need to know about the **Gay Geeks**, a discussion and social club for men and women. The central idea of the group is that brain power is the future life force in America. Members come together to have thoughtful discussions about significant topics *and* laugh and have fun. The **Lambda Amateur Radio Club** is open to anyone who holds an amateur radio license or who wishes to become licensed. And if you're a pilot, you could fly into a prearranged spot and find the **Golden Gate Flyers**, a group of aviation professionals and enthusiasts who have meetings and other activities as well.

You'll find continuing education groups, like the **Harvey Milk Institute**, where classes are held on topics of special importance to the gay community. If you're ready to "walk the walk," join an activism group to help the queer voice get heard.

Connecting through spiritual activities nurtures acceptance, understanding, empathy and love. **Dignity/SF, Golden Gate MCC**, and **Sha'ar Zahav** are only a few of the excellent church/temple organizations that offer both spiritual as well as supportive services.

Gay and Lesbian

High Eagle Canoeing, Tuolumme River. Photo by Marc Pierce

Activism

Alice B. Toklas Lesbian and Gay Democratic Club

P.O. Box 422698, San Francisco, CA 94142
(415) 522-3809
Activity Location: Piaf's, 1686 Market Street (415) 864-3700

Started in 1972 as the first lesbian and gay Democratic club, it continues to play an active role in shaping policy. Get involved in working on issues by joining this active and interesting group of politically-minded people.

☼ 2nd Monday/month ☎ 7pm

Amnesty International
Members for Lesbian and Gay Concerns (AIMLGC)

500 Sansome Street, Suite 615, San Francisco, CA 94111
(415) 291-9233 majordomo@io.org with message 'subscribe amnesty-L'
http://www.amnesty-usa.org or http://www.amnesty.org

Work on behalf of people persecuted for their sexual orientation and other human rights abuses. AIMLGC is part of Amnesty International, an organization which works to free prisoners of conscience, insure fair and prompt trials, and abolish torture and executions.

☼ 2nd Thursday/month ☎ 6pm

Gay and Lesbian Alliance Against Defamation (GLAAD)

1360 Mission Street, Suite 200, San Francisco, CA 94103
(415) 861-4588 http://www.glaad.org

GLAAD promotes fair media coverage of lesbians, gays, bisexuals and transgenders, fighting stereotypical portrayals in the print and electronic mediums.

International Gay and Lesbian Human Rights Commission

1360 Mission Street, Suite 200, San Francisco, CA 94103
(415) 255-8680 iglhrc@iglhrc.org http://www.iglhrc.org

The commission monitors, documents, and exposes human rights abuses of sexual minorities and people with HIV/AIDS worldwide.

Gay and Lesbian

Log Cabin Republican Club of San Francisco

P.O. Box 14174, San Francisco, CA 94114
(415) 522-2944   logcabin@cais.com

This is the voice of gay and lesbian Republicans who believe in personal responsibility, limited government and Republican candidates who support non-discriminatory practices.

☎ Scott

Business/Career

Bay Area Career Women (BACW)

55 New Montgomery Street, Suite 606, San Francisco, CA 94105
(415) 495-5393   http://www.bacw.com

Their vision statement says it best–"BACW's mission is to empower its members and all lesbians, to eliminate discrimination and prejudice, and to promote lesbian pride, leadership and visibility by providing network opportunities which bridge our diverse communities through education, philanthropic and social activities." The membership represents a diversity of people from a vast array of professions. About 50 events are offered each month where professionals can interact.

💰 $65/year membership

Golden Gate Business Association

1699 Van Ness Avenue, San Francisco, CA 94109
(415) 441-3651

GGBA, established in 1974, is the nation's oldest gay and lesbian business association. Comprising gay-owned businesses, professionals, artisans and individuals located throughout the Bay Area, this organization continues to thrive. Take part in their excellent business development programs and monthly networking events.

The Gay Macintosh Users Group

(415) 552-GMUG   *gmug@gmug.org*   *http://www.gmug.org*
Activity Location: St. Francis Lutheran Church, 152 Church Street
(415) 621-2635

Join GMUG to learn more about Macintosh computers and meet other Mac loyalists. Terrific discussions and presentations bring you up to speed on the wonderful features of the Mac. You may also win a new software product—raffled off at the general meeting.

☼ 3rd & 4th Thursdays/month   ⏰ 7:30pm
💰 Free to members; $5/non-members

Continuing Education

Harvey Milk Institute

548 Castro Street, Suite 451, San Francisco, CA 94114
(415) 552-7200   *http://members.aol.com/harvmilk*

The Harvey Milk Institute offers continuing education programs that feature topics of special interest to the gay community. Classes are usually offered on a semester basis but there are some one-day events and retreats. Call for a catalog.

☎ Kevin
💰 $10-$25/class

Dancing & Music

Baroque Buddies

(415) 648-4853

Aimez vous Bach? If so, this is a social group for those who enjoy music of the Baroque period. An event is held every other month at a member's house and features a potluck supper and a music program.

☎ Cath

Gay and Lesbian

Castro Folkdancers

(415) 507-1867

Activity Location: Eureka Valley Recreation Center, 100 Collingwood Street
(415) 554-9528

Join this international folkdance group to learn ethnic Line Dances. There is no need to have a partner and beginners are encouraged to give it a try. You'll be having so much fun by the end of the lesson that you'll want to stay for the general dance from 8-9:30pm. And what would stop you?

☼ Tuesdays   ☎ 7:30-8pm
☎ Andrew

Queer Jazz Club

(415) 922-3789

A group of music lovers who meet monthly for a potluck/social to share and play music following a given theme (vocalists, music from the 50s, etc.) that was chosen at the prior gathering. This is a mixed-gender club, open to anyone in the lesbian and gay community who loves jazz. All events are held at the members' houses for an informal and comfortable experience. Members range from practicing musicians to jazz neophytes. All are welcome.

☼ 1st Saturday/month   ☎ 7pm
☎ Roni
💰 $10/year membership

The Rawhide

280 7th Street, San Francisco, CA 94103
(415) 621-1197

Learn to Line Dance and Two-Step Waltz in this western club with a large dance floor. Country dance lessons provided with admission and no partners are needed.

☼ Monday-Fridays   ☎ 7:30pm
💰 $2

History

Gay and Lesbian Historical Society of Northern California

973 Market Street, Suite 400, San Francisco, CA 94103
(415) 777-5455   http://www.glhs.com

G et involved with this excellent organization which is run exclusively by volunteers. Stop by on Saturday or Sunday between 2-5pm to see the changing exhibitions or to explore the research center and archives. The society also hosts receptions, lectures and events throughout the year.

Hobbies

Golden Gate Flyers

584 Castro Street, Box 500, San Francisco, CA 94114
(415) 995-4938   Capnjfrank@aol.com
http://members.aol.com/mike0256/ggfl.htm

S hare your passion for flying! If you join this social organization for aviation professionals and enthusiasts, you can take part in the monthly fly-in where everybody flies into a selected spot. Call for their newsletter, *The Gayviator*, to learn how you can get involved.

💰 $25/year membership

Lambda Amateur Radio Club/Golden Gate

P.O. Box 14073, San Francisco, CA 94114
(415) 863-1196   http://www.geocities.com/westhollywood/2473/larc.htm

C onnect with others interested in ham radio. Membership is open to anyone who holds an amateur radio license or who wishes to become licensed.

☼ 2nd Thursday/month (except Nov. & Dec.)
💰 $15/year membership

Gay and Lesbian

Social

BFSF (BiFriendly-SF)

(415) 703-7977 ext.4
Activity Location: Muddy Waters Coffee House, 262 Church Street
(415) 621-2233

B FSG is a social group open to bisexuals and bifriendly people. Meet, talk and discuss timely topics of special interest to the bi community. The organized discussion is facilitated by a BFSG member and is quite enjoyable.

☼ 2nd Monday/month   ⏲ 7:30pm

Dyke Friends of SF

(415) 824-7892
Activity Location: Muddy's Coffee House, 1304 Valencia Street (415) 647-7994

T his diverse group interested in forming lasting friendships meets bimonthly to have coffee and get acquainted. Couples and singles are welcome.

G Forty Plus

(415) 552-1997
Activity Location: First Unitarian Church, 1187 Franklin Street, (415) 776-4580

T his club was established in 1972 for gay/bisexual men over 40 and their admirers. The events include a program and social hour.

☼ 1st & 3rd Sundays/month   ⏲ 2-4pm
☎ Jordan Lee

Gay Geeks

3181 Mission Street, #130, San Francisco, CA 94110
(415) 679-3680   dk@wco.com
Activity Location: Josie's Cabaret & Juice Joint, 3583-16th, (415) 861-7933

J oin this mixed-gender social club, formed with the gay intellectual and visionary in mind. Geeks meet for thoughtful and analytical discussions.

☼ 1st Saturday/month   ⏲ 2pm
💰 Free

Gay and Lesbian

MAX (Men's Associated Exchange)

2261 Market Street, Suite 431, San Francisco, CA 94114
(415) 442-1994
Activity Location: City Club of San Francisco, 155 Sansome Street
(415) 362-2480

MAX is a non-profit social organization for professional gay men. Join them at their "TGIF" after-work cocktail receptions held at the lovely City Club. Ask them about their travel, art, sport and career-oriented activities.

☼ 1st & 3rd Fridays/month   ☎ 6-9pm
☝ Free; $5/non-members

Men Over Forty

4104 - 24th Street, Suite 309, San Francisco, CA 94114
(415) 642-8000
Activity Location: Kairos, 2128 - 15th Street (415) 861-0877

If you are a gay man, 40 or older, you qualify to participate in these excellent and affordable one- and three-day retreats. Designed to help clarify personal priorities and goals, the sessions are conducted in a warm and supportive atmosphere by a licensed psychologist. Past retreat topics have included, "Successful Aging," "Building Healthy Self-Esteem," and "Developing Closer Relationships With Others."

☼ Saturdays   ☎ 10am-4:30pm
✆ David
☝ About $65/retreat

TV/TS & Friends

P.O. Box 426486, San Francisco, CA 94142
(415) 564-3246

An active and friendly transvestite and transgender group that sponsors seminars, workshops, costume balls, dances and support groups. They can also steer you to other TV/TS organizations around the Bay Area.

Gay and Lesbian

Spiritual

Dignity/SF

1329 7th Avenue, San Francisco, CA 94122
(415) 681-2491   dignity@aol.com   http://www.dignityusa.org

A faith community of lesbian, gay and bisexual Catholics and their friends and families. Call for further information and a newcomer packet.

Golden Gate MCC

1508 Church Street, San Francisco, CA 94131
(415) 642-0294   http://userwww.sfsu.edu~black/ggmcc.html/

A diverse, affirming and inclusive Christ-centered congregation. The church sponsors HIV support for women and men, couples communication groups, baptisms, commitment ceremonies and memorial services. Also, they present excellent music and drama programs.

☎ Rev. Sharna Sutherin

Sha'ar Zahav Shabbat Services

220 Danvers Street, San Francisco, CA 94114
(415) 861-6932

Jewish lesbian and gay congregation meets for services are held every Friday and every second Saturday at 8:15pm.

Sports & Games

High Eagle Flyfishing

628A Hayes Street, San Francisco, CA 94102
(415) 621-8254

Group for gay, lesbian, bisexual and transgender trout enthusiasts. Wade in your favorite rivers and scenic streams. Overnight trips usually involve camping and beginners are welcome.

☎ Marc Pierce

Different Spokes

P.O. Box 14711, San Francisco, CA 94114
(415) 282-1647   72150@compuserve.com

S taying active is easy with this biking group that will keep you
moving with their rides and socializing at the social events. After
attending a ride or two, riders are encouraged to support Spokes by
becoming members.

🐌 $18/year membership

Dyke Hackers

(415) 824-1453   Sandip@aol.com or sandip@best.com

J oin this group of lesbian golfers who like to golf with other lesbian
golfers in a relaxed, comfortable and fun environment. They do *not*
take themselves too seriously and all levels are welcome.

Gay and Lesbian Tennis Foundation

2215-R Market Street, Suite 109, San Francisco, CA 94114
(415) 863-7643   Dmckinsf@aol.com http://www.gltf.org/~gltf

G LTF has activities for players of all abilities, including singles
and doubles tournaments, clinics and social events. The membership consists of many beginning tennis players learning to play in a
comfortable environment, as well as those wishing to improve their game
by playing with advanced players.

☎ Lee
🐌 $40/year membership

High Eagle Canoeing

628A Hayes Street, San Francisco, CA 94102
(415) 621-8254

A group for gay, lesbian, bisexual and transgender canoeists. The
membership is approximately 50% men and women. Join the
beautiful and exciting two-day group paddles on the Russian, Eel,
Stanislaus and American Rivers and more. Beginners are welcome.

☎ Marc Pierce

Gay and Lesbian

Lesbian Bowlers

(415) 285-0641

Activity Location: Japantown Bowl, 1790 Post Street, (415) 921-6200

H ave fun bowling with women friends. The group offers a bit of free instruction. Call for more details and to confirm bowling alley and time.

☼ Sundays   🕐 5:30pm

☎ Sara

SAGA North

P.O. Box 14384, San Francisco, CA 94114
(415) 995-2772 Saganorth@logx.com   http://saganorth.com

I f you join this gay and lesbian ski club of all abilities, you'll enjoy out-of-town ski trips during the winter season. Every year they travel to the "Aspen Gay Ski Week," Vail and Jackson Hole, plus monthly ski trips to Lake Tahoe. During the summer the group is involved in river rafting, water skiing, biking, hiking, potlucks and more.

💰 $40/year membership

San Francisco Hiking Club

P.O. Box 14065, San Francisco, CA 94114
(415) 487-6410

T his non-profit, volunteer-run organization provides opportunities for the gay and lesbian community and their friends to explore and enjoy the outdoors together.

💰 $15/year membership

SF FrontRunners

584 Castro Street, Suite 300, San Francisco, CA 94114
(415) 978-2429

A social running and walking club for lesbians, gays and bisexuals and their friends. All levels are welcome in the competetive and non-competetive activities they offer, including a weekly run and a monthly Sunday run. This fine group is a staple of the famous "Bay to Breakers" running event.

💰 $24/year membership

SF Games

(415) 679-3678

Activity Location: Muddy's Coffeehouse, 1304 Valencia, (415) 647-7994

A well-known place to hang out and meet new folks while you try your hand at familiar card and board games like Hearts, Spades, and SCRABBLE. No experience is needed and everyone is welcome to join this informal games group. Look for them toward the center of the room.

☼ Wednesdays   🕐 7:30–11pm

🪙 Free

SF Tsunami

(415) 487-6614

G ay and Lesbian Masters Swim Team invites qualified master swimmers of all ages, races, genders and abilities to enjoy both competitive and non-competitive swimming. Join in meets, lake swims and many social events throughout the year.

Golden Gate Bridge/Presido. Photo by John Larsen.
Courtesy S.F. Conv. & Visitors Bureau

Health for Mind & Body

Fitness • Health Studies • Life Studies

Martial Arts • Meditation

Nutrition, Herbs & Healthy Food • Tai Chi

Yoga • Health & Fitness

Health for Mind & Body

Yoga students enjoying a moment of stretch and release at
The Mindful Body. Photo by Steve Savage

Members enjoying a game of squash at the San Francisco Bay Club

Health for Mind & Body

Taking good care of yourself goes way beyond the pursuit of achieving the perfect body. Many San Franciscans transcend the purely aesthetic desire to be the *buffest* by practicing a mind-body connection to good health and body image. Working from the perspective that how you feel as a complete entity affects your health, San Franciscans strive to find ways to lessen stress through physical release and peace through intrapersonal study.

We are as diverse in our methods of pursing good health as we are individualistic. What appeals to one will not work for another. Many are drawn to Eastern health methods, demonstrated by the abundance of practitioners of yoga, massage, tai chi chuan and herbology. For others, a traditional fitness club offering weight training, machines and cardiovascular classes is a better choice. Whatever your preference, the trick is to find *your* favorite ways to create harmony between your mental and physical health, and balance the activities in your professional life and personal life. If you can do this while toning up your muscles and reducing your waistline, all the better!

Many of the activities in this book will contribute to your good health and physical fitness, such as those listed in Chapter Seven: Games, Sports & Outdoors. Just reading the book and planning new ways to do interesting and pleasurable things contribute to your psychological health. However, the activities in this chapter are specifically concerned with the exploration of health issues. So if you want to do things that will be good for you, look at all the activities in the book. If you are ready to embark on your own healthy journey, the activities listed in this chapter can get you started.

Actually, there are two general types of activities in this chapter: *Classes* that teach better health practices, and *personal growth* activities which expand your physical, mental and/or spiritual experience. Some of the best and most reasonably priced classes in the area are sponsored by local hospitals, such as the **California Pacific Medical Center** which houses the **Planetree Health Library**. This medical library is a great resource for the general public with its collections of professional medical literature, health publications and alternative therapy information. Its **Office of Patient Services** provides free and low cost health, wellness and positive behavior-change programs to the public, such as

Health for Mind & Body

"Weigh To Go" or "Smoking Cessation" where you'll meet others struggling with the same issues. It also offers an "Evening Lecture/ Discussion Series," which can help you move on your path toward self-improvement through awareness. If you're really serious about that health change, you can see that help is available on a regular basis. Once there, you will find people who share both the wish *and* the gumption to get off their duffs and DO something about it. Are these the types of people you are hoping to meet? People who follow through on a wellness plan?

Personal growth activities abound in this region! No matter how you wish to pursue enlightenment, you'll find teachers and companions following a variety of growth practices. You could explore the programs in academic institutions like the **California Institute of Integral Studies** which sponsors lectures and discussions on the intellectual and spiritual aspects of Western and Eastern healing traditions. Other health communities emphasize massage as a way to relieve tired muscles and stimulate spiritual regeneration. **The Mindful Body** offers different massage techniques including Swedish, Esalen, Deep Tissue, Reflexology and Shiatsu in a class and workshop format.

Are you able to calm your mind in trying situations or do you feel torn by the stresses of life on a regular basis? **Psychic Horizons** will teach you meditation techniques to help you relax and stay grounded. Try their classes about topics that influence how we feel about ourselves, including relationships, prosperity, job satisfaction, creativity and self esteem. In a more unusual vein, have you heard of Breatherapy? The **Grove Center For Health & Creativity** offers this powerful and transformational technique of breathing that, once mastered, can be used to center yourself in any stressful situation. An additional benefit to these self-empowering discussions, workshops and classes are the friendships you may develop with other participants, even though you did not know them at all when you began.

Eating well is the right and privilege of every San Franciscan. It is our good fortune to reside in a region with an abundance of knowledgeable organic farmers who offer produce that is fresh, tasty and easy-to-find. Even markets that do not stock purely organic products provide outstanding, high quality goods throughout the year. And San Francisco is truly a mecca of specialty grocery stores that cater to every diet preference. The **Real Food Company** opened its first store in 1969 with the goal of providing the best organic and healthy foods available. The **Rainbow Grocery Cooperative** followed in 1975 as a bulk provider of grains and other products to the vegetarian community. Other markets offer seminars in healthy foods, communal dinners and bulletin boards loaded with notices of local classes, workshops and natural food organizations. If you're interested in meeting others who support a healthy and organic diet, be sure to check out your local healthy-foods market.

Vegetarians can find each other at the **San Francisco Vegetarian Society** that hosts many delightful evenings of diverse activities related to healthy eating. They have talks and discussions, dinners in, dinners out, speakers and trips. The newsletter is fantastic, with great-looking recipes, interesting commentary and a calendar of upcoming events. Also, **the San Francisco Life Food Society** meets monthly for an interesting program and potluck lunch that is strictly vegan. (Note from our cheese-challenged editor Kathy Sheehan: "By the way, do your readers know that 'vegan' means non-dairy, too?")

Food for the mind *and* body are offered by the **Green Gulch Farm Zen Center**. Located just north of San Francisco in a lovely valley opening onto the Pacific Ocean, Green Gulch includes an organic farm and garden which provides produce for the **Greens Restaurant**. You can visit during the day and take part in a Buddhist program, or simply spend time quietly in the gardens and stay overnight in the guest center.

Fitness clubs have a loyal and devoted following. They are also good spots to meet other regulars who enjoy a consistent workout. If you wish to be part of a gym with all the amenities (and your pocketbook agrees), there are several outstanding fitness clubs that offer a blend of athletic and social events. **The San Francisco Bay Club**, a full-service, coed, athletic and social club, sponsors a wide variety of sports and social activities. **Club One** has six locations downtown and membership reciprocity with clubs throughout the Bay Area. The **Pinnacle Fitness Club** includes nutritional assessment as well as weight training programs.

No chapter on health and fitness would be complete without a special mention of the **YMCA/YMHAs** in the community. They provide high quality, low budget fitness/sports programs for everyone's taste and are as much a part of the community as the library and the public school. Many also offer a wide range of group sports (e.g., volleyball,

Health for Mind & Body

tennis, group swimming) plus organized activities like dancing and karate. Some even sponsor singles groups. If you are interested in reasonably-priced fitness, check them out.

Groups providing emotional support for all types of addiction recovery are the 12-Step programs. These may be located in or near your neighborhood, often in a local church or synagogue.

As we said, taking care of yourself goes way beyond achieving a fancy body, Hollywood style. It's about an active program to be healthy—physically and mentally. Your smile will be brighter, you'll have a swing in your step and you'll be more open to the people around you. Around San Francisco, all the health and fitness you want is on your doorstep—along with the people whose commitment matches your own.

Living Tai Chi, Instructor Chris Sequeira

Health for Mind & Body

Fitness

Club One

360 Pine Street, 6th Floor, San Francisco, CA 94194
(415) 288-1010

With six locations downtown and membership reciprocity with clubs throughout the Bay area, Club One is a fitness network of full-service clubs. Strength and cardio-training, group exercise, swimming and rock climbing are just a few of the many activities and sports offered.

🐌 Initiation and monthly fee

In Shape At Andre's

3214 Fillmore Street, San Francisco, CA 94123
(415) 922-3700
Activity Location: Hayes Valley, 371 Hayes Street (415) 241-0203

Andre's has two locations where classes are offered in the morning and evenings. For your fitness program, take part in a step, spinning, cardio, or body conditioning class or a specifically designed class for moms and babies.

🐌 $10/class

Pinnacle Fitness Club

61 New Montgomery Street, San Francisco, CA 94105
(415) 543-1110 ext.206   *http://www.fitnessclub@dnai.com*

Full-service coed club with three locations downtown that offer complete weight training rooms, Cybex and Bodymaster free weights, rowing machines, nutritional assessment and much more. Pinnacle was voted "The Bay Area's Best Health Club" for three years in a row.

🐌 Initiation and monthly fee

Health for Mind & Body

The San Francisco Bay Club

150 Greenwich Street, San Francisco, CA 94111
(415) 433-2200

Full-service coed, athletic and social club that offers a wide variety of activities including squash, basketball, group exercise, yoga, taekwondo and Hydro-Fit. There are plenty of opportunities to meet other members and socialize at club-sponsored social events (member appreciation parties), athletic activities (biking and skiing) and educational events (language and wine tasting). Free parking and a shuttle from the financial district are also provided.

$ Initiation and monthly fee

YMCA

Branches throughout the Bay Area

Major organization for group physical activities on a community-wide basis. Local branches city-wide offer aerobics, weight training, tennis and sports, martial arts, swimming and some real jazzy classes like Modern and Ballroom Dance. Walking and running races are sponsored too. There are groups for singles only. Be sure to check out your local Y.

Health Studies

Citizens for Health

(415) 403-8057 (info line: hit #5)

Call the information line to find out about the following organizations that promote a plant based diet (Earth Save), people's rights to health care information (Citizens For Health), and the use of vitamins and minerals in mainstream medicine (National Health Federation). Call and learn more about these three fine organizations.

Health for Mind & Body

Planetree Health Library

2040 Webster Street, San Francisco, CA 94115
(415) 923-3680 (info line)
Activity Location: Institute for Health & Healing at Calif. Pacific Med. Cntr.

Planetree Health Library is the medical library for the general public. The collection contains professional medical literature, health publications and alternative therapy resources. You do not have to be a member to take part in the spring and fall Community Wellness Programs and the Evening Lecture Series.

☼ Tuesday-Saturday   🕐 11am-5pm;
💰 Free   Wednesday until 7pm

"Qigong" at the Immune Enhancement Project

3450 16th Street, San Francisco, CA 94114
(415) 252-8711
Activity Location: 50 Oak Street, 3rd Floor

Ongoing, traditional Chinese medicine class which teaches healing through breathing and gentle exercise. Wear something comfortable.

☼ Mondays & Wednesdays   🕐 5:30-6:30pm
💰 Sliding scale $1-$5

The Office of Patient Services

2100 Webster Street, Suite 100, San Francisco, CA 94115
(415) 923-3155

OPS is a non-profit group offering free and low-cost health education and counseling services to the Bay Area community. Take part in wellness and positive behavior change programs such as "Weigh To Go," and "Smoking Cessation," and meet others trying to overcome poor eating habits and smoking addictions. Also find many free classes that feature topics such as osteoporosis, prostate health and family programs.

☎ Nancy Boughey

Health for Mind & Body

Life Studies

California Institute of Integral Studies

9 Peter Yorke Way, San Francisco, CA 94109
(415) 674-5500 ext. 241   *http://www.ciis.edu*

Take part in these fascinating discussions that consider the intellectual and spiritual insights of Western and Eastern traditions expressing an "unifying vision of humanity, nature, world, and spirit." A treat for your mind. Call for a calendar of upcoming events.

💰 $10/general, $8/students, seniors, alumni

Sufi Order Of The West

(415) 355-3698
Activity Location: United Methodist Church, side door on 7th Ave., 3rd Flr., 4301 Geary Boulevard

All are welcome to attend a class in Sufi Studies, which include chanting, meditations and interesting discussions. Sufi is the highly-regarded mystical branch of Islam.

☼ Thursdays   🕗 7:45-9pm
☎ Paul Reinhertz
💰 Free

Center for Tibetan Buddhist Studies: Tse Chen Ling

4 Joost Avenue, San Francisco, CA 94131
(415) 339-8002   tclcenter@aol.com

The center offers its Basic Studies Program for the student who wishes to complete a full study program. If the complete program is more extensive than you wish, ongoing and individual classes, program events and mediation sessions are offered throughout the month. They are free to members; non-members pay a donation of about $10/event. Call for a calendar.

💰 $15/month

Health for Mind & Body

Zen Center

300 Page Street, San Francisco, CA 94102
(415) 863-3136

As soon as you walk through the door of the Zen Center, you can feel serenity in the atmosphere. People are moving at a peaceful gait, encouraging an awareness beyond their immediate vision. The center offers a wide range of classes, workshops, ceremonies, sittings, special lectures and guest events. Call for a calendar.

☎ Vicki Austin

Martial Arts

Aikido Center

1755 Laguna Street - c/o Social Hall of Konko Church, San Francisco, CA 94115
(415) 921-5073

Aikido is more than a self-defense technique—it's an activity that connects the mind and body through stylized movement. If you stop by, you can observe and talk with people who practice. Persons of all fitness levels are encouraged to attend.

💰 $40/3 week "Beginner's Course"

California Martial Arts Academy

2901 Clement Street, San Francisco, CA 94121
(415) 752-5555

Training in the martial arts is an excellent way for people of all fitness levels to get in shape and gain confidence. The academy focuses on teaching Kung Fu, the oldest form of the martial arts. Start with the Introductory Course that outlines the fundamental techniques, the philosophy and the self-defense skills of this art form.

💰 $10 /introductory lesson

Health for Mind & Body

Karate USA - Pacific Heights

2849 California, San Francisco, CA 94115
(415) 552-7283

Take part in a complimentary orientation session and learn more about Karate and its uniqueness as a martial art. This discipline relies completely on the body as both a weapon and potent defender. People of all levels of physical fitness are encouraged to attend.

ℬ About $49/2 lessons and free uniform

Meditation

Grove Center for Health and Creativity: "Breatherapy"

1739 O'Farrell Street, San Francisco, CA 94115
(415) 775-6145   grovecentr@aol.com   http:www.grovecenter.com

Try breatherapy, a powerful and transformational technique of breathing, taught by Surupa, a registered Breatherapist. You can use what you learn to calm yourself in many kinds of stressful situations. Also ask about other classes offered by this organization that focuses on personal growth.

ℬ About $25

Psychic Horizons

2240 Geary Boulevard, San Francisco, CA 94115
(415) 643-8800   http://www.psychichorizons.com

Everyone is welcome to attend this weekly meditation class with discussions about important topics that influence how we feel about ourselves, including relationships, prosperity, job satisfaction, creativity, self-esteem and more. Wear comfortable clothes.

☼ Tuesdays   ⌚ 7:30pm
ℬ Free

Health for Mind & Body

Sivananda Yoga Vedanta Center "Satsang"

1200 Arguello Boulevard, San Francisco, CA 94122
(415) 681-2731   sanfrancisco@sivananda.org   http://www.sivananda.org

S atsang is defined as meditation in the company of the wise. The
sessions are part silent meditation, part lecture and part mantra
chanting. The center also offers Vegetarian Cooking, Vedic Astrology,
Indian Classic Dance, Homeopathy classes and Hatha Yoga everyday.
Call for a calendar.

☼ Everyday 6-7:30am, Weds. 8-9:30pm, Suns. 6-7:30pm.
🕯 Free

Nutrition, Herbs & Healthy Food

Cooking with Chinese Herbs

1289 43rd Avenue, San Francisco, CA 94122
(415) 661-7160

L earn how to make delicious meals using traditional Chinese dietetics
with special attention to digestion. Subjects include Yin Yang Qi and
blood, food energetic, flavors, temperatures, and routes and actions of
foods. Chef Nam Singh, a Chinese herbologist, uses demonstrations,
lectures, field trips to Chinese markets and herbal pharmacies and
delicious meals that you help to prepare, as methods of instruction.

☼ Every other Wednesday (Beginners)   🕓 6:30-9:30pm
and Thursday (Intermediate)
☎ Nam Singh
🕯 About $30/class

Health for Mind & Body

San Francisco Market Collaborative

San Francisco, CA
(415) 772-0632
Activity Location: Ferry Plaza at the Embarcadero Center

Another great place to meet others interested in the pleasure of fresh, organic produce and products are the outdoor markets. The vendors are fast to start a conversation and soon everyone is talking. You never know which friends you might run into, and for anyone who is new to the city this is a wonderful way to begin to feel like home. Check out the Tuesday market at Steuart and Market Streets as well. It's a different crowd.

☼ Saturdays & Sundays   🖩 Sat 8am-1pm
🖢 Free   Sun 9am-1pm

Green Gulch Farm Zen Center

1601 Shoreline Highway, Sausalito, CA 94965
(415) 383-3134

Green Gulch Farm is a Buddhist practice center in the Japanese Soto Zen tradition. Located just north of San Francisco, it includes an organic farm and garden which provides produce for the Greens Restaurant. You can take part in a Sunday program which includes meditation instruction followed by tea, lunch and a question and answer period. Or go as a day or overnight guest and wander through the beautiful gardens.

Green World Mercantile

2340 Polk Street, San Francisco, CA 94109
(415) 771-5717

Wouldn't you like to learn about edible and medicinal (and dangerous!) herbs during a 3-hour walk through the Tennessee Valley Recreational Area? How about discovering the folk history, identification and uses of common 'weeds,' with take-home samples? Join herbalist Catherine Abby Rich, who gives these superb herb classes in conjunction with Green World Mercantile. By the way, Green World has fabulous natural and organically minded "goodies."

Health for Mind & Body

Rainbow Grocery Cooperative

1745 Folsom Street, San Francisco, CA 94103
(415) 863-9200

S tarted in 1975 as a bulk provider of grains and other products to the vegetarian community, Rainbow has evolved into a wonderful market for anyone who wants to eat in a healthy way. A wide range of organic foods are carried as well as macrobiotic items to fit the strictest diet. The staff are eager to answer questions for customers who come from all over the Bay Area. Before you leave, be sure to read the Bulletin Board for interesting postings. It's located by the customer service kiosk.

Real Food Company

1023 Stanyan Street, San Francisco, CA 94117
(415) 564-2800

S tarted in 1969 with the goal of providing the best organic and healthy goods available, Real Food has become a great source for fresh and tasty produce and health smart foods. They also have a store at 2140 Polk Street.

San Francisco Life Foods Society

662 29th Avenue, San Francisco, CA 94121
(415) 751-2806
Activity Location: Fort Mason Center, Bldg. C, Rm. 370,
Buchanan St. & Marina Blvd., San Francisco, (415) 751-4013

B ring a potluck dish for ten servings and have lunch with others who eat mindfully. Suggestions for your contribution are organic raw fruits and vegetables, nuts, seeds and juices; please, no cooked foods, meat, dairy products or processed juices. Bring eating/ serving utensils. A presentation follows the meal.

☼ 1st Sunday/month   🕐 1pm
☎ Darleen
💰 $15/year membership; $2 members; $4 non-members

Health for Mind & Body

San Francisco Vegetarian Society

P.O. Box 27153, San Francisco, CA 94127
(415) 273-5481   *http://www.vegan.org/sfvegsoc*

This group shares potluck meals, cooking classes and lectures, and excellent company. A bonus is the SFVS "green card" for discounts at participating restaurants. Call to receive one complimentary copy of the Vegetarian Calendar.

☼ 2nd Sunday/month
💰 $15/year membership

Whole Foods

1765 California Street, San Francisco, CA 94109
(415) 674-0500

This high-end healthy product market is a kind of hub of natural food activities in San Francisco. A bulletin board posts notices of natural living activities and healing groups in the area, and interesting 'wellness' literature is available.

Tai Chi

Tai Chi

Activity Location: Spreckels Lake, Opposite 36th Ave., at Golden Gate Park

Every Saturday and Sunday at 8:30am and 9:30am, free Tai Chi workshops take place. The group meets at the lake, creating a beautiful and tranquil setting to practice this ancient art form. When we stopped by to inquire about the group, they were very friendly and open to newcomers of all levels. Not an organization—just show up.

☼ Saturdays & Sundays   🕰 8:30am & 9:30am

Noe Valley Ministry "Living Tai Chi of Noe Valley"

1021 Sanchez Street, San Francisco, CA 94114
(415) 756-6857

Take part in a beginners class and start moving to this ancient art form that reduces stress, builds strength and improves your overall physical appearance and mind-set.

☼ Tuesdays & Thursdays   🕰 6pm
☎ Chris Sequeira
💰 About $8/class

Health for Mind & Body

Yoga

Integral Yoga Institute

770 Dolores Street, San Francisco, CA 94110
(415) 824-9600   IYISF@aol.com   http://users.aol.com/iyisfliyi.html

Drop-in Hatha Yoga Classes for all levels are offered as well as chanting and meditation workshops, concerts and other awareness events. Wear comfortable clothing, bring a towel and refrain from eating at least two hours before taking a class. A calendar is available.

🖐 $7/general; $4 seniors, students

The Mindful Body

2876 California Street, San Francisco, CA 94115
(415) 931-2639

Known as a center for movement, bodywork and personal inner work, they offer yoga, meditation and massage/bodywork sessions. Choose from a vast list of kinds of Yoga including Ananda, Gentle, Hatha, Integral, Kundalini, Power and Restorative. Different massage techniques, including Swedish, Esalen, Deep Tissue, Reflexology and Shiatsu are offered. Call for a calendar which lists upcoming workshops, classes and events, or stop by and take a look for yourself.

☎ Roy Bergmann

Yoga College of India

910 Columbus Avenue, San Francisco, CA 94133
(415) 346-5400

Learn all 26 poses of the Asana series. The class can be demanding but all fitness levels are encouraged to participate to the best of their ability. Students of all levels are welcome to participate on a drop-in basis for all classes. Bring a towel.

Health for Mind & Body

Yoga Society of San Francisco

2872 Folsom Street, San Francisco, CA 94110
(415) 285-5537

F eel free to drop in and take a Hatha Yoga class but please be on time. The classes include stretching, pranayama (breathing exercises), toning and deep relaxation meditation. Call for a calendar which outlines classes particularly good for beginners.

☎ Karen
💰 About $10/drop-in; $40/4 classes

Health & Fitness

Bay Area Naturally

1220 Sir Francis Drake Boulevard, San Anselmo, CA 94960
(415) 488-8160   cityspirit@aol.com

T his is a directory that features natural health and environmentally safe services and products. Structured like the Yellow Pages, it is easy and friendly to use. Listed inside are natural health care practitioners, holistic centers, natural food stores, spiritual centers, health spas, retreat centers and much more. The Calendar of Events and Restaurant Guide are loaded with interesting things to do and eat. Call to find out where to pick up your free copy.

💰 Free

Hobbies & Clubs

Antiques/Architecture • Collecting
Computers • Cooking
Food, Wine & Beer Groups • Gardening Clubs
Interest Groups • Nature Lovers
Sewing & Crafts • Style • Vintage Cars

Chapeaux lovers Judith Rubin, Bonnie Martin and Michael Teger of the San Francisco Hat Society. Photo by Jean-Marie Hawkins.

Isn't it amazing (and wonderful) that when you become interested in something new, you can almost always find a community that enjoys that interest as much as you do! It's probably human nature that we like to associate with others who share our passions, our curiosities and our areas of interest and knowledge. We like to meet with them, be active with them, tell interest-related jokes and develop a sense of "my group" with them. In fact, when we don't have such a group, we often feel a bit lonely, like something is missing.

Hobbies are often considered activities you do when you have an excess of leisure time. The notion conjures up images of someone spending hours involved in time-consuming (building miniature models) or costly (collecting rare books) pursuits. So many people have full-time jobs and hectic schedules that spill over into evenings and weekends. Others are busy with small children, aging parents or an otherwise full household. Who has time to have a hobby or join a club?

We know you can make very reasonable excuses about not having enough time for the activities you enjoy. Go ahead and deny the need to work in your garden or grab your telescope and head out to join others observing a waxing crescent or first quarter moon. But we think there are consequences. Pay attention. You may notice a lack of energy. Your temper may be shorter, your irritability greater. You might find that the only reason you look forward to Saturday is because you can stay in bed a little longer. Look around and you will see many whose lives (like yours?) are filled with too many commitments. Listen to an inner voice whispering, "Is this all there is?"

Then it happens. You meet people who seem to have it all. They may be involved as volunteers, club or hobby group members; they may do regular exercise or have a walking group. Yet they still maintain a full-time job and family. By hook or by crook, they have carved out a space, some time, to do their thing. It may not be much, but that time is *theirs*. You notice that their eyes twinkle when you talk to them. They don't swear in traffic jams or curse the check-out person at the grocery store for not moving fast enough. They don't worry that their lives are passing them by without having any fun. They go places where they feel a part of things, where they belong. They indulge their curiosity, thrive on learning new things, and value being involved with others who make time to do the things they love. They have gone the distance to create balance in their lives. As someone said—we all have the same 24 hours.

The choice is yours.

If you are ready to find a hobby of your own, you should enjoy this chapter. No matter how diverse your interests might be (or could be), we encourage you to let your imagination flow into whatever captures your fancy. San Francisco is teeming with an abundance of hobbies and clubs that you can explore and join. The following pages do not tell the whole story but, rather, give you an overview of the great and interesting *variety* of clubs in the area so you can see what's what. This is the beginning legwork, providing information to kick off *your* search. If an activity or group sparks a chord, go for it–and look for fellow enthusiasts!

So: what *do* we have in San Francisco?

Collecting things can be a terrific shared activity. There are clubs for people who hunt down and assemble collections of stamps, coins, model trains and all sorts of miscellaneous widgets. Some collectables are sizeable. Do you have a vintage car? If you do, you might want to know about the **Amici Americani Della Mille Miglia**, a group dedicated to finding and restoring nifty old cars and seeing that their owners have opportunities to drive them. Its biggest event of the year is the "California Mille," a 1,000 mile trek through California's back roads. We've heard it's a blast! We had to chuckle when we found out that the club also sponsors an annual "New Year's Day Anti-Football Run" which sounds like a great way to celebrate the new year. Also for the auto folks, the **Bay Area Chapter of the Model A Ford Club of America** is open to anyone with or without a car who has an interest in these antique gems. For train buffs, the **Golden Gate Model Railroad Club** maintains and operates one of Northern California's most extensive model railroads. Even if you're not a train collector yourself, be sure and stop by the **Randall Museum** to check out this remarkable miniature train world. For those interested in philately, **The Golden Gate Stamp Club** offers fellow stickers a bimonthly opportunity to share and swap stamps and socialize.

If your interests lean toward outdoor hobbies, members of the **San Francisco Model Yacht Club** invites both wind- and motor-powered model boat enthusiasts to join them for a sail on **Spreckels Lake** in **Golden Gate Park**. Or is your head in the stars? If so, then you'll want to

Hobbies & Clubs

know about the **San Francisco Amateur Astronomers** who meet monthly at the **Academy of Sciences of California Morrison Planetarium** to observe and enjoy the wonders of our celestial universe. You could also join the **San Francisco Sidewalk Astronomers** who prefer a more informal context for their explorations—the city sidewalks. If you want to join them peering into star clusters and interstellar matter on their favorite city street corners, you can take a look through their telescopes.

For those who love architecture, San Francisco has approximately 14,000 Victorians. These massive beauties reflect the Baroque and Gothic styles of ostentatious ornamentation and we love them. Why not join the **Victorian Alliance** which is actively involved in the preservation and restoration of buildings and artifacts that describe life in the city before the 1906 earthquake. Without them, San Franciscans would lose not only a famed tourist attraction but a window into the past. The **Architectural Foundation of San Francisco** will raise your awareness of the way architecture helped shape a city with world-renowned charm and character. Another fine organization, the **Art Deco Society of California**, is dedicated to the preservation of architecture, art, dance, fashion, film, music and modes of transportation from the period between 1919-1942. This group has a terrific time attending lectures, walking tours, picnics and dances. The annual Art Deco Preservation Ball allows you to step back into a scene reminiscent of *The Great Gatsby*. Overall, three excellent places for those who love history and culture and wish to participate in the magnificent heritage of San Francisco.

Flora was the goddess of flowers in Roman mythology. She still captures our heart and her followers include members of the **San Francisco Orchid Society** and **San Francisco Rose Society**. Both groups offer monthly programs on growing orchids and roses. Flora also describes the characteristics of plant life from a specific region. The **Strybing Arboretum Society** offers programs and classes for the amateur or professional gardener, as well as tours of its vast display of plant life garnered from specific regions of the world. Emphasizing the importance of flora from an environmental perspective, **The San Francisco League of Urban Gardeners (SLUG)** promotes greenery as a life source. The League sponsors many informative classes such as "Urban Composting" and "Growing Herbs For Health and Hearth," and hosts social events that raise our consciousness about the importance of urban gardening.

Hobbies & Clubs

Computers are more than merely business tools to San Franciscans, they permeate our culture. For many, they are the modern toy, er, hobby. Computer junkies hunch over coffee and get high about the latest upgrades like "XGA resolution," "TFT display," and "300MHz" that create hyper-quick, slim and constantly upgradable machines. Yes, we have a major subculture in the suburb of silicon city.

Computer clubs are great for people who are joined at the hip to their computers. They love being in the company of other computer users who know the language and understand the programs and the problems. The **Berkeley Macintosh User Group** (510-549-2684) is first class enjoyment, attended by stimulating people who impart everything you ever wanted to know about the MAC with a neat sense of humor to boot. (This book never would have happened had it not been for a MAC support group.) PC users can find their own at the **San Francisco Computer Society** or the **San Francisco PC User Group** for monthly meetings featuring lectures, discussions and demonstrations of the latest technology. Additional groups specialize in the use of specific software. The best place to look for a complete listing of computer user groups is in *Computer Currents*, a free publication distributed in boxes throughout the city. For those on the net, find information about computer groups from *Currents* at: http://www.currents.net.

Among the most popular clubs are food and drink groups. Why are we not surprised? After all, San Francisco has more than 3,300 restaurants and serves up wonderful products from the nearby California wine mecca.

The hobby of wine collecting is very cosmopolitan (and complex), requiring considerable information about soil, sun, production style, history of the region and type of grape. The happy task of drinking it is enhanced by your ability to sort through the flavors you are tasting and guess which wine it is. It's kind of a puzzle combined with sensual pleasure, all the more fun because you're in the company of others enjoying the same experience.

Learning about complementary wine and food combinations is the focus of the many fine food and wine clubs in the area, including the **American Institute of Wine and Food**, the **Dining Out Club**, the **International Wine Academy**, and the the **American Institute of Wine and Food**. You'll be participating with experts and newcomers in organized dinners, tastings, discussions and winery tours which are delicious and delightful. And wait until you see the homework!

The hobby of making one's own beer has its own loyal followers. The **San Andreas Malts** is a lively and fun group of homebrewers who come together sharing their variations of ales and lagers. Their events feature tastings, judgings and most importantly socializing above and beyond discussions on hops, malts and fermentation.

The pleasure of preparing a delectable meal is an activity that appeals to both men and women. Chefs of all levels learn through lectures, demonstrations and hands-on experience at the **HomeChef** where developing confidence and creativity in the kitchen is emphasized. For those who want to explore gourmet cooking, we suggest the **Tante Marie Cooking School**, known for its outstanding professional program. All inquisitive cooks can sign up for the school's one week comprehensive courses and biweekly demonstrations. The excellent **California Culinary Academy** offers weekend classes and a Sunday lecture series just right for beginners or experienced cooks. We didn't find any independent cooking groups operating as clubs, but think it sounds like a fantastic idea. Wouldn't you like to organize a cooking club that runs in the same way as a book reading group? Members could take turns demonstrating a new recipe followed by a group evaluation. Sort of a 'learning as you go' kind of thing. Let us know if you do. We'd love to come and check it out!

Please take some time thinking about *your* carved-out time, *your* niche. Sometimes people can be turned off by the idea of hobbies. They can sound so boring, like something you invent to while away your time. We think of them instead as organized interests where you indulge your curiosity, actively engage in something you love, and often join together with others around that activity. They provide a structure for ongoing relationships, where, because you have something in common, you know you belong.

International Plastic Modelers Society members at a monthly meeting sharing their models in progress and building techniques.

Hobbies & Clubs

Antiques/Architecture

Antique Journal "Show Goers Club"
1-800-791-8592

I f you love going to antique shows, join this club sponsored by the *Antique Journal,* a great source for information about antiques gatherings. All you pay is postage and handling to receive your badge which discounts your admission to countless shows in and around the Bay Area.

💰 $5/year membership

Architectural Foundation of San Francisco
130 Sutter Street, Suite 600, San Francisco, CA 94104
(415) 362-1492

T he foundation's goal is to "create a public awareness of the character and value of the city's architecture." Take part in organized events including golf tournaments, walking tours and the biennial Beaux Arts Ball.

💰 $75/year membership; $20 students

The Art Deco Society of California
100 Bush Street, Suite 511, San Francisco, CA 94104
(415) 982-3326

T he goal of this active group is the preservation of architecture, art, dance, fashion, film, music and various modes of transportation in American culture between 1919-1942. They have many wonderful activities including lectures, walking tours, picnics, dances and the annual Art Deco Preservation Ball. (P.S. Diane notes that Decorum, 1400 Vallejo Street, is a great place to find art deco artifacts and restored furniture, 415-474-6886.)

💰 $45/year membership

Hobbies & Clubs

Victorian Alliance

824 Grove Street, San Francisco, CA 94117
(415) 824-2666

This group supports the preservation and restoration of buildings and artifacts from the Victorian era. You can help to save the Painted Ladies and other less known Victorian architectural gems. Attend a monthly strategy meeting that is a combination business and social evening. In addition, there are other organized social functions and lectures throughout the year. Newsletter with location of meetings.

☼ Last Wednesday/month   ⏰ 7:30pm
💰 $20/year membership; $10 students/seniors

Collecting

Golden Gate Model Railroad Club

P.O. Box 37, Daly City, CA 94016
(415) 346-3303   http://www.jps.net/spassmo/ggmrc/ggmrc.htm
Activity Location: Randall Museum, 199 Museum Way (415) 554-9600

Members maintain and operate one of Northern California's most extensive model railroads. Persons interested in joining are encouraged to stop by on the 2nd and 4th Saturdays when members are sure to be at the museum, or call for more information.

☼ 2nd & 4th Saturdays   ⏰ 12:30-5pm
☎ Mike Stokinger

International Plastic Modelers Society, Golden Gate Chapter

(415) 507-0528
Activity Location: Gatehouse, Fort Mason Center, Buchanan Street & Marina Blvd.
(415) 441-3400

This group of modeling enthusiasts invites anyone interested in building scale models to bring and share their completed models or just stop by to chat. The meetings are relaxed and give opportunities to swap stories and tips. The Gatehouse is the building immediately on the right as you pass through the Fort Mason gate.

☼ 4th Thursday/month   ⏰ 7:30-9:30pm
☎ Hugh Silvis
💰 $20/year membership

San Francisco Coin Club

Activity Location: Knights Of Columbus, 2800 Taraval (415) 753-9595

This is an informal group that gets together to share their knowledge and passion for coins.

☼ 4th Tuesday/month   ⏰ 6pm

Stamp Francisco

466 8th Street, San Francisco, CA 94103
(415) 252-5975

Rubber stamps are great fun and are also beautiful and historical. Here is your chance to see antique rubber stamp sets and contemporary stamp art, plus you may purchase from a large selection for your collection.

The Book Club of California

312 Sutter Street, Suite 510, San Francisco, CA 94108
(415) 781-7532   *compuserve.76600,3562*

This group of book lovers and collectors are interested in the history and literature of the pacific coast and in fine printing and the graphic arts. Regular receptions, openings and weekly open houses are held at the Club. Membership is restricted to 1000 persons and a sponsor is necessary but if fine books are your sincere interest, this group would like to hear from you.

☎ James Nance
💰 $55/year membership

The Golden Gate Stamp Club

(415) 566-9699

Activity Location: Taraval Police Station Community Room, 2345 24th Avenue,
(415) 553-1612

Stamp collectors looking for fellow stickers can go here and find others interested in philately. Some stamps are magnificent!

☼ 2nd and 4th Monday/month   ⏰ 7:30pm

Hobbies & Clubs

Computers

Cyberworld

528 Folsom Street, San Francisco, CA 94105
(415) 278-9669   *http://www.cyberworldsf.com*

G rab a cup of coffee, relax on one of their comfortable couches or play your favorite computer game. A great place to have a meal, attend a lunchtime computer session or enjoy an evening party. Check it out—breakfast, lunch and dinner and the internet all with a panoramic view of the Bay Bridge.

INTERNET alfredo

790-A Brannan Street, San Francisco, CA 94103
(415) 437-3140   *al@ina.com*   *http://www.ina.com*

T his cybercafe provides computers for rent and exciting classes such as "Quark For the Real World," "Surfing 101," "Cyberinvesting," and "Optimizing Web Graphics." They also boast espresso drinks "served to perfection" in their 24-hour cyberlounge.

San Francisco Business Computers

110 Pacific Avenue, #153, San Francisco, CA 94111
(415) 788-5338   *sfbc@juno.com*

A n organization for anyone who uses computers in her/his work. Increase your computer knowledge base and get tips and answers to your questions. Guest speakers are featured at most events.

💰 $60/year membership; $10 visitors

San Francisco Computer Society

1280 Laguna Street, San Francisco, CA 94115
(415) 885-6202   *rforsberg@aol.com*

C PM and DOS novices are welcome. An excellent way to learn more about computers, meet others and find experts. Plus, the meetings are fun.

☼ 4th Monday/month   🕐 7pm
☎ Bob Forsberg

San Francisco PC Users Group (SFPCUG)

744 Harrison Street, San Francisco, CA 94107
(415) 777-1332   jmstern@mail.sfpcug.org   http://www.sfpcug.org
Activity Location: California Public Utilities Comm.Aud. , 505 Van Ness Avenue

M onthly meetings include presentations, discussions, a Q & A session and knowledgeable colleagues.

☼ 3rd Tuesday/month   ⏰ 7:30pm
🐝 Jerry Stern
💰 $4/non-members; students free

Cooking

California Culinary Academy

625 Polk Street, San Francisco, CA 94102
(415) 771-3536

T he academy's continuing education program for beginners and experienced cooks offers many delicious and innovative classes on the weekends. During the final hour of the day, you'll have a chance to meet and socialize with fellow students and chefs from other classes, while you enjoy an "ever-changing buffet that you helped prepare." They offer a fine Sunday lecture series as well.

💰 About $125/class

HomeChef

3525 California Street, San Francisco, CA 94118
(415) 668-3191   http://www.baychef.com

A wide variety of classes are offered for chefs of all levels. Students get hands-on experience and learn through demonstrations, discussions and homework. Truly a great way to improve your creativity and confidence in the kitchen.

Hobbies & Clubs

Tante Marie's Cooking School

271 Francisco Street, San Francisco, CA 94133
(415) 788-6699   *http://www.tantemaries.com*

This excellent cooking school offers classes and demonstrations designed to fit into your busy life. Take a weekend workshop, an evening series or a one-week comprehensive course. Try to attend an afternoon demonstration on Tuesday or Thursday given by one of their expert chefs. Call for more information.

☼ Tuesdays & Thursdays   🕐 2-4pm
☎ Mary Risley
💰 $40/demonstration

Food, Wine & Beer Groups

Dining Out Club

1978 - 23rd Avenue, San Francisco, CA 94116
(415) 731-8026
Activity Location: Various Bay Area restaurants

The Dining Out Club is a friendly and sophisticated group who like to explore new places to eat. Marti plans the menus and organizes the events which are absolutely delicious upbeat culinary adventures. All you need is an interest in fine dining and the desire to enjoy good company.

☎ Marti Sousanis, Director
💰 $130/year membership; $85/6 months
or $40/year membership + $10/event

International Wine Academy "Wine Lovers Bootcamp Series"

38 Portola Drive, San Francisco, CA 94131
(415) 6414767   *ayoung@sirius.com*

Call to find out about the intensive "Wine Lovers Bootcamp Series" offered in the Napa/Sonoma Valleys.

North Beach Palateers

556 Columbus Avenue, San Francisco, CA 94133
(415) 403-0666   mrg@sirius.com   http://www.sfnorthbeach.com

Sponsored by the North Beach Chamber of Commerce, the Palateers explore different restaurants in the area. Get on the mailing list and you can enjoy these delicious, organized dinners with them.

☎ Marsha Garland
💰 About $23/event

San Andreas Malts

P.O. Box 884661, San Francisco, CA 94188
(415) 731-8754   malts@majordomo.pobox.com   http://www.vav-nun.com/malts

This group of lively and fun homebrewers get together for beer tastings, beer judgings and socializing. Proust!

☎ Dave Kennar
💰 $15/year membership

San Francisco Brewcraft

1555 Clement Street, San Francisco, CA 94118
(415) 751-9338   sfbrew@sirius.com

If you want to get involved in the home brewing craze, call Steve. He will get you started with free brewing instructions and supplies that can be purchased. He is also a good resource who can put you in touch with others who share your brewing hobby.

☎ Steve Bruce

The American Institute of Wine and Food

1550 Bryant Street, Suite 700, San Francisco, CA 94103
(415) 255-3000   aiwfmemb@aol.com

Lovers of food and wine can join the Northern California chapter of this fine international organization. Take part in seminars, dinners, tours and tastings, demonstrations and friendly social gatherings.

💰 $75/year membership; $40 students

Hobbies & Clubs

Gardening Clubs

San Francisco League of Urban Gardeners
"SLUG'S Green Gardening Events"

2088 Oakdale Avenue, San Francisco, CA 94124
(415) 285-7584

E vents throughout the year including workshops such as "Urban
Composting" and "Growing Herbs For Health and Hearth." Call
for a calendar of upcoming events and don't forget to ask for their San
Francisco Gardens planting schedule. Some events are free to S.F.
residents.

💰 About $5/members; $10/non-members

San Francisco Rose Society

P.O. Box 563, Moss Beach, CA 94038
(415) 436-0497   *http://www.gardens.com*
Activity Location: Hall Of Flowers, Golden Gate Park, 9th Avenue & Lincoln Way

I f you simply love roses or want to learn how to grow outstanding
varieties, this delightful and friendly group of rosarians will welcome
you wholeheartedly. The monthly programs feature great discussions and
social mixers with refreshments served afterwards. A beginner's growing
class is held at noon in the Hall of Flowers before the monthly meeting.
The public is encouraged to attend.

☼ 2nd Sunday/month   🎟 1pm
☎ Donaldina Joung
💰 $10/year membership

Strybing Arboretum Society

Golden Gate Park, 9th Avenue at Lincoln Way, San Francisco, CA 94122
(415) 661-0668   http://www.mobot.org/aabga/member.pages/strybing

Take advantage of the comprehensive certification program which is offered for the amateur and professional gardener through the society. For a shorter time committment, you could attend the single day workshops, such as "Conifer Wreaths" offered around the holidays, and "Garden Furnishings and Furniture" in the spring. Expand your knowledge of botany and horticulture and meet others who share your hobby. Ask about the full moon walks. Non-members are encouraged to attend.

☎ Christine Landrum

💰 $40/year membership

The San Francisco Garden Club

640 Sutter Street, San Francisco, CA 94102
(415) 771-0282

The San Francisco Garden Club is the oldest garden club in California. The club is selective but if you truly love gardens and flowers, don't be dissuaded. Request to be on the mailing list, attend two events, and consider the application procedure that requires sponsorship by three members. Admittance to this club is well worth the effort.

The San Francisco Orchid Society

(415) 665-2468

Activity Location: San Francisco County Fair Building, Golden Gate Park,
9th Avenue & Lincoln Way

Anyone interested in orchids is encouraged to attend. Take part in the educational meetings that include lectures and slide shows about different aspects of orchid growing. If you become a member , you can sell to and purchase plants from other members.

☼ 1st Tuesday/month   🕐 7pm

💰 $15/year membership

Hobbies & Clubs

Interest Groups

Fort Point Historical Society

P.O. Box 29163, San Francisco, CA 94129
(415) 921-8193

Fort Point is directed to historic preservation and education at the Presidio. Take part and get involved with others who sponsor historical seminars, museum exhibits and historical research. Your participation will lend much-needed support the association needs to preserve the land as a national park.

💰 $30/year membership

Mycological Society of San Francisco

(415) 759-0495   *http://www.wco.com/~dale/randall.html*
Activity Location: Randall Museum, 199 Museum Way (415) 554-9600

Learn to identify mushrooms, both edible and dangerous. Join this group of mushroom hobbyists for lectures, shows and walks about a fascinating life form. Mushrooms are fascinating!

☼ 3rd Tuesday/month   🎟 7-9:45pm
(except June-August & Dec.)

National Maritime Museum Association

P. O. Box 470310, San Francisco, CA 94147
(415) 929-0202 ext.21   info@maritime.org   http://www.maritime.org

Join this group and enjoy a year of free admissions to the Hyde Street Pier, the USS Pampanito and more. Many activities are offered through the association including talks ("Seaman's Fare, Feast or Famine"), music and singing ("Chanty Sing"), slides/lectures and workshops ("Knotcraft"). Activities are open to non-members with Pier admission or as stated per event. Call for information.

✆ Labrina Harper
💰 $35/year membership

San Francisco Amateur Astronomers

(415) 566-2357 chelleb@aol.com http://www.members.aol.com/chelleb/sfaa.htm
Activity Location: Academy Of Sciences California, Morrison Planetarium
Golden Gate Park (415) 750-7145

The club has about 160 members who meet to observe and enjoy the wonders of the celestial universe. Find out more about their Star Parties where you can meet and socialize with members.

☼ 3rd Wednesday/month   🕗 8pm
💰 $20/year membership; $25 family

San Francisco Amateur Radio Club

P.O.Box 210269, San Francisco, CA 94121
(415) 752-8908   http://www.hooked.net/~youha/sfarc.htm
Activity Location: VA Hospital, Building #7, Auditorium, 4150 Clement Street

You don't have to be a member or have a license to attend the meetings of this group—just the desire to learn more about amateur radio.

☼ 3rd Friday/month   🕗 8pm
☎ Jorge Jo
💰 $25/year membership

San Francisco Model Yacht Club

(415) 386-1037
Activity Location: Spreckels Lake, Opposite 36th Avenue, Golden Gate Park

Accept the challenge and bring both wind and motor-powered model boats to sail on Spreckels Lake. All model yacht enthusiasts are encouraged to join.

☼ 2nd Thursday/month   🕗 8pm
☎ Tony Marshall
💰 $24/year membership; $10 initiation fee

Hobbies & Clubs

San Francisco Sidewalk Astronomers

1946 Vedanta Place, Hollywood, CA 90068
(415) 681-2565   *http://members.aol.com/raycash/sidewalk.htm*

Join this informal group of astronomy enthusiasts on their favorite corners around the city. The best time to set up is during a waxing crescent or first quarter moon when there is a planet or two for viewing, weather permitting. See you at: Noe Valley at the corner of 24th and Sanchez Streets; the Inner Sunset at the corner of 9th Avenue and Irving Street; the Outer Sunset at the corner of 24th Avenue and Irving Street; and Judah Street between 22nd and 23rd Avenues.

☏ Barry Hirrell
💰 $15/year membership

San Francisco Vultures

(415) 566-6393   *http://www.wco.com/~dale/randall.html*
Activity Location: Randall Museum Society, 199 Museum Way, (415) 554-9600

Join this model aviation group that builds and flies model planes of all types—electric, radio and glider. If you want to check it out first, you're welcome to drop in and watch the experts. Ages 12 to adult.

☼ 2nd Thursday/month   🕐 7:30-9:30pm
☏ Ralph Voorhees

Sports Car Club of America (SCCA)

301 Preston Court, Livermore, CA 94550
(510) 373-7222   *http://www.sfrscca.com*

Participation in this group really sounds exciting. How about volunteering at track events and being a starter, safety marshal or scorer? Many hands-on opportunities to fit your experience level. If your dream is to drive, then ask about the local regional road racing schools.

☏ Jean Burton
💰 $60/year membership

SS Jeremiah O'Brien

(415) 441-3101

Activity Location: Pier 32, The Embarcadero, San Francisco

If you love old ships and want to learn to sail the last intact Liberty Ship still in operation, contact the purser's office or tell the person at the ticket booth that you want to volunteer. Maintaining an historical ship with shipmates can be a n exciting step back in time.

Tal-y-Tara Tea & Polo Shoppe "Equestrians"

6439 California Street, San Francisco, CA 94121
(415) 751-9275

This charming combination equestrian shop and old world tearoom is a wonderful place to meet others who love horses. Tal-y-Tara is a hidden treasure to be discovered and shared.

The Young Collector Committee of the San Francisco Fall Antiques Show

450 Mission Street, 408, San Francisco, CA 94105
(415) 546-6661

Formed in 1995, this interesting group of people under 35 years of age provide an educational and social network for beginning collectors of antique fine art, decorative art and other collectibles. Call to get on the mailing list for upcoming events.

🍷 Cost of event

Nature Lovers

Golden Gate Audubon Society

2530 San Pablo Avenue, Suite G, Berkeley, CA 94702
(510) 843-2222   *http://www.audubon.org/chapter*

Join this avid group of bird enthusiasts on their many field trips and learn more about ornithology through their excellent workshops.

☼ 3rd Thursday/month   ⏰ 7:30pm
☎ Arthur Feinstein
🍷 $20/year membership

Hobbies & Clubs

San Francisco Aquarium Society

P. O. Box 34069, San Francisco, CA 94134
(415) 387-6626   sfas@aol.com   http://www.users.aol.com/sfas
Activity Location: California Academy of Sciences, Golden Gate Park
(415) 750-7145

Everyone interested in fish sciences is encouraged to attend, learn more and meet others who share an interest in the denizens of the deep.

☼ 1st Friday/month   ⏰ 8pm
☎ John Kepplin
💰 $15/year membership

San Francisco Hobby Beekeepers

2309 Lincoln Way, San Francisco, CA 94122
(415) 564-6518

This group is for honeybee hobbyists. Members keep bees individually and collectively. For your education, there is a course in Beekeeping as well as meetings and other programs.

☎ Paul Koski

Tamalpais Conservation Club

870 Market Street, Flood Building, Rm. 562, San Francisco, CA 94102
(415) 391-8021

This group has been active since 1912 preserving the wilderness of Mt. Tamalpais by retaining the land as public parks and nature preserves. Get involved and meet others on their scheduled "Trail Days."

💰 $5/year membership

Sewing & Crafts

San Francisco Quilters Guild

P.O Box 27002, San Francisco, CA 94127
(415) 647-9244
Activity Location: Bridgemont High School Chapel, 501 Cambridge Street

This diverse group comes together around their common love of contemporary and traditional quilts and needlework. They also reach out and make quilts for ill and homeless children. Don't forget to ask about the Saturday "Sewcials" that are held on the 3rd Saturday of each month from 9:30am to 3pm at Bridgemont High. Visitors are always invited ($3).

☼ 3rd Tuesday/month   ☎ 7:30pm
💰 $25/year membership; $15 seniors/juniors

The Embroiderer's Guild of America, Inc.

P.O. Box 210430, San Francisco, CA 94121
(415) 665-7737

Join this friendly group of all ages (20s to 80s) and experience levels to learn and share information about embroidering. Visitors are most welcome to attend two meetings before joining.

☼ 2nd Monday @7:30pm; 3rd Tuesday @ 10am
☎ Christine Anderson
💰 $35/year membership

The Sewing Workshop

2010 Balboa Street, San Francisco, CA 94121
(415) 221-7397   *http://www.sewing.wkshop.com*

Everything you want to learn about sewing is offered at this nationally recognized school. Visit an open house or check the catalog for an extensive list of classes.

Hobbies & Clubs

Style

Mr. Rick's Martini Club

236 West Portal Avenue, #376, San Francisco, CA 94127
(415) 566-2545

Join this group of "bon vivants who appreciate a certain style" and you will enjoy an "elegant evening out or a cozy night in with good friends and the perfect martini." Both singles and couples meet at the Martini Club for all kinds of gatherings, including supper club/swing dances, local artist entertainment and terrific cocktail hours. These club events have a 1930s-1940s feel to them. They say you'll feel like you're stepping into a classic movie!

☎ Laurie Gordon
💰 $20/year membership

San Francisco Hat Society

3141 Franklin Street, #6, San Francisco, CA 94123
(415) 241-8817   bhatgirl9@aol.com

This group of stylish women and men is composed of hat enthusiasts, designers, collectors, historians and shop owners who promote hats as fashion as well as significant artifacts of our social history. Enjoy interesting forums with lively conversation. Add to this group by bringing your enthusiasm and love of hats! Call to be added to the mailing list.

☎ Bonnie Martin

Vintage Cars

Amici Americani Della Mille Miglia

1701 Van Ness Avenue, San Francisco, CA 94109
(415) 292-2703   calmille@aol.com

This group finds and restores great old cars and helps to provide their owners with opportunities to drive them. Their biggest event of the year is "The California Mille," a 1,000-mile trek through California's back roads, through the Sierra foothills to Lake Tahoe, down into the Central Valley, then north to Eureka and back to S.F. This event is limited to 70 cars. Be sure to ask about the other events, including the annual "New Year's Day 'Anti-Football' Run."

☎ Dan Radowicz

Bay Area Chapter of the Model A Ford Club of America

181 Alpine Way, San Brian, CA 94066
(415) 285-5180
Activity Location: AAA Bldg.,100 Van Ness Avenue, 3rd Floor Conf. Rm.

All you have to have is an interest in Model A Fords to be part of this group. Many of the members have cars and take part in touring events scheduled throughout the year. If you have an interest in these lovely classic cars, the group will welcome you with or without a car of your own.

☼ 2nd Thursday/month   ☎ 8pm (except December)
💰 $20/year membership

Hobbies & Clubs

Members of Amici Americani della Mille Miglia preparing to start their engines for the annual run of the CALIFORNIA MILLE.

Dining Out club members savoring fine food and spirited conversation at a San Francisco Restaurant.

Music

Choral Singing • Classes • Classical Drumming & Guitar • Folk Jazz • Music Series

Music

The Anything Goes Chorus of the Community Music Center.
Photo by Claire Harmon

Most of us love music. We play our CDs or listen to the radio all the time. Music influences our moods, inspires us to dance and sing in our showers. It sets the stage for many of our activities alone and with others. But many of us don't know how to be active with music. We don't *do* music if you know what we mean. This chapter is for those of you who wish you were actively mixing it up in some way with the music you love.

People are making terrific music in San Francisco. What follows is a smattering of interactive music goings-on that will provide an entree into a variety of musical experiences, depending on your interests. They are all reasonable in cost and involve friendly, active people. For daily information, the *San Francisco Chronicle's "DATEBOOK* has outstanding listings for music events. Another way to learn more about your favorite music events is to go to one event of that type. The people there will know of others and the information will flow in your direction.

SINGING. Ah, singing! Like dancing and art, singing is something you do because you are human. It is your birthright to want to sing. You do *not* sing only because you have a beautiful voice or can "carry a tune." Those are performance standards some unhappy person thought up to keep us from having joyful fun. You sing because you want to make music or just because you feel good. There *are* places to sing where you must have a beautiful voice and read music, such as the choir of **Old Saint Mary's Cathedral**, the **San Francisco Lyric Chorus** or the **San Francisco Cable Car Chorus**. To sing with them you need to audition and sound very good. However, they are not professionals; they are semi-pros. And *you might be* that good. If you think you might be, try it out and see. No harm in that. (Ruth's voice is mediocre but she was admitted into a terrific Renaissance singing group because the group needed an alto and she didn't hurt the sound. How wonderful it was...So you never know.) For the rest of us, like Diane, who is more skeptical of her ability but still wants to sing, the **Community Music Center's Anything Goes Chorus** is a great choice. Community Center teaches beginners as well as seasoned singers the fundamentals of breathing, support and placement, harmonization and note reading. The best part about taking a class is that you will not be expected to be brilliant. Without that burden, you can sing happily along with others who also love to sing. And if you can't be a regular member of a group, you can sing Handel's "Messiah"

Music

at Davies Symphony Hall in December. It's an incredible experience to add your voice to the sound of the very fine singers singing one of the finest pieces of music ever written.

For a regular diet of folk singing, the **San Francisco Folk Music Club** sings together twice a month. Instrumentalists, folk dancers, new singers and listeners are all welcome in this informal group that loves music and stories. Since folk music is the music of cultural groups, don't overlook the many cultural centers noted in this chapter, such as German, Slovak and Irish, where singing and dancing are offered regularly.

PLAYING. One organization that offers a wide range of very inexpensive classes for instrumental music is the **Blue Bear School of American Music**. Blue Bear has been teaching musicians for more than 25 years and has classes for all student abilities. The Bay Area's oldest community arts organization is the **Community Music Center** where anyone interested in performing or learning more about music will find classes in reading and writing music, playing in ensemble or orchestra groups and private music lessons. Some instruments are hard to learn (violin) and some are easy (recorder) but all make terrific music and can be enjoyed in ensemble playing. For example, at **Amina's Studio** you will learn how to execute long, fast, rhythmic rolls on the Tabla (Egyptian drum). For you drummers who want to beat your skins without worrying about destroying your relationships or upsetting your neighbors, the **Drummers Only Studios** offers space where you can practice, jam with other musicians, and leave your equipment ready to play. The **Mission Cultural Center For Latino Arts** periodically offers affordable classes that include Capoeira and percussion along with a community of people who play together.

ENJOYING/LISTENING. Don't forget there are ways for you non-performers to be really active with music and meet others who share your musical interests. Some performances are followed by lectures, discussions and meeting-the-composer opportunities. For example, the **San Francisco Symphony** holds pre-concert lectures which are quite delightful, especially when Michael Tilson Thomas tells his wonderful stories. The **San Francisco Conservatory of Music** offers music-appreciation classes, such as "How to Listen to Opera" or the "History of Jazz." Ongoing programs at the **First Congregational Church** and **Old St. Mary's Cathedral** have a large following of regulars. After the concerts many people socialize and chat with the artists and each other. The **San**

Francisco Classical Guitar Society sponsors guitar concerts, recitals, workshops and discussions. These events are often informal and interactive, providing natural opportunities to talk to others who strum, play and appreciate guitar. So you don't have to sing or play an instrument to be involved in music. All you need is to decide what kind of music you prefer, find the regular activities that include some form of interaction, and you're on your way to building a community that shares your love of music.

There are also numerous social groups that surround music events. The **Bravo! Club, San Francisco Opera** is a group of young adults interested in building a new opera audience. Diane attended Bravo's pre-performance receptions and lectures and had a great time talking to people who also love fine opera productions. Singles can explore **Classical Occasions**, a club for single lovers of classical music and theater. It hosts monthly events that feature recitals and lectures given by professional artists, as well as several social and dinner events throughout the year. **Symphonix**, a young professional group, is only one of the twelve leagues of the **San Francisco Symphony** that sponsor fund-raising events, including the Black and White Ball, dinners, receptions and concerts. The leagues give you an opportunity to be supportive of the symphony and be actively involved with others in promoting the fine cultural arts we have in San Francisco.

Whether you are singing and dancing together, playing an instrument with a small group, taking a class or engaging in a discussion, San Francisco is an excellent place to find others people who love musical activities.

Symphonix members Connie Yeager, Pat Phelar, and Jeanne Miller.
Photo by Bob Merjano

Music

Choral Singing

Community Music Center
544 Capp Street, San Francisco, CA 94110
(415) 647-6015   *http://www.sfmusic.org*
Activity Location: (510) 482-9520

E veryone enjoys music at the Community Music Center. The "Any
thing Goes Chorus I & II" is for beginners who have little or no
experience, as well as the seasoned singer. Classes are available to learn
the fundamentals of breathing, support, placement, harmonization and
note reading. Advanced singers can work on improving their existing
techniques.
☏ Ellen Robinson

Old Saint Mary's Cathedral
660 California Street, San Francisco, CA 94108
(415) 288-3800

U nique choral opportunities are available in this lovely historic
church, including singing in the Sunday morning Choir, the
Saturday evening Vigil Choir or the Lunchtime Choir. Auditions
required. On Tuesdays and Thursdays, St. Mary's offers fine, predominately classical music, noontime concerts that attract a large group of
regular listeners.

San Francisco Cable Car Chorus
(415) 239-0746
Activity Location: Hall at Christ Church Lutheran, 1090 Quintara Street
(415) 664-0915

T he San Francisco Cable Car Chorus is a men's barbershop harmony
chorus that has great fun singing this lively music. If you have
experience harmonizing or are interested in attending upcoming performances, give them a call for further details.
☼ Wednesdays   ⏰ 7:30-10pm
☏ Gerry Costanzo

Music

San Francisco Lyric Chorus

(415) 775-5111

Activity Location: Trinity Episcopal Church, 1668 Bush Street, (415) 775-1117

This fabulous chorus needs singers for all voice parts. Participants meet weekly for rehearsals. Interested singers should call for further information or attend a rehearsal.

☼ Mondays ⏰ 7:15pm

The San Francisco Sweet Adelines

25 Lake Street, San Francisco, CA 94118
(415) 665-7960

A women's barbershop harmony chorus, the Adelines are looking for women who love to sing. No formal training is required to join. What a great way to learn about four-part harmony and blending voices.

☼ Thursdays ⏰ 7pm

Classes

Blue Bear School of American Music

Fort Mason Center, Building D, San Francisco, CA 94124
(415) 673-3600

This excellent non-profit music school has been around for over 25 years and continues to provide affordable and outstanding training. Take a class in one of the various subjects offered, including Music Theory, Guitar, Band Workshops, Voice, Ear Training, Songwriting and much more. There are opportunities for the serious music student as well as listeners-appreciators.

Community Music Center

544 Capp Street, San Francisco, CA 94110
(415) 647-6015   *http://www.sfmusic.org*

Established in 1921, this center is the Bay Area's oldest organization dedicated to community arts. They have a magnificent music program that is perfect for anyone interested in discussing, performing or singing music. One example is the "Beethoven Choral Workshop," open to people with all voice ranges with an interest in singing and a commitment to attend rehearsals.

Mission Cultural Center for Latino Arts

2868 Mission Street, San Francisco, CA 94110
(415) 821-1155

Check the schedule for classes being offered at the Mission Center, including theory classes such as "Listening and Rhythm." You'll need to bring your own instrument to join workshops in Capoeira and Percussion.

🐷 Free-$8

San Francisco Conservatory of Music

1201 Ortega Street, San Francisco, CA 94122
(415) 759-3429   http://www.sfcm.edu

Meet others who not only love music but want to learn about it. Take a class to understand "How To Listen To Opera," discuss "Maria Callas: The One and Only," or study "Jazz and Popular Vocal Technique."

Classical

Bravo! Club, San Francisco Opera

301 Van Ness Avenue, San Francisco, CA 94102
(415) 565-3285   http://www.sfopera.com

Join this group of young adults interested in building a new Opera audience. Membership includes free admission to the popular "Trio Series," pre-performance receptions and lectures, plus preferential invitations and seating. Enjoy the resurgence of this beautiful music.

$60/year membership

Deutscher Musik Verein (The German Band)

909 Hyde Street, Suite 228, San Francisco, CA 94109
(415) 474-7644   http://www.wco.com/~dale/randall.html
Activity Location: Randall Museum Society, 199 Museum Way (415) 554-9600

If you'd like to play in a concert band, this 30-member hobby band is always looking for new talent. Potential players are invited to stop by and join a rehearsal. Visitors are always encouraged to attend and listen.

☼ Thursdays   🎵 7:30-9:30pm
☎ Rick West

Music

First Congregational Church

432 Mason Street, San Francisco, CA 94102
(415) 392-2080

You'll love these fine chamber music concerts in the church on Union Square on mid-day Wednesdays. Go several times and you'll begin to recognize familiar faces. A great way to relax and find peaceful moments in the middle of the day, and it doesn't cost you a cent!

☼ Wednesdays   🎫 12:30pm
💲 Free

Old First Presbyterian Church

1751 Sacramento Street, San Francisco, CA 94109
(415) 474-1608   *http://www.oldfirstconcerts.org*

The "Old First Concerts" are wonderful music events to attend and enjoy. An ongoing favorite is the "Meet the Artists" series which includes a pre-concert discussion and post-concert reception.

💲 $9/general; $7 seniors/students

Symphonix of the San Francisco Symphony

Davies Symphony Hall, San Francisco, CA 94102
(415) 281-0700

The Young Professionals League is only one of twelve symphony leagues that help to sponsor many fund-raising events, including the Black and White Ball, dinners, receptions and concerts. This group holds enjoyable social events while supporting the orchestra. Check into the other eleven leagues also!

💲 $50/year membership; $90 couples

The San Francisco Classical Guitar Society

560 - 19th Street, San Francisco, CA 94107
(415) 221-9946   *ernest_culver@ci.sf.ca.us*
http://www.teleport.com/~kevinf/guitsoc.html

Explore classical guitar as an art form. Guitar concerts and recitals, workshops, discussions and lectures are frequently presented.

☎ Ernest Culver
💲 $20/year membership; $5/event non-members

Drumming & Guitar

Amina's Studio

829 Elizabeth Street, San Francisco, CA 94114
(415) 282-7910

L earn the subtle intricacies of drumming to Middle Eastern music. The class involves listening to and comparing Arabic songs and drum pieces while learning exercises that enable you to execute long, fast rhythmic rolls on the Tabla (Egyptian drum).

💰 About $10/class

Drummers Only Studios

(415) 334-7069

B ob Danielson has been the drummer in Beach Blanket Babylon since 1986 and is the founder of the Drummers Only Studios. Drummers of all levels can take private instruction and rent their own space where they can practice as often and as loud as they want. Perfect for the beginning drummer who doesn't want to make enemies by disturbing the peace.

☎ Bob Danielson
💰 About $18/half hour class

Rockenbach Music Studio

P.O. Box 20093, Piedmont, CA 94620
(510) 531-5625   guitar@sirius.com http://www.sirius.com/~guitar

R ockenbach Studio specializes in training for beginning and advanced musicians in guitar and bass lessons, songwriting, ear training, sight reading, solo transcriptions, improvisation and theory. Ask about the Ensemble Workshops where students form bands to play together. New members are invited into the group based on their playing level and musical tastes. Sounds like a great way to get a band together.

☎ Jock Rockenbach

Music

Folk

Irish Arts Foundation

44 Page Street, Suite 404B, San Francisco, CA 94102
(415) 252-9994   *http://www.iaf.org/~iaf/*

In the spring, the Irish Arts Foundation presents the Celtic Music & Arts Festival, a magnificent weekend festival of Ceili music with outstanding Irish musicians, cultural workshops, plus beginning and advanced step dancing. The foundation also offers concerts, readings and theater performances throughout the year.

☼ March

Plough & Stars

116 Clement Street, San Francisco, CA 94118
(415) 751-1122

Enjoy live folk music seven nights a week at this lively spot where there are plenty of people who are eager to enjoy the music, sing a few songs, and have a good time. Find yourself a cozy spot in front of the fire and sing away! Call for a schedule of upcoming events.

San Francisco Folk Music Club

885 Clayton Street, San Francisco, CA 94117
(415) 661-2217   *http://www.c2.org/harmony/folknik.html*

This is a group that shares a common interest in music they loosely define as "folk." Their primary emphasis is on group singing which everyone enjoys. Individual performers, instrumentalists, listeners, songwriters and folk dancers are all welcome to be part of these evenings of musical fellowship.

☼ 2nd & 4th Friday/month   🕐 9pm
💰 $7/year membership

Slavonic Cultural Center

60 Onondaga Avenue, San Francisco, CA 94112
(415) 584-8859

Balkan folk dances are flowing and wonderful! Visit these Balkan music and dance events, including the "Friday Music Series" and "Family Folkdancing," and see if you can resist taking part. Everyone is welcome.

Jazz

Jam Group

4104 24th Street, #115, San Francisco, CA 94114
(415) 552-1420   stinc1@aol.com

Y ou're invited to join these informal musical jam sessions and bring
your ideas, enthusiasm and "maybe even talent" to add to the mix.
The group founder is a guitar and piano player who acts as facilitator. All
skill levels and all instruments, including voice, guitar, piano, horns,
drums, and percussion etc. are welcome.

☎ Joe
& Free

Center for African and African American Art and Culture

762 Fulton Street, San Francisco, CA 94102
(415) 928-8546   caac@aol.com   http://www.caaac.com

S top by the last Monday nights in January, April and September for
these well-attended, free jazz events. This is really good music.

☼ Last Monday/month (Jan., April, & Sept.)   ⏰ 7-11pm

Gold Dust Lounge

247 Powell Street, San Francisco, CA 94102
(415) 397-1695

T raditional jazz is played nightly to a crowd of jazz aficionados. You
can always find the 'right' music in this friendly spot.

☼ 7 Nights   ⏰ 8:30pm-1am
& Free

Harry Denton's Starlight Room

450 Powell Street, San Francisco, CA 94102
(415) 395-8595

Y ou're probably thinking, "Sure we know about the Starlight Room,
but that place is for tourists." Not true. Many locals find it a great
meeting place and the entertainment is superb. Live bands fill the
calendar, plus a D.J. that spins the best tunes. Go on Wednesdays for the
weekly "Indulgence Party" (we'll keep you guessing) from 7-10pm and
you might meet Harry who stops by frequently to chat.

☼ Wednesdays   ⏰ 7-10pm

Music

Mark Hopkins Inter-Continental Hotel

Number One Nob Hill, San Francisco, CA 94108
(415) 616-6916   *http://www.citysearch.com/sfo/markhopkins*

M any exciting musical and dancing events are held monthly. You can attend alone, with friends or as a couple. The group dance lessons are popular ways to meet new dancers or you could go to hear the very fine vocalists and bands.

💰 About $6 until 9pm; $10 weekends

Radio Valencia Cafe

1199 Valencia Street, San Francisco, CA 94110
(415) 826-1199

C heck out these wonderful weekly jazz events that promote avant-garde and improvisatory music. The program is free on Friday and $3 on Saturday. Feel free to stop by alone or bring a friend and enjoy the music.

☀ Fridays & Saturdays   🕐 7-10pm
💰 Free-$3

San Francisco Jazz Festival

Four Embarcadero Center, San Francisco, CA 94111
(415) 398-5655   *sfjazzfest@sirius.com*   *http://www.sfjazzfest.org*

T his outstanding October music festival has been happening in San Francisco for more than 15 years. A great way to go to the festival and be involved with others immediately is to be a volunteer. Volunteers earn credits toward free tickets and an invitation to the post-festival volunteer party—which we have been told is quite a bash.

☎ Cynthia Taylor

Music Series

Market Street Association

870 Market Street, Suite 456, San Francisco, CA 94102
(415) 362-2500
Activity Location: In or near plazas around Market Street

The Market Street Association invites you to come out and hear the Bay Area's finest musicians performing everything from Rhythm & Blues to Retro-Rock. Give Lynn a call and she'll send you a schedule of events.

☀ Monday-Friday (July-September)   ⏰ Noon-1pm
☎ Lynn Valente
💰 Free

Noe Valley Ministry

1021 Sanchez Street, San Francisco, CA 94114
(415) 454-5238

The Noe Valley Ministry offers many excellent musical programs throughout the year. Be sure to take part in these wonderful concerts which support local artists. Get on the mailing list for more details about upcoming events that feature pre-concert lectures and post-concert receptions which are both informative and entertaining.

💰 Reasonable

The Luggage Store "Creative Music Mondays"

1007 Market Street, San Francisco, CA 94105
(415) 255-5971

An alcohol and smoke-free gallery environment that hosts "Creative Music Mondays" where the audience is treated to a variety of fine musical performers and genres. Give a call to hear a detailed description of upcoming performances and other events.

☀ Mondays   ⏰ 8pm
☎ Laurie Lazer
💰 $5-$10

 # Walk Thru'

DIVA "Donne Italiane che Vivono in America"

DIVA "Donne Italiane che Vivono in America" is a wonderful social club for women that meets once a month for Italian cultural events. You don't have to be of Italian heritage or speak the language to attend but you must bring your love and passion for Italy.

A different dimension of Italian culture is explored at every meeting. Events are held in members' homes and Italian restaurants as well as other cultural venues including the Istituto Italiano di Cultura. At most events a dinner featuring regional Italian cuisine is served, followed by a program spotlighting one of the group's talented members. Past programs included Tracy Fontana of *Quintessential Italy* who gave a slide lecture on "Magnificent Private Palaces and Villas of Italy." On another evening Elisabetta Fagioli, a wine expert, led a presentation and tasting of Italian wines, embellished with her own stories of growing up in Italy. Recently DIVA Liz Kraus, owner of *Toscana Ceramics*, hosted the group for a buffet and Italian wines reception. Following around-the-circle introductions, Liz treated the group to a talk and demonstration of "Italian Majolica," a magnificent style of pottery as an example of fine ceramic art. DIVA members were set loose to gather and choose Majolica platters, serving bowls, dishes and other pieces in glorious hues of deep blue, rich yellow, fiery red-orange at a special 20% discount.

The DIVAS is a great way to socialize with women who like learning, laughing and dreaming about all things Italian. Consider joining them for these great evenings of good food, wine and friends. Ciao!!

Seniors

Community Service • Lifelong Learning

Programs • Reading & Writing

Travel • Working

Elderhostel members enjoying a hike up Diamond Creek
in Peach Springs. Photos by Jim Harrison.

L et's make it clear that we don't think seniors need to be relegated to "Senior" activities. People are living longer and enjoying better health in their later years, creating a new idea of what it means to be a senior. Many are opting to postpone retirement by starting second careers, volunteering, and engaging in working/learning travel vacations. And why not? Many of us (Ruth here!) over 55 are able-bodied, cognitively active persons who don't want to surrender to stereotyped ideas about old age.

Sometimes, however, it's nice to be in the company of people who share our years: mature people with similar life experiences that come with our age or generation. Official senior Ruth says, "Sometimes I want to be with people who not only remember *where they were* the day that Kennedy was shot, but who also remember what they *thought* about it because they were adults with a political philosophy to frame the event." Sometimes seniors want to hang out with 'their own,' no matter what the activity, even though they do many things with the community-at-large. Thus, this is a listing of places for seniors to find other seniors to enjoy.

The activities described in this chapter require what many seniors have more of than most people: discretionary time. Many of the experiences described in this chapter are with **travel groups** (often reasonably priced), **community service** and **volunteer groups**, and a combination of the two: **working (service) vacation groups.** The travel group we've been hearing about for years from very satisfied participants, including friends and family, is **Elderhostel**. It surely deserves special mention as an outstanding seniors program. As you will see by reading the action-packed catalog, the activities are fabulous—you almost can't wait to be 55 to qualify (or 50 with a spouse of 55). Just think about studying Alpine ecology while living in a rustic dorm at Colorado State and hiking into the beautiful hills each day for classes. Or exploring Oregon around the Klamath Basin to describe the largest concentration of bald eagles. How about studying light opera at the Peabody Music Conservatory in Maryland? A week-long Elderhostel there costs less than $500, everything included! They also have working/service vacations which include collaboration with various service communities, such as **Habitat for Humanity**, so you can 'give back' while you expand your geographical and personal horizons. Examples of these programs are teaching English to Jamaican schoolchildren, two weeks in Peru studying the effects of the human population on dolphins, or studying the Howler monkey ecology in the Yucatan Peninsula. Sounds incredible, doesn't it?

Who will you meet as you plant trees in the Bayou? Certainly not self-absorbed "the world owes me a living" folks. No, you're more likely to find people who want to grow in exciting and challenging ways in the second part of their lives; they believe that all it requires is the enthusiasm to do so. Traveling in an organized group while going to destinations you choose offers security and a community network that shares an interest and unites around the experience. No longer do you have to drag unwilling friends or family members who will never let you forget about that "horrible place" you made them go. (Be sure to check the Chapter 17: Vacations for more vacations focused on specific interests.)

Community Service opportunities organized for seniors try to capitalize on seniors' skills. The **Service Corps of Retired Executives (SCORE)** recruits retired experts who are interested in helping small business owners/managers identify and analyze successful business practices. It's a win-win situation for both you and the recipient. For you, it's a great way to stay in touch with the business community and be useful to a struggling entrepreneur. The person you counsel reaps the rewards of your experience and finds a mentor who really cares about the success of his/her business. Another fine program is the **Retired Senior Volunteer Program (RSVP)** which coordinates volunteers for non-profit organizations, schools, libraries, hospitals and museums. You'll receive training, support, recognition and a limited transportation reimbursement as part of this program.

Another advantage to being a senior, besides having more time, is having your mind available for things other than work. Do you remember how tired your mind was when you got home from work every night? How you only wanted to do what was absolutely necessary before collapsing in front of the tube or crawling into bed with a book before (quickly) going to sleep? If you're lucky enough to retire, especially in your energetic years, you'll wonder what kinds of things you can do to keep your mind vigorous and expand yourself in exciting ways. Well, wonder no more! There are many opportunities in the Bay Area to learn just about anything you want, and many are earmarked for seniors. For example, more than 45 branches of the **Older Adults Department of City College** offer free high quality classes for persons who are 55 years and older on a variety of topics. **The Fromm Institute for Lifelong Learning** sponsored by the **University of San Francisco** is an outstanding program that welcomes persons who are at least 50 years old, regardless of their prior educational background, to its "multi-generational college environment." We have seen first-hand the excited faces of young and mature students all around the campus discussing what they have learned, enjoying each other's company in the cafeteria and doing research together in the library. If you choose, you may waive taking exams. Imagine—the university experience without the stress of exams!

For people interested in learning more about the aging process and other issues pertinent to a person over the age of 65, try the **Office of Patient Services**. It is a non-profit health education and counseling service with free classes covering topics such as "Marriage After 65," "Medications Management," and your "Traveling Health." These classes are designed to enhance your health and quality of life and are an excellent venue to meet others your own age. Participating in lifelong learning experiences is a great way to stay involved with the community around you. What we kept hearing from retirees was, "So much to learn and do and not enough hours in the day. I don't know where I ever found the time for work."

As you will see in this directory, there is an abundance of exciting interest groups in the city. How about getting involved in a book reading group? Duke Edwards, a lover of the classics himself, moderates a **Great Books** group that meets bi-monthly at the **Doelger Senior Center**. He is knowledgeable and receptive to calls for information about his group. (Also check Chapter 5: Discussion Groups for other book groups that would welcome your participation.) Why not take up or practice your ballroom dancing steps through the ongoing classes offered through the **Park and Recreation Department?** Or see a free movie on the first and third Tuesday of the month at **St. Mary's Hospital.** If you're looking for active compadres, the **Fifty-Plus Fitness Association** sponsors beautiful ocean walks and runs along the Lands' End Trail. The distance is approximately four miles and there is no fee; membership with the group is not required for participation. You'll find many exciting and pleasurable things to do when you explore activities that suit your interests, time,

Seniors

budget and physical needs.

Remember, too, there are very fine programs for seniors in every neighborhood, located in city-sponsored senior centers, in churches, synagogues and community centers. They may provide transportation, meals and assistance with information about basic health care and life services for seniors. And, very importantly, they help seniors link up with other seniors for friendship and social activities.

Community Service

American Association of Retired Persons Volunteer Talent Bank

601 E Street NW, Washington,DC 20049
(800) 424-3410

If you are retired, you can volunteer through AARP to help community service programs in the area or across the U.S. This national organization for active retirees (50and over) will gladly welcome your participation and give you leads to organizations where you can be of help.

Retired Senior Volunteer Program (RSVP)

1125 Quintara Street, San Francisco, CA 94116
(415) 731-3335

This local group coordinates and places volunteers 55 and over in non-profit organizations such as schools, libraries, hospitals and museums. You'll receive training, support, recognition and limited transportation reimbursement.

Service Corps of Retired Executives (SCORE)

455 Market Street, Suite 600, San Francisco, CA 94105
(415) 744-6827

Retired executives are needed to be SBA/SCORE counselors. Help small business owners and managers analyze and identify basic management problems. Use your diverse background and share your knowledge with others in personal counseling sessions. Being part of this organization is a good way to keep in touch with the business community while enjoying retirement.

Lifelong Learning

Center for Learning in Retirement, U. C. Extension Center

55 Laguna Street, San Francisco, CA 94102
(415) 863-4518

The University offers terrific opportunities for learning and intellectual stimulation. Take part in study groups or workshops that explore the many facets of art, literature, music, history, science, and economics, as well as many other stimulating and timely topics. Participate in upcoming programs, monthly walks and tours, the fall picnic and a winter holiday party.

🐌 $195/year membership

Older Adults Department of City College

106 Bartlet Street, San Francisco, CA 94110
(415) 550-4415

Classes are open for enrollment at any time during the semester to anyone over 55. Just order a schedule, choose your class, and show up to register. There are no fees, and classes are held throughout the city at more than 45 locations. It couldn't be easier.

☎ Dr. R. Wood Massi

San Francisco State University, Urban Elders Programs

#22 Tapia Drive, San Francisco, CA 94132
(415) 338-2127

If you are over 60, you qualify to participate in "60 Plus" and "Eldercollege," two excellent programs for older students. Decide if you want to take credited classes for a nominal fee and work towards completing a degree, or simply audit classes on a non-credit basis. Involvement in university life is a good way to keep an open social network and be part of social events sponsored by the program. Call for a brochure of classes.

☎ Celia Sullivan

The Fromm Institute for Lifelong Learning, U. S.F.

2130 Fulton Street, San Francisco, CA 94117
(415) 422-6805   *http://www.usfca.edu/fromm/home.html*

Regardless of your educational background, retired persons (50+) are welcome to participate in these university classes. There are no tuition fees but you may pay for a membership program which entitles you to take four courses a session. USF is a multi-generational college environment where people of all ages and cultural groups come together to learn.

☎ Robert Fordham
💰 $250/year membership

Programs

Central YMCA

220 Golden Gate Avenue, San Francisco, CA 94102
(415) 447-2555

You don't have to be a member of the Senior Program to stop by and enjoy lively conversation, coffee and tea, magazines, books, puzzles and games for free. Lectures, writing sessions, a hiking club, line dancing, language classes and an excellent exercise facility are also available but require membership.

☼ 8am-4pm Sunday-Friday; 12-5pm Saturday
💰 $20/year membership; 18/month dues

Diamond Senior Center

117 Diamond Street, San Francisco, CA 94114
(415) 863-3507

This is a great way to get out and meet new and interesting people. What's stopping you from taking part in an organized trip, or/and playing bridge or bingo? Keep your mind alert by learning a foreign language, and your body active by learning new dances. Enjoy a hot, nutritious lunch on weekdays with the companionship of others. Check for an extended schedule of hours.

☼ Monday-Friday   🍽 12pm (Lunch)
☎ Betty Garvey
💰 About $1.25 donation

Seniors

Fifty-Plus Fitness Association

P.O. Box D, Stanford, CA 94309
(415) 566-2542

Activity Location: Meet at the Seacliff lookout platform at El Camino Del Mar and 32nd Avenue

Join others on these beautiful ocean walks and runs along the Lands End Trail. The distance is approximately four miles and there is no fee. Membership with Fifty-Plus is not required to participate.

☼ 2nd Saturday/month   🕐 8:45am

Parks and Recreation Department

111 Lake Merced Boulevard, San Francisco, CA 94015
(415) 991-8002

Activity Location: Doelger Senior Center, West Lake Meeting Rm.
101 Lake Merced Blvd., Daly City (415) 991-8012

Be part of these excellent, ongoing Ballroom dance classes which are offered for dancers of all levels. Isn't it time to learn some new dancing steps?

🕐 Monday 7-8:30pm, Wednesday & Thursday 4-5:30pm.
💰 $2/class

San Francisco Senior Center, Downtown Branch

481 O'Farrell, San Francisco, CA 94102
(415) 771-7950

Who needs to learn about computers? You do! Take advantage of The Computer Learning Center and become a cybersenior. But you also like traditional social activities? Get involved in Ballroom and Folk Dance, Knitting or Choral Singing. Don't miss the hot, delicious lunch which is served daily, but be sure to make a reservation. Check for an extended schedule of hours.

☼ Everyday   🕐 12pm (Lunch)
☎ Mary Alice Stevenson
💰 About $1.25 donation

San Francisco Senior Center

890 Beach Street, San Francisco, CA 94109
(415) 775-1866

S an Francisco has many excellent senior centers and this one is terrific. The beautiful location in Aquatic Park will make you feel good about yourself, others and the city. Once through the doors, you'll discover all the fabulous ways to get involved. For starters, you can take an art, dance, foreign language or writing class. Sit down for a bridge game or just stop by to socialize. Lunch is served everyday but Saturday. We were told you should get there no later than 11:15am to ensure a lunch.

☼ Everyday but Saturday   🕐 12pm (Lunch)
💰 About $1.25 donation

St. Francis Neighborhood Senior Center

152 Church Street, San Francisco, CA 94114
(415) 621-2635

A great way to spend your Wednesdays is at St. Francis Center. The weekly program includes an informative or entertainment program, a hot delicious lunch and a sing-along. Sometimes you'll take excursions to interesting places. A lot of good reasons to be out and about.

☼ Wednesdays   🕐 10am-2pm
☎ Clayia Hamilton
💰 Free–$2/lunch

St. John's Presbyterian Church
"Hula Dancing for Seniors"

Arguello Boulevard, and Lake Streets, San Francisco, CA
(415) 751-1626
Activity Location: 1411 26th avenue (415) 753-5393

G et into the swing of things and hula with others who love to move to music. Beginners are taught the steps in the first ten minutes of this class of about 25-30 people, 55 years and over. Wear regular clothes, but look forward to performing the Hula in full costume when you perform!

☼ Thursdays   🕐 9:30am-11:30pm
☎ Deedee Richardson
💰 $2

Seniors

St. Mary's Hospital
220 Hayes Street, San Francisco, CA 94117
(415) 387-5361
Activity Location: Morrisey Hall (415) 750-5800

Take advantage of free movies offered for seniors. Call for the upcoming movie schedule.

☼ 1st and 3rd Tuesday/month   🕐 1:30pm
☎ Helen Johnson

Reading & Writing

Great Books Council
(415) 285-8409
Activity Location: Doelger Senior Center, 101 Lake Merced Blvd., Daly City
(415) 991-8012

This group reads and discusses two classics a month, delving into the work of the greatest writers and thinkers of all time.

☼ 1st and 3rd Thursday/month   🕐 1pm
☎ Duke Edwards
💰 Cost of reading material

Montefiore Senior Center, "Pen to Paper"
3200 California Street, San Francisco, CA 94118
(415) 292-1262

It's never too late to start writing. "Pen to Paper" is an excellent writing class that might prompt you to start working on the book you always wanted to write. Whether you're working on a novel, a short story or a research paper, a writing group is what you need for support and feedback about your work.

☼ Thursdays   🕐 1pm
☎ Margo Perin
💰 About $2.50/members; $5/non-members

Travel

Backroads

801 Cedar Street, Berkeley, CA 94710
(800) 462-2848 goactive@backroads.com   http://www.backroads.com

D oes pedaling through a sunny hilltop town in Tuscany sound like fun? How about cross-country skiing in the Canadian Rockies? Maybe a hike and safari trip to South Africa? Backroads, an active travel company, features about 90 multisport (e.g., hiking, bicycling, cross-country skiing) vacations around the world. People of different ages and fitness abilities are encouraged to find an itinerary and destination that is right for them. Selected trips are designed exclusively for seniors.

Elderhostel

75 Federal Street, Boston, MA 02110
(617) 426-8056   http://www.elderhostel.org

E lderhostel has an awesome program of thousands of educational adventures in all parts of this country and abroad. In San Francisco, join an Arts and Humanities Seminar which features a weekly cultural excursion. Travel to Oregon to the Klamath Basin to study the largest concentration of bald eagles, or to Washington to witness the changing tides and currents. In the process you'll discover local history and folklore. Elderhostel also offers volunteer working vacations, listed in another *Elderhostel Service* catalog.

Global Volunteers

375 E. Little Canada Road, St. Paul, MN 55117
(800) 487-1074

G lobal Volunteers offers a special program for older hostelers. This is a non-profit group with ongoing projects in Russia, Poland, Indonesia and other locations abroad as well as in the U.S. Call for a catalog of wide-ranging volunteer opportunities.

Seniors

Golden Age Travellers Club

Pier 27, The Embarcadero, San Francisco, CA 94111
(800) 258-8880

The club provides social and travel events information for people 50+. GAT also has a special listing for single travelers who are looking for roommates for cruises and tours.

💰 $10/year membership; $15 couples

Working

Life Plan Center

5 3rd Street, Suite 324, San Francisco, CA 94103
(415) 546-4499

An organization that helps persons over 50 face transitions in their work and personal lives. Orientations are held every Tuesday from 12-1pm and alternating Monday evenings from 6-7pm.

☎ Shireen Burns
💰 $70/year membership

National Council on the Aging

870 Market Street, #785, San Francisco, CA 94102
(415) 982-7007

If you aren't ready for retirement, check out this organization that helps people 55 and over reenter the work force.

☎ Nicholas de Lorenzo

Singles

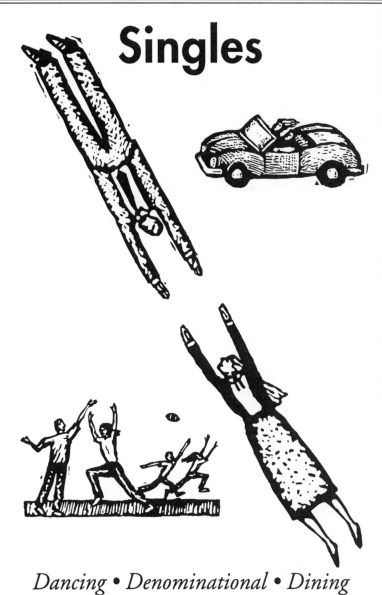

Dancing • Denominational • Dining
Miscellany • Music Lovers • Social Clubs
Sport Clubs • Travel

Singles

Meet and connect with other playful, active singles at
Fun Stuff For Singles or at a Recess! A Play Night For Grown-Ups
presented by Sue Walden & Co.'s ImprovWorks.

Who doesn't cringe when people talk about the "Singles Scene?" Don't we all get an unpleasant image of some dark smoky place with very loud music, where they serve drinks with little parasols and everybody is dressed up in his or her Hollywood best. These places give off a sort of adolescent feeling—and only those of us who still *look* kind of Hollywood adolescent look forward to it. We suppose it might be fun to step back into the excitement of the "promise of Friday night," testing our seduction skills (safely, of course) with the best of them. That's ok every now and then.

But the purpose of this resource book is to offer alternatives to those kinds of places. We want to suggest places where you can find all kinds of compatible people, single and attached, who are doing interesting activities together in the fresh air of daylight. We think that these will be your favorite people.

In our Singles chapter, however, we suggest activity places meant only for single people. If you are single there are times when you feel like being with people who are also single. After all, they are in the same situation with respect to relationships as you are, who think and talk about some of the same issues about socializing that you do, and who frequently are available (and willing) to go to a movie or nightspot on a Saturday night. There are also times when you, as a single person, do not feel like being in a situation where everyone else is coupled.

And there are times when you feel like meeting *new* men and women to have fun with, outside of your usual group of friends. These times may even include adventuresome moments when you feel like looking for candidates for a permanent love relationship. In other words—you're ready to stretch, risk a bit and expand your boundaries.

Nothing wrong with that.

So, **where are they?**

Where are the single people *you* want to meet? They *could be* in that dark smoky place. Never can tell. Problem is, it's also hard for *you* to tell. After all, what can you tell about a person in the dark except that she has pretty legs or he has nice broad shoulders (No, that's *not* enough). You might glean some other information from the brief shouting discussion you have, or by how he or she dances in a cramped space, but probably not much else. What you likely can discern is whether you feel any animal magnetism. That's important, but in and of itself it's not a great predictor of a solid, long-term relationship.

When people talk about some deep, dark, psychological propensity they have for choosing the wrong people, we ask where they meet them. Often they say they meet them in clubs. In such a case, the deep, dark propensity probably has more to do with the deep, dark club— where they did the best they could to choose with no information about true compatibility factors. Don't get us wrong—clubbing can be a lot of fun—but it's not a great way to find a compatible partner.

Not to worry.

There are many groups for single people, or mostly single people, that are activity-based. Taking part in organized activities like dancing, skiing, dining out, musical events and discussions makes interaction between people easy and natural. There are even activities established for specific populations, such as certain age groups, vegetarians, religious denominations or people of a particular size and height. Really, there are more groups out there than you can imagine. Problem is, where do you start?

One place to start is with the **Professional Guild,** the largest social singles group in California, where you surely can expand your circle of single friends in the Bay Area. The local branch sponsors two or three events a month around San Francisco, including mixers, parties, dances and workshops. The Guild will also inform you about events taking place throughout the state. It has never been easier to meet attractive and interesting people who could be lots of fun to pal around with on a Friday night. And after that, who knows?

Ski clubs are often all-around social groups. The **San Francisco Ski Club** is a year-round ski and social club for active single adults and they welcome skiers (and socializers) of all levels. Even if you've never hit the slopes, don't be dissuaded because the club offers terrific programs for beginners as well as advanced skiers. Other activities include white- water rafting trips, cycling tours, volleyball at the Marina Green and a weekly social event held at Gabbiano's Restaurant behind the Ferry Building. If you're single and looking for a place to be active with people on the move, this is a great place to start.

If you love fine food, interesting wines and stimulating dinner conversation, why not check out the **Dining Out Club**, the **Single Gourmet**, or the **Singles' Gourmet Soiree**? We really like culinary groups because you're bound to have *some* fun (eating) and it gives you something to do besides stare at somebody while you talk. Also, there are lots of people there, so you don't have to carry the ball the whole time. It's fun to listen to people talk to *each other*, too. You learn a lot and also find out who the good listeners are. Since the events are planned well in advance, you'll know the menu ahead of time, as well as whether to expect a speaker as part of the program. These are quite lively affairs and we've had delicious fun with these folks.

There are many mixed (not just for singles) organizations that sponsor special activities for single people or where the majority of people in attendance are single. Going dancing alone is easy at the **Metronome Ballroom** because you can meet new dancers at a group class followed by a dance party. Look in the Metronome calendar for the events held occasionally for singles only. You can really kick up your heels at **Recess! A Play Night For Grownups**, where up to 25 people, including many single people, participate in "get-to-know-ya" mixers and story, word and guessing games. Your creativity will be challenged by ingenious theater games designed to stimulate understanding of universal human situations. The **Bravo! Club** of the **San Francisco Opera** is a great venue for opera lovers to meet other opera lovers at the many pre-performance receptions, lectures and fund-raisers. Board the "Mambo Cabaret on Wheels" and go club hopping to local Latin and Caribbean clubs with **The Mexican Bus**—a great way for singles (and others) to explore hot clubs within the security of a group.

Who will you meet in these places?

The people who go to group events enjoy being active and are interested in finding a network of active friends, just as you would be if you joined them. Also we've found that people who are open to going to events for singles are aware and up front about looking for new single friends to socialize with, as well as hoping to meet romantic partners.

The 50 percent divorce rate guarantees that people are coming and going all the time in singles groups, so there are many different people attending from week to week. That means there are plenty of new people for you to meet each time you go, as well as acquaintences you might have seen/met at a prior event with whom you can comfortably start a conversation.

Some people comment on the "desperate losers" who go to singles events, including clubs. We're never sure why. Are people who are unattached more likely to be losers than people who are attached? In our travels around these organizations, we have found engaging people who are enthusiastic, gentle, kind, sexy and interesting as well as people who are not so appealing. We found them similar to the attached population except that the single people were often a little more friendly. Studies of cross-cultural experience show that you often find what you expect to find. If the only people you are meeting seem "boring," you might wonder about the signals that you're sending and if there are worthy people you are screening out.

Keep in mind that each person you meet at an activity comes with her connections to all the other activities that she enjoys. So when you meet others and talk with them about their pleasurable pursuits (and *do* ask them!), you open up a world of possibilities to explore—with them or on your own.

One of the golden opportunities that comes with being single is that you can move freely in the active world. You don't have to get approval or coordinate your movements with anyone. You can explore a multitude of things with new people using your personal criteria as your only boundary. It can be a very exciting time to explore the world—and yourself!

Dancing

Bachelors 'n' Bachelorettes Square Dance Club

(415) 731-1712
Activity Location: Ebenezer Lutheran Church, 678 Portola Drive
(415) 681-5400

Remember how much fun Square Dancing is? From the title of the club, you can see that singles are encouraged to learn some fancy do-si-dos. The people are friendly and welcoming and there is no need for concern about your skill level even if you're a beginner. Stop by and watch a session and see if you don't come back!

☼ Fridays
☎ Shirley
💰 $2.50

📅 7pm lesson,
dancing 7:30-9pm

Belles & Beaux Social Club

P.O. Box 143, Kentfield, CA 949141
(800) 858-2443

Take part in these organized dance events with live band music held in various locations in San Francisco and the Bay Area. All ages are welcome with a majority of the group between 30 and 60. Past dances have featured Big Band Swing music, R & B Motown and fabulous tunes from the 50s and 60s.

☎ Melissa Bradley
💰 About $20

Metronome Ballroom

1830 17th Street, San Francisco, CA 94103
(415) 252-9000

A great place to find experienced partners! Group classes, private lessons and dance parties featuring Ballroom, Latin and Swing dancing are held in this San Francisco treasure. Friday is Newcomer's and Argentine Tango Night, Saturday is West Coast Swing and Jitterburg Night, and Sunday is Ballroom, Swing and Latin Night.

💰 $10/lesson & party; $8 party; $6 students

Singles

Mr. Rick's Martini Club

236 West Portal Avenue, #376, San Francisco, CA 94127
(415) 566-2545

M r. Rick's is a great venue for meeting single people although the club is not exclusively for singles. Join this group of "bon vivants who appreciate a certain style" and you will enjoy an "elegant evening out or a cozy night in with good friends and the perfect martini." Both singles and couples meet at the Martini Club for all kinds of gatherings, including supper club/swing dances, local artist entertainment and terrific cocktail hours. These Club events have a 1930s-40s feel to them, like stepping into a classic movie.

☎ Laurie Gordon
💰 $20/year membership

The Mexican Bus

(415) 546-3747
Activity Location: Chevys Mexican Restaurant, 150–4th Street
(415) 543-8060

B oard the "mambo cabaret on wheels" and go club-hopping to local Latin, Caribbean and African music hot spots. The cost includes your transportation and cover admission charges. This is a great way to explore new clubs and meet people. You must be 21 and reservations are required because space is limited, so please don't just show up.

☼ Most Fridays & Saturdays   🕐 9:45pm-2am
💰 $30/person

Three Babes and a Bus Nightclub Tours

(415) 552-2582
Activity Location: New Joe's Restaurant, 347 Geary Street, San Francisco
(415) 397-9999

T his is an outstanding way for men and women to experience some of San Francisco's hottest dance clubs. If you don't know which ones they are, these folks do! Not for singles only but many single people are aboard. You must be 21 and advance reservations are *required.*

☼ Saturdays   🕐 9:30pm-1:30am
💰 $30/person

Denominational

Jewish Community Federation, Young Adults Division

121 Steuart Street, San Francisco, CA 94105
(415) 436-0711

Singles of all ages can find events that are right for them through the federation. One subgroup of the organization is YAD with more than 2,500 Jewish young adults between the ages of 21-39. They enjoy social activities, religious and cultural education, leadership development and community service opportunities. Be sure to ask about the book club.

☎ Dan Lavin

Singletarians

(415) 821-7865

Activity Location: First Unitarian Church, 1187 Franklin Street, San Francisco
(415) 776-4580

This group of single persons 40 years and older are members of all faiths. They attend concerts, video parties, picnics, potluck suppers and lunches and enjoy dining out and other happenings. The best way to meet the group is at the potluck lunch that is held every second Sunday. If you are under 40, look into the Young Adults Group.

☼ 2nd Sunday/month　　　　　　🕐 1:00pm
☎ Karen Grech
💰 $20/year membership

St. Vincent de Paul

2320 Green Street, San Francisco, CA 94123
(415) 522-9242

This is an active young group of Catholic singles who enjoy all types of socializing activities. Call the telephone bulletin board for more information about the Young Adults Group.

☼ 2nd & 4th Monday/month　　　　🕐 7:30pm

Singles

Dining

Dining Out Club
1978–23rd Avenue, San Francisco, CA 94116
(415) 731-8026

A friendly group of people, approximately 25-65 years of age, who like exploring restaurants in the Bay Area. While it's basically a social club open to anyone, singles are especially encouraged.

☎ Marti Sousanis

💰 $130/year membership or $40/year mbshp plus $10/event

Singles' Gourmet Soiree
(510) 653-0583   *Lvestanen.aol.com*

E njoy wonderful dinners in San Francisco and around the Bay Area with other intelligent, like-minded singles. Events are also open to non-members. If you'd like to attend, call and leave your fax or email information only. The group has stopped taking mail or voice message requests.

☎ Laura Vestanen

Singles Supper Club
P.O. Box 60518, Palo Alto, CA 94306
(415) 327-4645   *ssc@best.com*

T he Supper Club holds excellent dinners, dances, and other social throughout the Bay Area. This is an enjoyable group.

💰 $125/year membership

The Single Gourmet

P.O. Box 4427, San Rafael, CA 94913
(415) 472-0904

J oin this dining, travel and social club for "discriminating single adults" in the Bay Area. The organization schedules a variety of restaurant dinners, cocktail parties and travel, sporting and cultural outings. Another benefit of membership is automatic reciprocity with more than 20 affiliated chapters around the U.S. so you can meet new active singles in different cities when you're traveling.

☎ Julie Garfield

💰 $99/year membership, plus event costs

Miscellany

Cafe Latte II

4 Embarcadero Center, San Francisco, CA 94111
(415) 982-2233

S top by and meet others at these friendly Happy Hours for single professional people. Jazz and Blues music played from 5-8:30pm. No cover.

☼ Wednesdays-Fridays   🕐 4:30-6:30pm

First Unitarian Church - Singles Forum

1187 Franklin Street, San Francisco, CA 94109
(415) 776-4580

A group of single men and women (roughly between 35 and 50 years) who meet twice a month to discuss issues relevant to being a single person. Past discussion topics have included "Respecting Personal Boundaries In A Relationship" and The Importance of Feeling Whole As A Single." This is not a church-related religious service. At the time of publication, this group was reorganizing. Please call to confirm their activities.

☼ 2nd & 4th Sundays/month   🕐 9:30-11am

Singles

Parents' Place

3272 California Street, San Francisco, CA 94118
(415) 563-1041   *http://www.jfcs.org*

Discover this excellent organization that sponsors programs and workshops for single moms and dads. Sharing your questions, experience and knowledge with others in the same situation can be invaluable and great for friendship building. Child care programs are available for your child while you are there. Call for a catalog.

SAN FRANCISCO BAY GUARDIAN

520 Hampshire Street, San Francisco, CA 94110
(415) 255-7600   *http://www.sfbg.com*

The *BAY GUARDIAN* sponsors get-togethers for singles interested in placing personal ads. There is no charge to attend the party or to place a free 40-word personal ad with voice mail. You could have real fun with this!

SF WEEKLY

185 Berry Street, Suite 3800, San Francisco, CA 94107
(415) 541-9556   romance@sfweekly.com   http://www.sfweekly.com

Writing and placing a personal ad has lost the stigma of being something that only desperate people do. People use them for finding romance or for finding platonic companions with whom to do activities. The parties are always great fun in places such as SF MOMA, Harveys and the Stroke of Genius. Don't worry about your writing skills because there are romance writers at the party to help.

☎ Wendy Ervin

Sue Walden & Co.'s ImprovWorks
"Fun Stuff For Singles"

1801 Franklin Street, #404, San Francisco, CA 94109
(415) 885-5678
Activity Location: Fort Mason Center, Building C,
Buchanan Street & Marina Boulevard (415) 979-3010

Participate in communication games, discover your special talents, and enjoy a night exploring the world of improvisational theater while meeting other many single people. These activities *are* fun!

☎ Sue Walden   🕰 7:30-10pm
💰 About $120/4 events

Music Lovers

Bravo! Club, San Francisco Opera

301 Van Ness Avenue, San Francisco, CA 94102
(415) 565-3285   http://www.sfopera.com

Building a broad opera audience is the primary focus for this largely young adult group with many single members. Membership includes free admission with a guest to the "Trio Series," pre-performance receptions, lectures, preferential invitations and seating. Expand your network of opera buddies while you enjoy these musical perks.

💰 $60/year membership; $100 for 40+ years

Classical Occasions

P.O. Box 170248, San Francisco, CA 94117
(415) 923-9431   rnmosher@compuserve.com
http://ourworld.compuserve.com/homepages/rnmosher

A wonderful club for single lovers of classical music and theater. Bimonthly events feature recitals and lectures with a social hour that precedes the program. Several dinner evenings are held throughout the year.

💰 $80/year membership

Singles

Symphonix, San Francisco Symphony
Davies Symphony Hall, San Francisco, CA 94102
(415) 281-0700

The Young Professionals League of the San Francisco Symphony is a social organization with many single members. The group promotes the symphony by helping to sponsor events such as dinners, receptions and concerts taking place throughout the year. Keep an eye out for the now famous Black and White Ball which is held every two years—the next scheduled for 1999.

💰 $50/year membership; $90 couples

Social Clubs

The Bachelors of San Francisco
P.O. Box 26237, San Francisco, CA 94126
(415) 905-4525

You must be a single male to join and maintain membership in this organization that sponsors social functions throughout the year. The annual Bachelors' "Drinks Under The Dome" is a blast! Single ladies are encouraged to attend events.

☎ Daron Craft

Golden Gate Tip Toppers
(415) 281-5664

Men must be 6'2"+ and women must be 5'10"+ to qualify for membership in this social club for tall people. A lively group of mainly single people who get together for organized dinners, house parties, dances and other social events.

The Professional Guild
1107 Kennedy Place, Suite 3, Davis, CA 95616
(800) 870-7072   (916) 700-0000   *http://www.ns.net/singles*

They say they are California's largest single social group and they are right here in the Bay Area. If you join, you will meet many interesting and attractive single people at two to three events each month, including mixers, parties, dances and workshops.

💰 About $12-$20

Widows'/Widowers' Network

2116 N. Main Street., #B, Walnut Creek, CA 94596
(510) 256-7952

An excellent organization of volunteers who provide support, conversation and friendship to widowed persons. They sponsor many social events as well as a travel club for members.

Sport Clubs

Mile High Adventures & Entertainment

74 New Montgomery Street, San Francisco, CA 94105
(415) 974-5776   *http://www.pacificfun.com*

A membership club for singles who are interested in meeting others for adventuring fun. Over 50 events are planned monthly, including backpacking, dancing, skydiving, skiing, golf, scuba diving, card games, progressive dinners and more. No couch potatoes here!

San Francisco Ski Club

450 Silver Avenue #3, San Francisco, CA 94112
(415) 337-9333   *http://www.sfskiclub.org*
Activity Location: Gabbiano's Restaurant, 1 Ferry Plaza (415) 391-8403

A year-round ski and social club designed for active single adults over 21. This group has seasonal activities throughout the year, including summer white-water rafting and spring cycling, as well as fabulous skiing excursions. This is a great place to meet upbeat people in beautiful surroundings. Check out their web site.

☼ Tuesdays (September–May)   ⏰ 7:15pm
    Summer: 1st & 3rd Tuesdays
☎ Steve Noetzel
💰 $50/year membership

Singles

Single Cyclists

P.O. Box 656, Kentfield, CA 94914
(415) 459-2453   jbradbury@polka.macuser.ziff.com
http://users.aimnet.com/~harry/sc/schome.html
Activity Location: San Francisco and Bay Area

This group of active singles loves bicycling, and also do a variety of non-athletic social events together. The monthly mountain and road rides are rated for difficulty, eliminating the guess work you might have to do about what is physically required. You'll find organized dinners, informal potlucks, theater excursions and much more listed in their calendar.

💰 $30/year membership

Travel

Club Med

P.O. Box 4460, Scottsdale, AZ 85261
(800) Club Med   http://www.clubmed.com

These well-known get-away vacations offer many wonderful single friendly activities at terrific resort locations throughout the world. All meals, sports and entertainment are included in a one-price fee so you can forget about money once you get there. Surf to their site or call for a catalog which outlines Club Med resorts that are particularly designed for single people.

Single Travelers

(510) 420-1381
Activity Location: Upstairs banquet room, Gaylord India Restaurant
Ghirardelli Square (415) 771-8822

A group that gets together and plans faraway adventures. Converse with other single people who love to travel while eating hors d'oeuvres in pleasant surroundings.

💰 $7

Theater

Classes • Public Speaking

Shows Miscellany • Volunteer Involvement

Bay Area Theatresports (BATS) actors
Regina Saisi, Stephen Kearin and Tim Orr.
Photo by Workmaster.

Theater

Theater is strong in San Francisco, from traveling Broadway shows to experimental comedy. In any given week you have the choice of seeing shows produced in large houses with ample budgets to small, thinly-financed plays that struggle to open but excel in quality. As the number of theater productions expands, so does the active theater community. If you'd like to take part, you'll find opportunities for interactive audience drama experiences as well as stage production and acting.

There are many ways to be connected to the theater and its eclectic community. If it is a whole new world to you and you're the type who likes to *know* what you're doing, there are excellent schools that teach theater skills. Some of these are related to well-established theaters such as the **American Conservatory Theater (ACT)** which offers its Studio A.C.T. part-time, professional activing program for adults. You will be challenged to learn lines and perform ("Introduction To Acting"), participate in stage design ("Backstage At The Geary"), or interpret Elizabethan prose ("Shakespeare for the 1st Time") depending on the class you choose. Learning solid drama skills will help you to overcome stage fright as you move toward an accomplished performance. And if time or money for classes is holding you back, try the fine theater classes at the **San Francisco Recreation and Park Department**. You'll likely find good pals, aspiring thespians like yourself, in either place. And if you're new, you'll find other nervous beginners who are learning and experimenting. With expert classes and good energy, you'll be more accomplished than you ever dreamed in no time.

San Francisco is known for its outstanding improvisational theater. Improv differs from traditional theater in that the actors don't depend heavily on a playwright's script. Rather, they tap into the spontaneous and creative sides of themselves to develop a scene without the aid of elaborate sets or costumes. They predict, respond to and develop the scene based on their fellow actors' actions and words. An exciting difference between regular theater and improv is that with improv, the direction and finale of the play is not pre-determined. Simply put, improv is built on spontaneity rather than pre-established outcomes.

Taking an improv class or watching scenes come to life is exciting, and it's the best way to understand this unique theater genre. Many excellent organizations offer improv classes. One of the biggest is the **BATS Center for Improvisational Theatre.** Since no experience is necessary and there are different levels of classes for the beginner, don't be too worried about giving it a try. BATS students range in age from 16 to 80 and we have heard only glowing reports about faculty and classes. In conjunction with the school, scheduled improv performances are produced through **Bay Area Theatresports**—a wonderful choice to see and understand the art of improv. The popular "Audience Choice All Stars" is an interactive event where audience members are encouraged to scream, yell, talk among themselves, and vote for the best scene. Everyone chats freely at intermission following such an engaging, reactive experience to the drama, making this a great overall venue for people who go alone as well as couples and groups.

Improv games are fun! They are non-competitive activities and drama where group interaction and teamwork take place in a safe and supportive environment. We think they are among the few places where adults have a chance to get together to play and take gentle risks without feeling self-conscious. Try **Recess! A Play Night For Grown-Ups** and/or **Improv Game Night**, which offers a pot-luck supper and games in a social gathering. What kinds of games do they play? One common game is the group story. Each person adds one bit onto the last person's thoughts. Creativity is encouraged and there are no wrong answers. But you have to go yourself to understand the range of these innovative activities. We'll just tell you that with this terrific combination of theater and games and good leaders, you haven't had so much fun in a long time.

Explore theater as movement. **Hoodlums and Heroes** invites actors and non-actors to drop-in to warm up their bodies and stretch their non-verbal communication skills by learning staged movement and theatrical combat. In this class about the subtleties of movement on stage, your body will learn to talk without the use of words. The theatrical combat aspect of the class involves the techniques of exchanging combative gestures without really executing the maneuver. Randall, the instructor, calls it: "...creating aesthetically pleasing mayhem safely." Participants are professional actors as well as non-actors. Wear comfortable clothing and be prepared to have a lot of fun.

Explore circus as theater. The **San Francisco School of Circus Arts** invites you to "join the circus" without leaving the city. This real circus school, where you can take drop-in flying trapeze, trampoline and clown classes, will give you a window into the experience of a circus performer. Wow! You can master a new performance art or just fulfill the dream of "flying through the air with the greatest of ease," with safety nets of course. (Tell us, really, that you never wanted to do that.) It doesn't surprise us that the flying trapeze class attracts an active and very social group of loyal followers.

All theaters depend on volunteers. As a volunteer you'll see the productions unfold before your eyes and know that your part in it helped make it happen. You'll also receive free or reduced priced tickets, and take part in receptions, parties and informal theater gatherings. Ushering is the simplest way to get involved, and the method that requires the least amount of commitment. We think of ushers as greeters as they help people find their place as part of the audience and perhaps chat during intermission. Just a sample of theaters that will welcome you as an usher include the **American Conservatory Theatre (ACT), Asian-American Theater Company, Cable Car Theatre, Jon Sims Center for the Performing Arts, Lorraine Hansberry Theatre** and the **San Francisco Mime Troupe.**

If you'd rather be behind the scenes, try a production activity like set design, costume making, playing music, script work, lighting, ushering/ticket taking and promotion. Making a performance happen is the result of many peoples' work, not just the on-stage performers. The experience of working *together* on such a cooperative venture is as an exciting way to network. Another nice thing about working on a production is that it is a time-limited commitment. You are part of an ongoing group that agrees to meet and work together to put a play together, but you are only committed for the life of the play which is usually about 6 to 8 weeks. If you wish, you can leave after that, or you can sign up again and leave after the *next* production. Then again, you may just love it and stay in the theater for years, where you'll have a new depth of understanding and love for plays people have loved for centuries. And, again, you'll meet others who love them too.

If your interest in theater has more to do with being an active

Theater

audience member and learning about drama, perhaps you'd like to find others who are also interested in a theater-goers network. Read on! The **Musical Theatre Lovers United** is a group of musical theater lovers who celebrate the show tunes of Gershwin, Porter, Berlin, Sondheim and more. They are a fun bunch who meet for sing-alongs, attend productions, and really enjoy the company of other musical theater enthusiasts. Another venue to meet others who are interested in a theater-goers network is the weekly stage reading presented by the **Playwrights' Center of San Francisco**. After the reading the audience critiques the playwright's material and that encourages natural audience interaction. Express your views or chat with others who share your interest in theater.

San Francisco has exceptional interactive theater activities. You only need to reach for them!

Hoodlums and Heroes students Erik Flom, Stephen Bass, Kurt Bodden, Megan Marx, Alf Adams and Marion Gothier in action.

Classes

BATS Center for Improvisational Theater and Bay Area Theatresports tm

Fort Mason Center, Building B, San Francisco, CA 94124
(415) 474-8935   improbats@aol.com   http://www.projectcool.com/bats
Activity Location: Bayfront Theater

S tudying improvisational theater at the BATS Center is a terrific way to have fun and exercise. Students range in age from 16 to 80, many with no previous experience. Also at BATS is "Theatersports," in which a lively, interactive audience votes to decide the winner of the weekly improv scene competition. It's a lot of fun to meet others through inter-audience interaction, and the shows are a stitch. For info about Theatersports, call (415) 665-5527.

Hoodlums and Heroes

P.O. Box 591358, San Francisco, CA 94159
(415) 751-9263   hero@sirius.com
Activity Location: Jon Sims Center For The Performing Arts, Studio #3
1519 Mission Street (415) 554-0402

A ctors and non-actors are invited to warm up their bodies and stretch out their non-verbal communication skills by learning staged movement and theatrical combat. Wear comfortable clothes and prepare yourself to have a lot of fun while "creating aesthetically pleasing mayhem safely."

☼ Mondays   ☎ 11:30am-1:30pm
☎ Randall Miller
🖒 $10/drop-in

Improvisational Open Workshop

Activity Location: Fort Mason, Building C, Rm. 370, Buchanan St. & Marina
Blvd. (415) 453-9092

O ngoing workshops feature theater games and scene work. People of all acting levels are welcome to participate. Stop by and check it out for yourself.

☼ Saturdays   ☎ 1-4pm
☎ James Cranna
🖒 $5

Theater

San Francisco Recreation and Park Department

50 Scott Street, San Francisco, CA 94117
(415) 554-9523
Activity Location: Various recreational centers

H ave you secretly wanted to take acting classes but were not prepared to make a major time or money commitment? If so, you can
join one of the fine and reasonably priced classes offered through the
Recreation and Park Department.

San Francisco School of Circus Arts

755 Frederick Street, San Francisco, CA 94117
(415) 759-8123
Activity Location: West Polytechnic Gymnasium

H ere is your chance to join the circus without leaving the city. This
real circus school offers flying trapeze, trampoline and clown
classes and much more. Drop-in classes are offered as well as a professional studies program. Everyone is invited to master a new art or fulfill a
dream.

🐷 About $25/class

Studio A.C.T.

30 Grant Avenue, San Francisco, CA 94108
(415) 439-2332   *http://www.act-sfbay.com*

S tudio A.C.T. is an evening and weekend part-time acting program
for adults offered through the American Conservatory Theater.
Classes are designed for beginning through professional level students in
courses ranging from Improvisation and Voice and Speech to Stage
Combat, Singing, Acting, Shakespeare and On-Camera Acting. Four
ten-week sessions are offered each year beginning in January, March,
June, and September.

The Next Stage

1695 18th Street, #313, San Francisco, CA 94107
(415) 826-6505   *kimmelltns@aol.com*
Activity Location: Trinity Episcopal Church, 1668 Bush Street (415) 775-1117

Get involved and take a class or one-day seminar at this excellent school and theater company. Immerse yourself in improvisational training in a "safe space" for the beginner and a challenge for the more advanced actor. Ask about "Improv Games Nights," high energy evenings utilizing improvisation and theater fundamentals in a noncompetitive, teamwork environment. The potluck dinners make Games Nights both creative and social gatherings.

☎ Marcia Kimmell

Theater of Yugen

2840 Mariposa Street, San Francisco, CA 94110
(415) 621-0507

Learn more about Kyogen, the comic art form performed between the highly stylized Noh Plays. Kyogen addresses such worldly concerns as greed, vanity, lust and is played out to produce embarrassing and unexpected results. Open to all interested students. Call for the dates of the next workshop.

Public Speaking

Toastmasters

(415) 437-4029 tminfo@toastmasters.org   http://www.kudonet.com/~d4master

Toastmasters is an active, supportive, national club network devoted to the art of public speaking. Taking part in this group requires you to attend meetings and prepare material, but the rewards of increased confidence are substantial. There are over 40 groups in San Francisco, so you will likely find one near to you.

Theater

Shows Miscellany

Josie's Cabaret and Juice Joint

3538 16th Street, San Francisco, CA 94114
(415) 861-7933

Stop by during the day for a bite to eat because the crowd and the vegetarian food are good. Stop by in the evening for great entertainment. Past performances have included a lesbian detective comedy and a hilarious drag show featuring performer and drag star Musty Chiffon. Predominately light and funny gay themes.

☼ 8pm & 10pm (Friday & Saturday); 8pm only on weeknights

Musical Theater Lovers United

1606 Church Street, #2, San Francisco, CA 94131
(415) 552-2222   *http://www.enchanting.com/mtlu.htm*

Join this group of musical theater lovers who celebrate the showtunes of Gershwin, Porter, Berlin, Rodgers, Sondheim and more. Enjoy sing-alongs and excellent productions in the company of other musical theater enthusiasts. Non-members are encouraged to attend events.

Playwrights' Center of San Francisco

P.O. Box 460466, San Francisco, CA 94146
(415) 626-4603   *playctrsf@aol.com*   *http://www.playwrights.org*
Activity Location: Fort Mason Center, Blue Bear Theater, Building D
Buchanan Street & Marina Blvd. (415) 979-3010

A staged reading of a new and original play is presented for a live audience each week. The audience critique becomes an amusing, interactive experience between artist and audience. Anyone is welcome (members and non-members) to perform a scene at the monthly "Scene Night." Also ask about the annual DramaRama competition for the best new play.

☼ Fridays   🕐 7:30pm
☎ Laura Smith
💰 $3/members; $5/non-member

Sue Walden & Co.'s ImprovWorks
"Recess! A Play Night For Grown-Ups"

1801 Franklin Street, #404, San Francisco, CA 94109
(415) 885-5678

Activity Location:Fort Mason Center, Building C, Buchanan Street & Marina Blvd.
(415) 979-3010

Go to a "Recess" for improvisational training in a noncompetitive and playful atmosphere using exercises and games. This is your chance to leave the work world behind and act like a kid again. If you find that improv is for you, improv training classes are available.

☎ Sue Walden   🕑 7:30-10pm
💰 $15

The Luggage Store

1007 Market Street, San Francisco, CA 94105
(415) 255-5971

An alcohol and smoke-free gallery environment that hosts a weekly comedy open mic hosted by Tony Sparks. Everyone is welcome to participate. Be there by 7:30pm to sign up, and don't forget to ask about "Creative Music Mondays" and the current visual installation exhibits.

☼ Tuesdays   🕑 8pm
☎ Laurie Lazer
💰 $1-$3

The Marsh

1062 Valencia Street, San Francisco, CA 94110
(415) 826-5750   sawmarch@aol.com

Known as the "breeding ground for new performance," the entertainment is outstanding and fresh. The Marsh is quickly becoming a major spot for the theater crowd, especially since the addition of the Mock Cafe, located next-door at 1070 Valencia Street. The combination of the two venues creates more space for varied performances. Get on the mailing list.

Theater

Theater Bay Area

657 Mission Street, #402, San Francisco, CA 94105
(415) 957-1557   tba@best.com   http://www.theatrebayarea.org/

A resource center for working (or aspiring) film and theater actors who gather here for information about current auditions, casting calls, workshops and more. Membership is required to take part in the professional activities. The monthly magazine *Call Board* is published by TBA.

🏛 $37/year membership; +$12/year for *Call Board*

Venue 9

252 9th Street, San Francisco, CA 94103
(415) 626-2169   ftloose@best.com   http://www.ftloose.org

Venue 9 is a multi-use performance space that features independent and experimental films and videos, as well as comedy and musical theater productions. Check out their calendar of reasonably priced exciting events. People attending Venue 9 are the cognoscenti of theater goers.

💰 About $6-$10

Volunteer Involvement

11th Hour Productions

756 San Jose Avenue, San Francisco, CA 94110
(415) 647-4464

This theater would appreciate hearing from people interested in ushering or working at the concession counter. If you become involved as a volunteer, you might be spurred on to audition for an upcoming role.

American Conservatory Theater (ACT)

30 Grant Street, San Francisco, CA 94108
(415) 439-2349   http://www.act-sfbay.com

Interested in seeing productions for free and being involved in the theater? Ushering at ACT is a great way to see shows and meet other theater lovers in the process. Call for more information.

Asian-American Theater Company

1840 Sutter Street, Suite 207, San Francisco,CA 94115
(415) 440-5545   aatc@weret.net
Activity Location: Noh Space, 2840 Mariposa Street
(415) 621-7978

Give a call and learn more about Asian-American Theater. They need show helpers to work in the box office as well as ushers and backstage production volunteers. Shows are held at the Noh Space.

Cable Car Theater

430 Mason Street, San Francisco,CA 94102
(415) 587-6747

Volunteering gives you an inside look. Give your time as an usher, work in the box office or at the concession stand. Some backstage technical work is available, especially for those with previous experience. A great way to get involved in the theater community.

Chamber Theater

3717 Buchanan Street, San Francisco, CA 94123
(415) 346-3107

Try your hand at working backstage with props, or helping to build and paint sets. Ushers and concession stand volunteers are also needed before and during intermissions to support these fine performances.

Jon Sims Center for the Performing Arts

1519 Mission Street, San Francisco, CA 94103
(415) 554-0402

Volunteers are welcome to get hands-on experience producing experimental and other theater performances.

Lorraine Hansberry Theater

620 Sutter Street, San Francisco, CA 94102
(415) 288-0320

Find out about ushering and other volunteer opportunities in this high quality theater that continues to produce wonderful shows.

Theater

San Francisco Mime Troupe

885 Treat Avenue, San Francisco, CA 94110
(415) 285-1717

A great chance to learn more about mime as an art form. Help build sets for the three shows produced yearly.

Recess! A Play Night For Grown-Ups
hosted by Sue Walden & Co.'s ImprovWorks.

Vacations

Artist Residency Program • Biking

Environmental Volunteering

Museum Study Tours • Outdoors

Personal Growth/Retreats

A group enjoying a gourmet cycling adventure with Country Spokes

This is the chapter that is *not* about San Francisco. By definition, it is about places away from San Francisco—vacation places, where San Franciscans can meet compatible people. What distinguishes *these* vacations is that they are not lying-on-the-beach trips. They are active, learning, collaborating, building and moving experiences. At the heart of them all is interaction with others.

The friends you make building a soft bridge in Ecuador can support a social life connection in San Francisco. First of all, you might maintain phone (or on-line) contact with the people you meet on your trip or have an occasional reunion. You might even arrange to go on vacation with them next year. Secondly, you could be entering into an interest group/network that extends to the Bay Area and meet others, not on the trip, who share that interest. At the very least, you will be "out there," meeting compatible people and expanding your social network—something you would miss if you went on a safe vacation to the beach (again) with your friends.

So where to go?

Let's start with several premier groups that specialize in outdoorsy adventurous trips for small groups that usually have some kind of learning built in to the experience. **REI**, out of the beautiful Pacific Northwest, has trips all over the U.S. and abroad. They backpack, kayak, mountain climb and engage in other rigorous activities in a variety of *gorgeous* locations. The **Sierra Club** has similar activities but includes programs that educate participants about our natural resources, such as a weekend expedition to watch bald eagles. **Outward Bound** offers "safe adventure-based courses" designed to stimulate personal growth through group cooperation. You build self confidence and strengthen self-reliance while learning survival skills through expeditions. Locating water sources while desert backpacking or scaling a mountain with your climbing team in the Rio Grande are good examples of their trips, designed to be suitable for people of all ages and adventure levels.

In the outdoors arena are numerous programs specializing in one or another type of activity. For example, you could try biking with **Country Spokes** which offers tours for the energetic beginner or the intermediate rider. Choose between a two-day weekend or five-day midweek trip,

Vacations

(both van-supported for tired legs or flat tires). You'll be spending your days bicycling the lovely California countryside, and your nights camping in dome tents, safely situated in scenic campgrounds. Sounds like a good balance between challenge and comfort.

Your vacation can be a personal growth experience. The well-known **Esalen Institute**, located on the breathtakingly beautiful Big Sur coast, provides space for a personal retreat. They offer outstanding workshops including: "Managing To Have Fun: The Power of Humor in Business," "Being Single" and "Relationship as a Spiritual Path." Esalen participants we've talked to say they return to their lives refreshed and renewed. The **Green Gulch Farm Zen Center**, located just north of the city, is a Buddhist practice center open to the public. Take a traditional Zen mediation retreat (one-day, five-day or seven-day) or simply go as a guest. You'll meet others whose idea of a vacation is a walk through the fragrant, colorful and delicious organic gardens or along the glorious Pacific coast.

Traveling as a volunteer allows you to become *part of* a culture or environment you might never experience otherwise. **Earthwatch** recruits volunteers to assist scientists in field operations, from monitoring mountain lion populations to excavating 26,000-year-old mammoth bones in South Dakota. The catalogs will knock you out with dynamic interactive adventures in incredible places. **Global Service Corps** is looking for people interested in environmental and community development, to commit two or three weeks as volunteers in such countries as Costa Rica, Guatemala, Kenya and Thailand. In most cases of volunteer travel, you are responsible for paying your own travel expenses, but costs are kept to a minimum.

Some vacation groups and trips are organized for specific types of travelers: seniors, singles and women. (Please check those chapters for more information.) **Elderhostel** is a very large and well-established program offering thousands of exploratory trips. The quality is outstanding and people report that the trips have changed their lives. Programs include the "The Ceramics of Mexico" and "The Volcanoes of Costa Rica" and many others in the United States. Single people can learn sports like tennis, skiing, and scuba diving at one of the many **Club Med** resorts catering to the single traveler. Through the **Call of the Wild**, adventurous women can participate in organized hiking and camping trips around the Bay Area or explore remote wilderness destinations in the company of like-minded women.

Artists who dream of having the chance to work full-time on their art can look into **Villa Montalvo** in nearby Saratoga which offers one- to three-month residencies for writers, visual artists, musicians and composers. Taking part in this program allows the self-motivated artist to be around others but have plenty of independent work space. This is a true artists' colony where interaction between residents is natural and supportive.

Some Notes of Encouragement

Vacations are an excellent time to develop exciting *new interests*. This is true for a number of reasons. You have more open time and energy and less general stress. Also, you have the chance to learn something and get involved in doing it for a concentrated period of time without the distractions of routine demands. Further, you will be doing these things in new, exciting and beautiful settings that can expand your perspective and stimulate your interest. To top it off, being actively engaged in something new is often quite restorative, so you could return from your vacation quite refreshed.

Vacations are also a great time to take a fresh look at yourself and your life. There is something liberating about not being at home where you are bound by your regular surroundings and your usual ways of being. Things often look different when you're away. They take on a different cast. Psychologists call this changing your "set." Its encourages you to expand your perspective. Being away is also a great time to experiment with your usual ways of *behaving*. For example, you can get up earlier and think or meditate. When you meet others at breakfast you can talk quietly and peacefully about the lovely view (instead of how you usually act in the morning...). Or you can *risk* more than you usually do at home (where people will remember forever if you fall on your face) and talk more (or less), take leadership (or following) roles, ask someone that interests you to lunch (or let them ask you)—something different. It's a chance to extend your experiences, to try on other ways to be with yourself and others. Fun. Interesting. Watch yourself. How do you like it? If you don't, you can go back to your usual ways when you get home and not confuse your friends!

To learn more about specific places you might want to go, try your local travel book stores, such as **Rand McNally**. They offer excellent travel lectures and are friendly and helpful. Have a great trip!

Walk Thru'
Esalen Institute

Esalen Institute
Photo by
Margaret
Livingston

Esalen has been a mecca since 1962 for world-renown artists, religious thinkers, philosophers, psychologists and all people interested in personal growth. The workshops and seminars are of the highest quality in areas such as group process, personal exploration, meditation, and spiritual studies for weekend and five-day programs. Esalen is staffed by long-term scholars who give their time in exchange for tuition.

Many come simply for the experience of repair and renewal relaxing in natural hot springs and quiet meditation and yoga along the California sea coast. The property is perched atop a cliff with lush lawns, vegetable and flower gardens and wind-blown Cypress trees throughout. The view is a wide expanse of ocean blues with the boiling ocean surf below. It is truly a magical spot.

Mealtime is a lively interactive experience with conversations running the gamut between traditional and progressive ideas. Food is outstanding, prepared from fresh fruits and vegetables cultivated and harvested from the garden.

Standard accommodations are shared housing with two or three people per room. Couples can request a private room. Wear comfortable clothes that allow for ease of motion and sitting on the floor.

Artist Residency Program

Villa Montalvo

15400 Montalvo Road, Saratoga, CA 95071
(408) 961-5900

Villa Montalvo offers free one- to three-month residencies for writers, visual artists, musicians and composers. Montalvo is meant for the self-motivated artist who wants to work on a project but does not want to be either in isolation or committed to a communal experience. This community affords relaxed and natural interaction. The application process requires samples of your work.

Biking

Country Spokes

P.O. Box 30131, Walnut Creek, CA 94598
(800) 544-0226   cspokes@ccnet.com   http://www.ccnet.com/~cspokes

Everyone from the energetic beginner to the intermediate rider will find these two-day weekend or five-day midweek van-supported tours unforgettable. Spend your days bicycling the California countryside and your nights camping in dome tents with screened windows, safely situated in scenic campgrounds with full amenities. Healthy, energizing gourmet meals are an added pleasure. Meet other active folks, get some exercise and see the backroads of California.

☎ Jill Okyle or Joe Bailey

Scenic Cycling Adventures

1324 NW Vicksburg, Bend, OR 97701
(800) 413-8432   info@scenic-cycling.com   http://www.scenic-cycling.com

These are trips for bicycle enthusiasts who want a first-class touring experience that is also affordable. All tours include lodging, two support vehicles (for tired legs or flat tires), excellent tour leaders, small groups and touring companions with similar physical stamina levels. Tours are available in Arizona, Colorado, Idaho, New Mexico, Oregon, Utah and Washington State. A challenging outdoor sports experience with just the right amount of luxury.

Vacations

Environmental Volunteering

Earthwatch

Box 403, Watertown, MA 2172

(617) 926-8200   info@earthwatch.org   http://www.earthwatch.org

E arthwatch sponsors programs of volunteers and scientists working together to improve significant environmental problems. Past projects have included trips to study Israeli desert floods, humpbacks off Hawaii, an ancient Iberian village and a Bahamian reef survey. Call or email for a catalog.

Global Service Corps

300 Broadway, San Francisco, CA 94133
(415) 788-3666   gsc@earthisland.org
http://www.earthisland.org/ei/gsc/gschome.html

H ow about working in Costa Rica, Guatemala, Kenya or Thailand on a two- or three-week volunteer program? If you are interested in being active in environmental or community development, this is an opportunity to do so and discover parts of the world you might not visit otherwise. Longer placements can be arranged. Global Service provides the program and you cover your own expenses.

☎ Tom Parker

Global Volunteers

375 E. Little Canada Road, St. Paul, MN 55117
(800) 487-1074

G lobal Volunteers is a non-profit volunteer organization with ongoing projects in 15 countries. Why not take a two- to three-week service learning trip and learn firsthand about another culture or community while doing some good? You can teach English (no teaching experience is required), work in the rain forest or donate your professional skills. Choose a destination from the catalog, renew your passport and you're ready to go.

Oceanic Society Expeditions

Fort Mason Center, Building E, San Francisco, CA 94123
(800) 326-7491   http://www.oceanic-society.org

Taking part in an expedition is an exciting way to explore the natural world while supporting environmental preservation. The Society offers two types of expeditions. The Natural History group includes soft adventure educational experiences led by Oceanic Society naturalists and local guides. These trips are designed for anyone in good health. The Research Expeditions are designed to support scientific research. You work as part of a team with field biologists collecting data and logging information.

☎ Jennifer Austin

Museum Study Tours

American Museum of Natural History Discovery Tours

Central Park West at 79th Street, New York, NY 10024
(800) 462-8687   discovery@amnh.org

Pricey but high-quality educational trips. Look at these extraordinary destinations: "Borneo: A Natural History Paradise," "The Amazon: Discovering Untamed Wonders," "Lands of Pharaohs and Prophets: Egypt, Israel and Jordan," "Big Cats of the Serengeti" and many more. These are amazing adventures with travelers eager to learn.

Smithsonian Study Tours and Seminars

1100 Jefferson Drive SW, Room 3077, MRC 701, Washington, D.C. 20560
(202) 357-3030   http://www.si.edu/tsa

The Smithsonian offers classes at the museum in Washington, D.C. as well as learning tours all over the world. They are all fantastic. You can study "American Popular Music" in New Orleans, "Living and Design" in New York City, and the Revolutionary War at Valley Forge and Brandywine, PA. Also, their international tours are outstanding. Just look at the catalog.

Vacations

Outdoors

Backroads

801 Cedar Street, Berkeley, CA 94710
(800) 462-2848   goactive@backroads.com   http://www.backroads.com

Does pedaling through sunny hilltop towns in Tuscany sound like fun? How about cross-country skiing in the Canadian Rockies? Maybe a hiking and safari trip to South Africa is your dream. Backroads is an active travel company that features about 90 multisport (hiking, bicycling and cross-country skiing) vacation destinations around the world. These exciting trips are geared for people of all ages and fitness levels.

Mountain Travel Sobek

6420 Fairmount Avenue, El Cerrito, CA 94530
(800) 227-2384   info@mtsobek.com   http://www.mtsobek.com

These tours are moderate to expensive but to many it's worth the money to have expert guides who guarantee that their trips run smoothly. The result is stress-free travel to such exotic destinations as South America (the Galapagos Islands), Polar Journeys (Expedition Antarctica), Europe (Hiking Hidden Spain), Africa (Kilimanjaro & Beyond), South Africa (Zambezi River Expedition), Asia (Trekking & Tigers) and the Pacific (Australia Wildlife Safari).

Outward Bound

690 Market Street, San Francisco, CA 94104
(888) 882-6863   http://www.outwardbound.org

OB offers five schools where wilderness outings are taught and experienced. Participants take part in a safe adventure-based course designed to encourage personal confidence and self-reliance and the development of a close knit group. Choose from courses such as Desert Trekking, Sea Kayaking, Whitewater Rafting, Mountaineering, Seamanship and many more. For all ages and varied physical competency.

REI Adventures

P.O. Box 1938, Sumner, WA 98390
(800) 622-2236   travel@rei.com   http://www.rei.com/travel

REI organizes mountain biking, kayaking, backpacking, climbing and walking trips all over the U.S. and the world beyond. Learn outdoor skills on your adventure and experience the world from an active perspective. REI has a special commitment to responsible travel, and emphasizes the need to respect the environment and the local people.

Road Runner Worldwide Hostelling Treks

6762A Centinela Avenue, Culver City, CA 90230
(800) 873-5872   americanadventures-roadrunner@postoffice.worldnet.att.net

An organized hostelling trek is a great way to travel affordably within the safety and camaraderie of a small group. There is no age limit but most participants are under 35. Choose from trips offering different adventures in exciting destinations. You just might find yourself passing the tropic of Capricorn in Austria or viewing the Atlantic and Indians Oceans from Cape Point in South Africa. (P.S. Hostelling International, (415) 788-2525, can get you plugged into more than 5,000 hostels in 70 countries worldwide.)

The American Alpine Club

710 10th Street, Suite 100, Golden, CO 80401
(303) 384-0110   getinfo@americanalpineclub.org
http://www.americanalpineclub.org

This national mountaineering and climbing organization was established in 1902 and is a very good source for the serious climber. Visit their web page for further information on expeditions and other climbing related activities.

Vacations

Yosemite National Park Field Seminars

P.O. Box 230, El Portal, CA 95318
(209) 379-2321   yose_yosemite_association@nps.gov   http://yosemite.org

A Yosemite Field Seminar is an unrivaled learning vacation in
Yosemite Valley, Wawona, and Tuolumme Meadows that covers a
variety of natural and human history and art-related subjects. Past
seminars have included: "Where Glaciers Roamed–Geology of the
Yosemite Sierra," "Mammals of the High Sierra," "Alpine Ecology" and
"Young Lakes Beginner Backpack." All seminars include free camp-
ground space and cabins can be reserved. Simply beautiful.

☼ February–November
💰 About $120-190

Personal Growth/Retreats

Esalen Institute

Highway 1, Big Sur, CA 93920
(415) 644-8476   http://www.esalen.org

E salen is truly a special place. Artists, religious thinkers, philosophers,
psychologists and persons interested in personal growth have been
drawn to Esalen since 1962. You feel more peaceful from the moment
you enter the space resting on the spectacular cliffs high over the Pacific.
The organic garden and natural hot spring baths add to the special
experience. The best ways to discover Esalen are to take a weekend or a
five-day workshop as a seminarian.

💰 Moderate-expensive

Green Gulch Farm Zen Center

1601 Shoreline Highway, Sausalito, CA 94965
(415) 383-3134

Green Gulch Farm is a Buddhist practice center in the Japanese Soto Zen tradition. Located just north of San Francisco, the center includes an organic farm which provides outstanding produce for the Greens Restaurant. Go for the Sunday program with meditation instruction, a tea ceremony and a question and answer period followed by a delicious lunch. You can also stay as an overnight guest. For renewal, wander through the gardens and down to the ocean and interact with others as much or as little as you like.

💰 Moderate

Harbin Hot Springs

P.O. Box 782, Middletown, CA 95461
(707) 987-2477

Harbin Springs is a fantastic place to go alone or with others. You can join interesting workshops or simply spend time bathing in the mineral pools. Harbin is not a traditional spa; rather it is a spiritual and transformational hub where the human condition is explored and respected. Go to be involved with the community or go to be alone— whatever you need to replenish your spirit.

💰 Moderate-expensive

Tassajara

300 Page Street, San Francisco, CA 94102
(415) 431-3771

Tassajara is a Zen monastery about five hours from SF that operates as a resort from May to September. Guests are treated to fine vegetarian meals and the hottest (around 140°F) and richest mineral hot springs in the U.S. Here is a working Buddhist community that invites guests to participate in "zazen" (meditation sittings), go hiking, read a book or swim in the spring-fed pool. Go for tranquility and peace in a heavenly setting. No formal participation is required.

💰 Moderate-expensive

Global Volunteer team members work with local townspeople
on a project in Mexico

Writing & Poetry

Author Readings • Discussions

Poetry Readings • Publishing Arts

Writing Groups

National Poetry Association. Photo by Rob Lee.

Writing & Poetry

San Francisco is the home of the staged poetry reading. Close your eyes and let your imagination flow back in time. You are in a smoky cafe in North Beach. A young man dressed in black with shockingly long hair walks to the front of the room and takes center stage. The audience is filled with young smiling faces that gradually grow silent. The young man begins a recitation describing ills that reach deep into the social fabric of America. He says words that no one would say in "polite society"—but make sense to his listeners. They come to drink in his unspeakable words. Words that rock the conservative collective consciousness of the 50's. Words that are poetic in their accusations.

Using poetry as an instrument, the Beatniks challenged the status quo. By 1956, word of a subversive movement in San Francisco was filtering throughout the country, but it wasn't until Lawrence Ferlinghetti, the publisher of Allen Ginsberg's poem *HOWL*, was arrested for distributing "obscene" literature that the Beatniks and their work received national notoriety.

The debate was noisy but the drama was settled in a courtroom. The voices of many distinguished literary and academic witnesses persuaded Judge Clayton Horn that *HOWL* was not obscene and that it had "redeeming social significance." With that ruling, the rules regarding freedom of speech were changed.

More than 40 years since the Beats passed through San Francisco, their legacy continues. During any given week, you can hear a poetry reading in a coffeehouse or cafe somewhere in the city. The poets' clothing styles continue to change and their words might seem tame or lascivious, but the literary art form is etched in the city's soul.

Writing and poetry tell our stories—stories about our loves, our mothers and children, our travels and adventures, our dreams and travesties and the reaches of our souls. When we write, we connect with others and tell about ourselves. We also learn about new ideas, ways of doing things and places to go. Writing activities appeal to people who like to think. Through these experiences we expand our knowledge and interests, both by listening to others' works or by taking pen (or computer) in hand ourselves.

You can enter writing and poetry activities through hundreds of doors. You can browse in a bookstore and sit at a cafe table with your book choices, drinking a cappuccino. (We always glance over our books to see what other people are reading—do you?) You can go to readings and chat with the authors and the listeners. If you're feeling brave you can read your own writing and poetry out loud and test your work with audience feedback. You can participate in conferences to learn special writing skills. You can join clubs that meet regularly to read certain types of books (e.g., mysteries) or be part of a writer's group for mutual support and thoughtful criticism. Our favorite is the pleasure of the "music" of an author reading her works to you. We think it's reminiscent of the old days of bedtime stories—soothing, comforting—wonderful!

Writing and poetry can be enjoyed on a spectrum of risk levels. You can participate at a very safe and soothing level or in a high exposure, challenging way. If you choose the latter and read your works to an audience, you may experience a special connection with others who are willing to come forward as well. We think both ways are truly fulfilling and definitely worth doing. Especially when there is such a rich and diverse writing environment in which to do it.

Another thing we like about writing events is that they are often free or dirt cheap. Where a movie costs $8.50 and a play $15 and more, an excellent author will read to you free of charge. Also you can find writing and reading events in many areas of the city. This fortunate situation is largely because of the emergence of bookstores as more than retail outlets, with a new mission to draw patrons together into the reading/writing experience.

So how and where?

You can hear authors at **Borders** or **Barnes & Noble** almost every night of the week. These authors will be talking about how to find or end relationships, Japanese gardening, the best vitamins to prevent cancer, how to play "**Go**," and how to land a publishing job. You'll hear terrific contemporary fiction like *Stones from the River* and the classics. Bookstores also sponsor music on most weekends as well as games and other interactive events. (Ruth got killed in the Go match. You might do better!) You can plan the events you don't want to miss by checking the *San Francisco Chronicle's* "DATEBOOK," the *BAY GUARDIAN* and the *SF WEEKLY* for complete listings of authors and topics, or check in the bookstores for their monthly newsletters describing new books and upcoming events. These programs are high quality and a lot of fun.

Don't forget to keep a close eye on the non-chain bookstores for enlightening evenings as well. The **Clean Well-Lighted Place for Books** was packed for Cindy Crawford and is a great place to stop by after the attending an event at the Herbst Theater, symphony or opera. **City Lights Bookstore** continues to be the premier literary meeting place. It sponsors readings and other events that draw a mixed crowd of downtown professionals and artists of considerable sophistication.

You'll be pleased with the excellent programs to be found at the **San Francisco Public Library** which sponsors a wide diversity of speakers on a regular basis for little or no cost. And if you still haven't seen the new main branch, you're really missing something. It's an architectural wonder. Pick up a calendar of events at your local branch while you're choosing your free video or before attending your book discussion group.

If you are an aspiring writer, you will have company galore and many opportunities to share your work. Beside the above mentioned places that invite local writers, there are informal salons such as the **Ad Hoc Writers**, a group of science fiction and fantasy writers, where you can read your writing and be informally critiqued. The **Sunset Writers' Workshop** has been active for more than 10 years and explores all forms of fiction and nonfiction except poetry. Barbara Griffith, the facilitator, told us that after posting their page on the net, she has been forced to start a waiting list to manage the large number of interested people.

Our experience is that writing groups have become very popular. If you can't find one that is right for you, you could probably start your own. Post a notice at different bookstores about the group you hope to establish and soon you may find you have a group tailor-made to your particular interests. For example, **Sisters In Crime** is now a well-established group supporting the development of women mystery writers.

Have you thought about taking a creative writing class? Try **City College** or **San Francisco State University,** keeping in mind that they will require a commitment of two classes a week plus homework. For a less structured class, **Bernal Book's** writer-in-residence offers a series of classes called "Pen To Paper" that is enjoyable and structured with less pressure to produce. For you potential screenwriters, **The Studio** offers practical classes such as "Screenwriting 101," "Selling Your Script" and "Creating Characters." These classes are perfect for someone who wants to learn more about the film craft in a climate that is both supportive and professional.

Writing & Poetry

And for POETS!

San Francisco teems with places to read and listen to poetry—such as **Cafe La Boheme, Sacred Grounds Cafe, Polk Street Beans and Cafe.** Here's your chance at an open mic! Also, the **San Francisco African American Historical and Cultural Society** hosts a poetry reading every second Thursday with refreshments.

If you want to know more about the San Francisco poetry community, the **National Poetry Association** is the key. Also, pick up a copy of *Poetry Flash* (we get ours on the second floor of **City Lights** in the poetry section) for a complete listing of monthly poetry events.

Writing and poetry activities are a great way for all of us, not just published writers, to listen, think and talk together about prose and poetry, contemporary issues and art. The cafe-salon venue for people to meet and connect is for you and me. Let's go for it and keep it alive!

A San Francicso Literary Soirée in full swing-members recording for KALW radio at a Graham Greene evening. From left to right are Peter Robinson, Norman Macleod, Brigid McCartney and Carol Goodman.

Writing & Poetry

Author Readings

Barnes and Noble

2550 Taylor Street, San Francisco, CA 94133
(415) 292-6762

B arnes and Noble Bookstores encourage patrons to attend book
signings and poetry readings in the store, as well as browse and read
with a Starbucks from their cafe. Their newsletter is out early so you can
choose the authors/programs you want to attend ahead of time. Often
the programs are interactive, giving you a chance to talk to others about
their/your favorite books. Lovely music events as well.

☼ Everyday   🕐 9am–11pm

Borders Books

400 Post Street, San Francisco, CA 94102
(415) 399-1633

B orders carries a huge selection of book titles. It's also a great place to
meet others who are mulling around reading books, enjoying author
signings, lectures, demonstrations, participating in reading groups or
drinking coffee in the cafe. Late hours make this a good destination for
to enjoy the company of other adult readers when you're browsing by
yourself. Find their complete newsletter in the store.

☼ Everyday   🕐 Open 9am; Close Mon-Wed 11pm;
                                        Thur-Sat 12am; Sun 9pm

City Arts and Lectures, Inc.

1415 Green Street, San Francisco, CA 94109
(415) 392-4400
Activity Location: Herbst Theater, 401 Van Ness Avenue

A variety of "Literary Events at the Herbst Theater" are sponsored by
the Friends of the San Francisco Public Library. Prose writers and
poets such as John Updike, Joan Didion, Maya Angelou, Ruth Rendell,
Tobias Wolff are featured. Tickets can be obtained through the City Box
Office, 153 Kearny Street, Suite 402, SF 94108.

Writing & Poetry

Intersection for the Arts

446 Valencia Street, San Francisco, CA 94103
(415) 626-2787   *http://ecstatic.com/orgs/intersection*

Any contact you have with this quality organization will nurture your artistic side. They sponsor the outstanding "Writers-in-Residence" program designed to aid writers in developing, promoting and experimenting with their writing. Audiences have the opportunity to follow the artists and the development of their work at the Tuesday Night Reading Series. Call for a catalog and confirm dates of events.

Stacey's

581 Market Street, San Francisco, CA 94105
(415) 421-4687   events@staceys.com   http://www.staceys.com

For you downtowners who want to see an author or hear a lecture during your lunch hour or right after work, Stacey's is a good place to go. The crowd is predominately professional and friendly. FYI: Bay Area non-profits and reading clubs can use Stacey's new events meeting space at no charge.

☼ Scheduled dates   🕰 12:30pm & 5:30pm
☎ Colleen Lindsay

The San Francisco Public Library

100 Larkin Street, San Francisco, CA 94102
(415) 557-4400

Library branches throughout the city offer a monthly calendar of literary programs and events. Past programs have included dramatic readings of the classics; slide and lecture presentations featuring Californian historians; art exhibitions and much more. These are excellent free programs.

Writing & Poetry

Discussions

The San Francisco Literary Society

1 Weatherly Drive, Suite 402, Mill Valley, CA 94941
(415) 381-9091
Activity Location: Northern Trust Bank, Conf. Rm., 580 California, Suite 1800
(415) 765-4400

Involvement in the Literary Society is an excellent way to keep your reading up-to-date and enjoy interesting speakers (writers, poets and dramatists). The Thursday program includes a buffet (7pm), a guest speaker (7:30pm) and concludes with an open discussion where everyone is encouraged to participate. Discounts on all events including the literary soirees at the Hotel Rex are added benefits of membership.

☼ Scheduled Thursdays ⏰ 7pm
✆ Peter Robinson
💰 $225/year membership; $400/year family

Poetry Readings

Cafe La Boheme

3318 24th Street, San Francisco, CA 94110
(415) 643-0481

Poetry readings are held regularly on Fridays at 8pm but should be confirmed because the dates change. Cafe La Boheme is a great venue if you want to read your original work or share your favorite poems. If you want to read, call ahead to get on the reading schedule. If you just want to listen, just show up.

Writing & Poetry

City Lights Bookstore

261 Columbus Avenue, San Francisco, CA 94133
(415) 362-8193

Lawrence Ferlinghetti is a major American poet and publisher and the creator of City Lights, the first paperback bookstore in America. City Lights also has been a premier literary meeting place since 1953. You can find the classics from Ginsberg, Kerouac and Burroughs, and contemporary avant-garde writers as well. Be sure to go upstairs, sit back and read some poetry, and pick up a copy of *Poetry Flash*.

☼ Open everyday   🕰 10am-11:45pm

National Poetry Association

934 Brannan Street, 2nd Floor, San Francisco, CA 94103
(415) 552-9261   *gamuse@slip.net*   *http://www.slip.net/~gamuse*

Poets and aspiring poets: Here is a forum where all styles and levels of writing are appreciated. NPA supports the promotion and appreciation of poetry by offering outstanding live poetry programs, events, readings and workshops. Everyone connected with this poetry community is upbeat and helpful. If you don't know about the annual Cafe Arts Month (November) sponsored by NPA, check the newspaper for readings and performances for the entire month.

Paradise Lounge

1501 Folsom Street, San Francisco, CA 94103
(415) 861-6906

Sunday night "Poetry Above Paradise" is a popular weekly event with featured readers presenting a variety of verse. If you are interested in presenting your work at the open readings, sign-up time is 7pm. You must be over 21 to attend.

☼ Sundays   🕰 8pm
💰 Free

Polk Street Beans and Cafe

1733 Polk Street, San Francisco, CA 94109
(415) 776-9292

O rganized poetry readings are followed by an open mic, available to all comers for free expression.

☀ Thursdays   ⏰ 7pm
💰 Free

Sacred Grounds Cafe

2095 Hayes Street, San Francisco, CA 94117
(415) 387-3859

J oin this ongoing poetry gathering to hear some great verse followed by an open mic.

☀ Wednesdays   ⏰ 7:30pm
💰 Free

The San Francisco African-American Historical and Cultural Society

762 Fulton Street, San Francisco, CA 94102
(415) 292-6172

Activity Location: Center For African Art and Culture

T hese Thursday night poetry readings feature special guests who read and discuss their writing after which audience members are encouraged to share theirs. Refreshments are part of these very nice evenings for people who want to hear, read and discuss poetry and find a community that shares that interest.

☀ 2nd Thursday/month   ⏰ 7pm
☎ Eric DuPree

Yakety Yak

679 Sutter Street, San Francisco, CA 94102
(415) 885-6908

Y ou can be part of the program by reading your original work or your favorite poems. Sign-up time is 6:30pm.

☀ Fridays   ⏰ 7-9pm
💰 Free

Writing & Poetry

Publishing Arts

Media Alliance

814 Mission Street, Suite 205, San Francisco, CA 94103
(415) 546-6334   ma@igc.org   http://www.media-alliance.org

The Media Alliance is a resource center for persons interested in or professionally employed in a media-producing capacity. They hold excellent classes, including newswriting, magazine writing, proofreading, photography, online publishing, graphic design and Mac computer instruction. Be sure to ask about their publication *People Behind the News.*

San Francisco Bay Area Book Council

123 Townsend Street, Suite 260, San Francisco, CA 94107
(415) 908-2833   sfbook@best.com   http://www.sfbook.org

A wonderful organization that promotes literacy through cultural programs including the annual San Francisco Bay Area Book Festival. A don't miss event that features bookstore, publisher and library exhibits, author readings and signings, children's activities and publishing seminars. Volunteers are always needed.

The San Francisco Center for the Book

300 De Haro Street, San Francisco, CA 94103
(415) 565-0545   info@sfcb.org

A good resource for professional and semi-professional writers, and self-publishers interested in "the art of the visible word" through the writing, production and craftsmanship of books. Many high quality classes are available to help you get started with *your* book. If you're in the middle of a novel and your characters are in a jumble, ask about the free Friday book clinic. Free receptions, readings and lectures are held throughout the year.

☎ Kathleen Burch

Writing & Poetry

Writing Groups

Writing Group

337 Elsie Street, San Francisco, CA 94110
(415) 282-0794
Activity Location: Bernal Heights Library, 500 Cortland Avenue
(415) 695-5160

A small, informal writing group that meets to share their work, generate ideas and lend support and friendship. Fiction, non-fiction, poetry and essay writers are all encouraged to attend. The group's meeting places rotate between the Bernal Heights Library and Bernal Books (401 Cortland Avenue), so call before you go.

☀ 1st & 3rd Tuesday/month   ☎ 7pm
☎ Eileen McCann
💰 Free–About $5/donation (to cover costs)

Ad Hoc Writers

2636 East Avenue, Hayward, CA 94541
(510) 582-1549

A group of science fiction and fantasy writers that meet about every three weeks on Saturday afternoons from 1-5pm. They rotate meeting locations between SF, South Bay and East Bay. Give a call and start creating your own science fiction fantasies!

☎ Jim Van Scyoc

Bernal Books

401 Cortland Avenue, San Francisco, CA 94110
(415) 550-0293   bernalbks@aol.com

Margo Perin, the bookstore's current writer-in-residence, offers "Pen to Paper," a series of creative writing classes. Advanced sign-up is requested and there is a small fee. Bernal Books is also a great place for book readings, informal talks and author appearances.

☀ Wednesdays   ☎ 7pm

Writing & Poetry

California Writers' Club, Peninsula Branch

303 Delmar Way, San Mateo, CA 94403
(415) 615-8331   http://www.asesur.com/us.cwc

The Peninsula Branch is active from San Francisco to Palo Alto and welcomes writers who have been nationally published. They also sponsor the annual Jack London Writers' Conference on the second Saturday in March. Published as well as nonpublished writers are encouraged to attend. If you are not a professional writer but take your writing seriously, attending the writers' conference is a good way to learn more about the industry and meet other writers.

☎ Lucinda Crisp
💰 $35/year membership

Clean Well-Lighted Place for Books

601 Van Ness Avenue, San Francisco, CA 94102
(415) 441-6670

A friendly bookstore that encourages you to take your time looking at and browsing the books. Check the wall behind the register for all kinds of interesting reading and writing groups that are looking for new members. A nice place to stop by after the opera, symphony or an evening at the Herbst Theater.

☀ Everyday   📅 Open 10am;
                              Close Sunday-Thursday 11pm;
                              Friday & Saturday till midnight.

Mystery Writers of America, North California Chapter

615-F Willow Street, Alameda, CA 94501
(510) 865-3022   Jgdawson@ix.netcom.com or Mwanorcal@aol.com
http://user.aol.com/mwanorcal/

If you have been writing mystery stories and want to join the world of professional mystery writers, this group is for you. Mystery fans and writers who are unpublished can apply for one of a limited number of Affiliate memberships. The group wishes to include those with a serious interest in the mystery writing area.

💰 $65/year membership

Writing & Poetry

San Francisco Mystery Bookstore

4175-24th Street, San Francisco, CA 94114
(415) 282-7444   sfmyboks@aol.com   *http://www.mysterynet.com/sfmb*

Visit this wonderful bookstore that caters to mystery enthusiasts, where new, used and out-of-print books are available for purchase. You can meet others who share your passion for crime fiction here, especially at the frequently held signings and readings. You just might find yourself chatting with a fellow mystery lover about what really happened on that dark and stormy night!

Sisters in Crime, North California Chapter

211 Orange Street, Oakland, CA 94610
(510) 834-5055   charcook@aol.com

Welcome to the world of women mystery writers. Membership is open to all persons who have an interest in mystery writing, and wish to support women writers. At their bimonthly meetings you'll meet local published authors and be involved in some safe, but scary mystery related discussions.

☏ Charlotte Cook
💲 $40/year membership

Society of Children's Book Writers, North California Chapter

536 Thomas Circle, Suisun, CA 94585
(707) 426-6776

For writers or potential writers of children's books, this group will help you develop your hobby into a profession. The event locations vary but are held throughout the Bay Area. You'll meet others at the quarterly programs, through the newsletter and at the annual retreat.

☏ Bobi Martin
💲 $50/year national membership; $15/year local membership

Writing & Poetry

Sunset Writers' Workshop

3365 Sacramento Street, San Francisco, CA 94118
(415) 929-1651

This fine writing group, active for over 10 years, explores all forms of fiction and nonfiction prose writing. Newcomers are asked to call first because the group size is limited to maintain manageability. (A "cookie" contribution of $1 is asked to help with light refreshments!)

☼ 2nd & 4th Wednesday/month   ☎ 7:30-10:30pm
☎ Barbara Griffith

The Studio, Creative Workshops for Screenwriters

582 Market Street, Suite 2008, San Francisco, CA 94104
(415) 789-7399   sasent@sirius.com   http://www.sirius.com/~sasent

Do you want to learn more about the screenwriting craft? The Studio offers practical and useful classes such as "Screenwriting 101," "Selling Your Script" and "Creating Characters," presented in a professional and supportive environment. If you're a fiction writer, why not learn what goes into writing a screenplay compared to writing a novel? You might find yourself dusting off that manuscript.

☎ Sam Scribner

Appendix:

Interesting Information

(We're having trouble ending this book.)

Dog (and owner) Places

There is no denying that San Franciscans love their dogs. Dog lovers stop to chat as their canines sniff, growl and maneuver themselves within their doggy hierarchy. We have been told by several of San Francisco's professional dog walkers that the following places are special dog/people friendly spots. But *please* be considerate and pick up after your dog so these public places are nice for all of us to visit.

Alta Plaza - Steiner & Clay Streets

Crissy Field - Off Marina Boulevard

Fort Funston - Off Skyline Boulevard

Huntington Park- California & Taylor Streets (small dogs)

Lafayette Park - Sacramento & Gough Streets

Mascone Recreation Center - Laguna & Chestnut Streets

Mission Dolores Park - Dolores & 20th Streets

Cigar Places

Cigar enthusiasts are an active bunch who enjoy living the good life. Starting a conversation with someone from this group is easy—just ask them what kind of cigar they are smoking! This list is but a sample of places where cigar smokers won't be escorted to the door.

Balboa Cafe, 3199 Fillmore Street, (415) 921-3944

Big Four Restaurant, 1075 California Street, (415) 771-1140

Cypress Club, 500 Jackson Street, (415) 296-8555

Essex Supper Club, 847 Montgomery Street, (415) 397-5969

Maxfield's Bar & Grill, Sheraton Palace Hotel,
2 New Montgomery Street, (415) 546-5020

Morton's of Chicago, 400 Post Street, (415) 986-5830

Redwood Room, Clift Hotel, 495 Geary Street,
(415) 775-4700

Ritz Carlton Dining Room Bar, 600 Stockton Street
(415) 296-7465

Eating Alone

We hear constantly that people hate going out to eat alone. If you're new to the city, without a significant other or on your own for the night, there will be times when you want to go out for a meal alone. Diane's personal favorite is the U.S. Restaurant located at 431 Columbus Avenue (415) 362-6251. The place is very comfortable, full of nice regulars and the waitresses enjoy knowing many of the customers by their first names.

About You

We are interested in knowing more about you, including your favorite places to eat alone and any clubs or groups that you would like included in upcoming editions of CISF. You can contact us directly by email at Drdecastro@aol.com or Ruthymar@aol.com or through OFFTIME PRESS, (415) 292-5230, 41 Sutter Street, Suite 1763, San Francisco, CA 94104.

We are interested in hearing from you because this book was created with you in mind. Knowing who you are specifically helps us provide better information and service. Also, by responding, you will be added to our mailing list for upcoming events, workshops and newsletters. We look forward to hearing from you.

See you out there!

Diane & Ruth

Index

Did You Borrow This Book? Have one of your own!

If you have your own copy of
Connecting In San Francisco: 693 Great Places To Enjoy Yourself And Meet New People, you can make notes in it and refer to it whenever you're on the go. You can obtain your personal copy from local bookstores or by completing and returning the form below. For more information, contact us at (415) 292-5230 or via email at Drdecastro@aol.com or Ruthymar@aol.com.

_____ YES, I'd like _____ copies of
Connecting In San Francisco: 693 Great Places To Enjoy Yourself And Meet New People.
Please allow 30 days for delivery.

Name _____

Address _____

City/Sate/Zip _____

Phone (___) _____ Email _____

_____ book(s) at $12.95 each $_____

Add 8 1/2% sales tax:$1.10, $2.20, $3.30,etc. $_____

Shipping and Handling @ $3.00/Book. $_____

Total Enclosed $_____

Make your check payable to:

OFFTIME PRESS
41 Sutter Street, Suite 1763
San Francisco, CA 94104

Bulk Orders Invited

For bulk discounts or special handling, please contact our
Special Markets Department, OFFTIME PRESS
(415) 292-5230.

Workshops

_____YES, I'd like to receive a free notice of upcoming
events, workshops or newsletters.

Other Books

_____YES, I want to purchase a copy of

*Connecting In Philadelphia: 512 Great Places
To Enjoy Yourself And Meet New People*
by Ruth B. Harvey.
($9.95 plus $3 shipping & tax)

_____YES, I want to purchase a copy of

Philly NiteLife: 40 Friendly Philadelphia Nitespots
by Ruth B. Harvey.
($8.95 plus $3 shipping and tax)

Contact:

OFFTIME PRESS
41 Sutter Street, Suite 1763
San Francisco, CA 94104

About Us

Ruth Harvey, Ph.D.

Psychologist turned author, **Ruth Harvey, Ph.D.** has been writing about connecting through the activities we love since 1981. As a self-publisher (Offtime Press), she also wrote and produced the regional best seller *Connecting in Philadelphia* (1994) and *Philly NiteLife* (1996), with San Francisco as the second of many major cities to be included in the *Connecting* series.

A college teacher and counseling psychologist in another life, Ruth is now a full-time writer, speaker and workshop leader in communication and building social networks. Her ongoing workshops in *Social Interaction*, based on the concept of connecting through your interests, are well-known in the mid-Atlantic region. A popular professional speaker, she also appears regularly on local TV and radio programs exhorting people to take time out, relax and laugh, meet more people, grow with the challenges of exciting adventures and find meaningful connections.

Diane de Castro

After researching and writing about *Connecting in San Francisco*, **Diane de Castro** knows more places to interact and socialize around the Bay Area than do most native San Franciscans. Throughout the development of the book, she thrived on exploring the city, meeting its diverse people, and trying new activities with the resulting satisfaction of feeling connected.

Diane graduated *Summa Cum Laude* from the University of San Francisco where she was awarded the prestigious *Outstanding Student Scholar Award in Communication.*

Theatrical by nature, Diane is an experienced actress. She has more than ten years of acting experience, including theater productions, films and TV commercials in Chicago, New York, Washington, D.C. as well as San Francisco. Diane has studied and performed with the well-known improvisational troupe, *Second City,* in Chicago and now enjoys acting periodically with the San Francisco mystery theater troupe, *Murder On The Menu.*

When not involved with acting, teaching and book promotion activities, Diane is writing a suspense romance novel and developing a television show that will enable her to continue exploring the city.